The Changing Vampire
of Film and Television

The Changing Vampire of Film and Television

A Critical Study of the Growth of a Genre

TIM KANE

McFarland & Company, Inc., Publishers
Jefferson, North Carolina, and London

LIBRARY OF CONGRESS CATALOGUING-IN-PUBLICATION DATA

Kane, Tim, 1971–
   The changing vampire of film and television : a critical study of
the growth of a genre / Tim Kane.
      p.   cm.
   Includes bibliographical references and index.

   ISBN-13: 978-0-7864-2676-8
   ISBN-10: 0-7864-2676-4
   (softcover : 50# alkaline paper) ∞

   1. Vampire films—History and criticism.   2. Vampires on
television.   I. Title.
PN1995.9.V3K36   2006
791.43'675—dc22   2006025564

British Library cataloguing data are available

On the cover: (left, top to bottom) Images from the the films
Nosferatu, Dracula (1931), *Dracula* (1958), *Fright Night, Blade* and
Underworld; and (right) the television series *Dark Shadows* and
Buffy the Vampire Slayer

Manufactured in the United States of America

McFarland & Company, Inc., Publishers
   Box 611, Jefferson, North Carolina 28640
      www.mcfarlandpub.com

To my wife, Kate.
Her support and endless knowledge of horror cinema
made this project possible.

I would also like to acknowledge the
advice and support of Paul Majkut,
the one responsible for guiding me to this path,
for better or worse.

CONTENTS

PREFACE

I grew up watching monster movies—vampires, werewolves, and the giant creatures from Toho. I have always been attracted to the dread they inspire, all the way back to the boogeyman hiding in my closet or under the bed. This fascination endured into my adulthood in the form of avid movie consumption. When I was considering the capstone project for my master's degree at National University, professor Paul Majkut noticed my fascination for the macabre. He suggested I try something along the lines of horror films. That was all the incentive I needed. I returned by the end of the week with an outline for my thesis.

I had noticed a trend in the cinematic and televised depictions of vampires. Both the appearance and demeanor of the cinematic vampire had changed drastically since its introduction with Bela Lugosi in 1931. As I watched countless vampire films, these tendencies became more concrete. The evidence indicated that there were three distinct periods of vampire narrative, breaking roughly along historical lines. The first period comprised the Universal films. In this period, the vampire dressed formally and remained foremost a villain. Next came the films of Hammer, the hugely successful television series *Dark Shadows*, and the remaining films of the 1970s. These depictions of the vampire showed more human aspects. Though still an isolated noble, the vampire demonstrated distinct emotion toward several of his female victims. The third period began in the 1980s and continues up to the present day. The examples of this last period—*The Lost Boys, Interview with the Vampire, Buffy the Vampire Slayer,* or *Underworld*—seemed to be horribly incompatible, yet I sensed that they belonged together.

The final piece of this puzzle lay with genre. The current published research indicated that genre was a static concept. Source after source quoted classic examples and failed to acknowledge any degree of change. The bulk of genre research involved including or excluding films based on a predetermined set of parameters, and these parameters were often based on a limited number of films. None of the research had attempted to study a range of films, over the period of decades, to see how the characteristics of a single genre held true, or even possibly changed.

Movie studios have churned out vampire-oriented films nonstop since the 1931 *Dracula*. That's over seventy years of celluloid just waiting to be exploited. In terms of genre studies, it constituted a gold mine!

I set out to look at these films, as well as some overlooked, yet influential television series. I used Rick Altman's research into semantic-syntactic approach as a guide to analyzing these vampire narratives. I fashioned seven areas of study that I felt both embodied the vampire narrative and carried through all three historical periods. These seven areas were (1) how the vampire looked at the victim to exert a kind of hypnotic control, (2) the act of the vampire biting the victim, (3) the process of the victim's infection by vampirism, (4) the physical appearance and demeanor of the vampire expert, (5) the physical appearance and demeanor of the vampire, (6) the act of presenting a cross to a vampire, and (7) the destruction of the vampire. I would look examine each of these seven areas when viewing the films or television series. Any element, however minor, that fell within the scope of one of these areas was included and subsequently analyzed.

This book is not about holding specific examples up for praise. Several of my most favorite films were excluded because they did not match the scope of the investigation. Additionally, some films that I find difficult to watch were included, because they had a tremendous influence on subsequent narratives and the genre as a whole.

I hope that the importance of this research in terms of genre studies is not overshadowed by the bias against the study of horror cinema. Often academics look down their noses at vampires and their ilk, regarding them as infantile. History has shown that horror films are dependable box-office earners, and these films have, more than once, saved a studio from bankruptcy. If we are to accept that the success of a film or television series has at least something to do with its popularity with the viewing public, then horror must be considered a major force, and should not be so lightly discounted. This study's examinations into the nature of genre can easily be applied to other areas—the Western, the gangster films, or the musical. See this book as it was intended, an adventure into truth; be it ever so small or simplistic, it is valuable nonetheless.

INTRODUCTION

The Evolution of the Vampire

If a vampire were to come to your house and knock on the door, what would you expect to see? A man with a widow's peak, decked out in a cape and tuxedo? Or perhaps you would expect him to have fangs, dripping with blood, and a malevolent gaze to freeze you to the bone. Maybe you would find yourself face to face with a young man in a tattered denim jacket, his face misshapen into a demonic visage. All of these vampires existed in the minds of audiences at one time. The expectation for the vampire in horror cinema has evolved from Bela Lugosi in *Dracula* to Kate Beckinsale in *Underworld,* from villain to hero.

The purpose of this book is to track the evolutionary changes in genre. As a case study, I have selected vampire narratives (a sub-genre of horror) for the focus of this book. Not only is horror the longest lived of any genre, vampire narrative films have been consistently produced since *Dracula* in 1931. The current state of genre criticism leaves many questions unresolved. All current theory acknowledges that genres do indeed change over time, but none details explicitly how or why. This book is essential to determining the factors that cause a genre to change.

In *The Cinema Book,* Pam Cook and Mieke Bernink track the progress of films from their beginning to modern day. They state that even from its inception, genre criticism viewed genres as fixed entities. Examples of genre are often called "classic" and held as the standard by which all others are judged. "New films often deny accepted definitions and appear to the genre critic to mark a decline from 'classic' examples" (138). Early genre criticism focused on defining characteristics of genres and the formation of the "'classic' moment," which films either moved toward or, after a classic period, moved away from into decline. Yet even these early critics conceded that genres were not wholly static. Genre scholar Laurence Alloway insisted that genres are "fluid" and are run in "cycles" (quoted by Cook and Bernink 138).

3

The classic image of the vampire as portrayed by Bela Lugosi in Dracula *(1931, Universal). Here Dracula carries Mina (Helen Chandler).*

During the 1980s, prominent genre critic Stephen Neale concluded "genres work on the terrain of repetition and difference" (quoted by Cook and Bernink 143). He describes alternating cycles of audience expectation, which is either in a state of "equilibrium" or "disruption" (143). Either the audience sees what it expects or it is surprised. Since that time, Rick Altman derived his semantic-syntactic approach to genre criticism, which looks at films from a structuralist viewpoint. He agrees that genres do change over time and even questions the reasons for this change: "But what is it that energizes

A more modern image of vampires displaying monstrous faces for preying on victims: Willow (Alyson Hannigan) and Xander (Nicholas Brendon) from Buffy the Vampire Slayer *(1977–2003).*

the transformation of a borrowed semantics into a uniquely Hollywood syntax? Or what is it that justifies the intrusion of a new semantics into a well-defined syntactic situation?" (Altman 222). Instead of exploring this avenue of genre transformation, Altman shifts his focus onto the ritual and ideological viewpoints of genre criticism. Furthermore, Altman goes on to speak of a "relatively stable generic syntax," which he implies can take years to develop. I'll discuss more of Altman's semantic-syntactic approach later.

Genre critics have danced around the question of whether genre is stable or mutable since the inception of its study. Several critics, notably Altman, Neale, and Crane, acknowledge that genres shift and change over time, yet none seem willing to examine how these changes take place. The desire to see some kind of stability in genre is overwhelming. As Altman himself states, "a fundamental problem of genre studies stems from the ever-present desire for a stable and easily identifiable object of analysis" (84). He goes on to define genre as a "complex situation," and ultimately concerns himself with where to locate genre, whether within the text, the audience, or the institutional production. Altman's concepts operate at a highly abstract level. What we need is a case study, where the "complex situations" of genre evolution can be documented.

I will use Rick Altman's semantic-syntactic approach to examine nineteen vampire narratives (in film or television) spanning seventy-two years, from 1931 to 2003. By identifying seven common semantic and syntactic elements, I can track how these elements appear and change through the films. The interplay of these elements will reveal the complex situations of genre overlap, repetition, equilibrium and disruption in the film genre.

At this point, the terms semantic and syntactic need to be defined. A semantic approach looks at the genre's building blocks, specifically things that can be counted and easily labeled. Altman quotes Marc Vernet's detailed list of building blocks that go to make up the semantic elements of a Western:

> Vernet outlines general atmosphere ("emphasis on basic elements, such as earth, dust, water, and leather"), stock characters ("the tough/soft cowboy, the lonely sheriff, the faithful or treacherous Indian, and the strong but tender woman"), as well as technical elements ("use of fast tracking and crane shots") [220].

This approach would align with Saussure's paradigmatic axis. These semantic elements are the building blocks of the genre narrative. The cowboy of the Western uses a six-shooter, not a machine gun or a sword. Those weapons would imply a wholly different genre. When I refer to semantic elements, it is to these building blocks of genre that I am referring: atmosphere, props, characters, and technical elements.

Syntax is a far more difficult concept to nail down, and I must admit I've struggled with defining it precisely. It aligns with Saussure's syntagmatic axis in that it refers to how the basic semantic elements combine to create the whole narrative. Altman pulls from Jim Kitses's work on the Western and states that syntax "emphasizes not the vocabulary of the Western but the relationships linking lexical elements" (220). Altman goes on to explain how the syntax sets up semantic expectations:

> In Western texts, regular alternation between male and female characters creates expectation of the semantic elements implied by romance, while alternation between two male characters through a text has implied—at least until recently—confrontation and the semantics of the duel [225].

Thus syntax is more related to "plot structure, character relationships or image and sound montage" (89). Syntax is a hard concept to pin down, precisely because it constitutes a relationship. Additionally, syntax relies heavily on semantic elements that make it up. The semantic elements can be changed, but this drastically alters the syntax. Take the confrontation example above. The Western duel presupposes two male characters on the opposite ends of a dusty street, each with a six-shooter strapped to his waist. These are the necessary semantic elements to enable the syntax: two gunslingers, the dusty street, and the six-shooter. Alter these elements, exchange the six-shooter for a machine gun, and the syntax is altered. Conversely, the mere inclusion of these elements (six-shooter, cowboys, a dusty street) does not constitute a Western unless they are aligned with the syntax of the duel.

I will use the relationship of syntax to semantic elements to track changes in the genre. For example, take the syntax of presenting the cross to a vampire. At its earliest introduction into film, Van Helsing holds a crucifix in his palm, and Dracula cringes, hiding his face behind a cape. This does not establish the syntax as pure or classic, but merely a starting point. Hammer films regularly used the same syntax (the vampire cringing away) but with different semantic elements (Van Helsing uses two

Count Alucard (Lon Chaney, Jr.) in Son of Dracula *(1943, Universal) cowers in the face of a cross, held by Professor Laszlo (J. Edward Bromberg).*

objects to create a cross). Later, in John Badham's 1979 *Dracula,* we see the same semantic elements (a Van Helsing character presenting a crucifix) but with an altered syntax (the vampire grips the cross and it burns). These alterations of either syntax or semantic elements underpin the evolution of the genre. Most often these changes are subtle, but occasionally, intense mutations of the syntax or semantic elements occur. Whether these mutations are taken up and repeated by other films shows the relative success of such mutations. The fact that many other films used (and often parodied) the Hammer style of crossing two objects to form a cross speaks of it as an enduring syntactic element in the vampire narrative. On the other hand few other films have taken up the syntax of the vampire laughing at the crucifix. Therefore this mutation failed to be added to the genre of vampire narratives as a whole.

The scope of this work tracks vampire films over a long period of

Dracula (Frank Langella), no longer afraid of it, grabs a cross held by Jonathan Harker (Trevor Eve) and it instantly ignites, in this scene from Dracula *(1979, Universal).*

time, from 1931 up until 2003. I have made a conscious choice to divide the vampire narrative corpus into three cycles of films, which roughly align to historical periods: The Malignant Cycle (1931–1948), the Erotic Cycle (1957–1985), and the Sympathetic Cycle (1987–present day). There are many other divisions I could have made. For instance I might have divided along purely historical lines, and split the films up by decades, but I felt this was too arbitrary and ignored groups of films which clearly shared a common thread or even a series of films (such as Hammer) that spanned several decades. Another system might be to break the films along studio or national lines, like Universal films, Hammer films, or Mexican films. This too has its limitations. It would ignore standalone works like *Return of the Vampire*, and would also become mired in the individual films of the 70s, 80s and 90s, after the collapse of the Classic Hollywood studio system.

The film cycles I have chosen are based on a shared syntax. In other words, they fit together as a whole, exploring some of the same themes, and repeating semantic elements. Additionally each cycle is followed by a slump in the industry in which few new vampire narrative films were being made. By making this division along structural and historical lines I can break the films in cohesive yet manageable groups for study.

The next obvious question is which movies to include or exclude? Rick Altman explains that "nearly every genre critic offers a long list of films, but only treats a few of them. Sometimes this restriction is done consciously and openly" (24). In order to avoid rampant genre overlap and extreme taxonomy, I have had to exclude certain films. This is not to say that these films do not share certain semantic or syntactic elements with vampire films, but the line has to fall somewhere. As a whole I have excluded pornographic films, and films where the vampire is based entirely on an alien creature (e.g. *Planet of the Vampires*). Additionally, the list of films includes only vampires who drain blood and not life-force (e.g. *Scanners*).

I have further culled the list down to nineteen films, all of which evolve from the original vampire mythology as set down by Bram Stoker's novel *Dracula*. Again, I am not saying that this is the classic example of the vampire narrative; far from it. Instead I wish to follow the evolution of the supernatural vampire through the genre. This means that I have had to exclude several films from the book that I hold in the highest esteem. According to Altman, "all genre terms are implicitly authored; that is, they are always the product of a specific user group" (99). With this in mind, I must separate myself as the viewer from myself as the critic. Although the viewer in me might include certain films, I have to exclude them if they do not fit the scope of this book. Four example films will help define what constitutes a vampire film for the purposes of this book.

There is no doubt that Friedrich Wilhelm Murnau's *Nosferatu, Eine Symphonie des Grauens* (*Symphony of Horror*) is a piece of landmark cinema, both for its Expressionist filmmaking and its unique treatment of the vampire as plague. It, however, carries little weight when the historical exhibition of the film is considered. The film was exhibited for a short time in Germany and Budapest during 1922 through 1925. Afterward, under the persistent influence of Florence Stoker, the film was believed to be destroyed. It managed to resurface in 1929, playing to audiences in New York and Detroit. However, preeminent Dracula scholar David J. Skal writes that the film "was not taken seriously" (103) and that most audiences considered it "a boring picture" (100). *Nosferatu* was purchased by Universal to "see what had already been produced" (108) and Skal believes that the film "almost certainly [had] been studied by all the key creative personnel" (128) leading to the Universal production of *Dracula* in 1931. J. Gordon Melton, author of *The Vampire Book* traced the survival of the original *Nosferatu* film. An abridged version was aired on television in the 1960s as part of *Silents Please,* and subsequently released by Entertainment films under the title *Terror of Dracula,* and then again by Blackhawk Films under the name *Dracula* (Melton 499). Blackhawk also released the original version to the collector's market under the title *Nosferatu the Vampire.* An unabridged copy of the movie survived Florence Stoker's death warrant and was restored and screened at Berlin's Film Festival in 1984.

Despite its influence on the making of the 1931 *Dracula, Nosferatu* has few syntactic descendants (aside from the revised and condensed re-releases of its original text). The syntax of vampire as a scourging plague has only been seriously taken up by two films: the 1979 remake by Werner Herzog, *Nosferatu: The Vampyre,* and the 1979 television miniseries of *Salem's Lot,* directed by Tobe Hooper. The fact that this syntax has been so seldom explored highlights the fact that it is tangential to the vampire narrative genre as a whole. Perhaps if the original *Nosferatu, Eine Symphonie des Grauens* had been allowed regular release, this would not be the case. Thus, for the purposes of this book, the syntax of vampire must have had a significant effect on the genre at some point (that effect may have faded by present day). In other words, it needs to be repeated by subsequent films or television series at some point.

The next two films are included in nearly all canons of important vampire films, despite the fact that neither contains a true supernatural vampire: Tod Browning's 1927 *London After Midnight,* and its remake, released in 1935 as *Mark of the Vampire.* The reasons for inclusion are no doubt tied to the direction of Tod Browning in both films, and the appearance of Bela Lugosi in the 1935 version. However, neither film offers up a true undead villain; in each case the villains are a troupe of actors pretending to be vampires. Therefore, for the purpose of this book, only vampires exhibiting supernatural abilities will be considered.

Melton considers Mario Bava to be responsible for "several of the most memorable vampire films of the 1960s" (44). His most "important" and "classic" vampire film is *La Maschera del Demonio* (released in the United States as *Black Sunday*) (45). This is the closest Bava ever comes to portraying a vampire fashioned off the mythology as set forth by Bram Stoker. Although a drop of blood returns Asa, the vampire of the film, back to life, she drains her counterpart, Katia, through touch rather than bite. The transfer drains life-force rather than blood, and Asa appears to take on the role of a resurrected witch more so than a vampire. As for Bava's later efforts, the 1961 *Ercole al Centro della Terra* (*Hercules in the Haunted World*) is linked to vampirism simply by casting Christopher Lee in the role of Hades, while *Terrore nello Spazio* (released in the United States as *Planet of the Vampires*) falls more into the genre of science fiction than horror. With these limitations in mind, the vampire of this book must consume blood to live.

There are quite a few films that meet all of the above specifications for a vampire (repetition of syntax throughout the genre, the exhibiting of supernatural abilities, and the need to consume blood), and yet still must be eliminated

Bava's film was also released under the title The Devil's Commandment. *The movie poster stated: "The Mad Scientist Who Killed for Fun!"*

The film The Fearless Vampire Killers; Or Pardon Me, But Your Teeth Are in My Neck *is a spoof of the Hammer Dracula films.*

from our study. The film *Cronos* by Guillermo del Toro is an apt example. In this film a mechanism (a product of science) creates the condition of vampirism. Likewise, Bava's *I Vampiri* functions under the same "scientific" principle. The blood from the victims is used to keep the Duchess alive via a machine that resembles many of the atomic and mad-scientist instruments of the 1950s movies. Therefore, the vampires of this book need to be supernatural in their creation as well as existence. It is upon these limitations that I have formed the list of nineteen films.

Finally there are some wonderful additions to the genre in the form of comedies, notably Andy Warhol's Dracula, *The Fearless Vampire Killers, Love at First Bite,* and *Once Bitten.* Although these films are worthy of consideration, I must take into account the adaptations made in order to create a comedy. The lead character (in most cases the vampire) must be softened and made sympathetic in order for the comedy to work. This bypasses much of the syntax built into the genre, replacing it with a parody of the vampire syntax or borrowed syntax from the genre of comedy.

Within this narrow scope of films I endeavor to answer the question of how and why genres transform over time. What semantic or syntactic elements repeat, and how do new syntactic elements originate? Where is the separation point between syntax and the semantic elements that support it? In order to tackle these questions we must consider whether genre films change at all, and how genre criticism has handled the fixed notion of the "classic." An overview of genre criticism as a whole is needed. By seeing the problems faced and overcome within the area of genre study, the answer to these current questions can be better addressed.

The State of Genre Criticism

Clearly genres change. Despite critics who expound the mythic qualities of horror movies, modern audiences do not view older films in the same way. Horror genre critic Jonathan Lake Crane exemplifies this idea when he states that the Universal films "are not" scary and "do not" attract modern audiences (26). Yet even with this obvious evidence in place, many critics seem to shy away from the question of just what makes a genre transform. Most understand that genres reflect changes in society. Genre critic Leo Baudry (quoted in Hayward 162) likens genre to a "barometer of the social and cultural concerns of cinema-going audiences." But exactly how does this barometer work? If genre is not static, then why are words like classic or stable still used to describe genre?

The notion of a static genre is illustrated through how critics view the genre of horror. Both Andrew Tudor and Brian Murphy (quoted in Cook and Bernink 195) see horror as ahistorical, simple, and static. For Murphy the genre is governed by "absolutely inflexible laws," such as werewolves transforming "always on nights of the full moon," and vampires always having an aversion to garlic. The idea that any genre must impose a syntax of "always" is a frightening concept. It dooms the genre to endless repetition. Furthermore, Tudor distances horror from genres that "inform and deepen," like the Western, because of the "rigid simplicity of the horror film's conventions."

Rick Altman pins the core instigator of a static genre on the critic's desire for synchronic analysis. A synchronic analysis means that a critic will analyze a genre through a series of discrete films—a bit like examining a film only a frame at a time. Even when a genre like the Western is tied to history, it is only through "a discontinuous succession of discrete moments" (221). In other words, critics still view and analyze genre by studying individual films. Altman suggests that rather than deal openly with an evolving concept of genre, critics have created "categories designed to negate the notion of change [...]. Westerns and horror films are often referred to as 'classic.'" Altman calls this system of genre study "insulated" from the "flow of time."

Even when critics do acknowledge that genre films require some variation, they do so with one of two restricted paradigms, both related to organic metaphors (Altman 21). The first treats genre as a living being, "with individual films reflecting age brackets." Critics like Jane Feuer, Thomas Schatz and John Cawelti speak of the "life cycles" of films. These critics simply rename the "classic" period of the genre under the new heading "coming of age." Altman quotes Cawelti on the ages of the adventure genre as moving from a time of "innocence," to "experience," and then "disillusionment."

Perhaps the reason this metaphor is so pervasive is due in part to genre study being limited to the Western, musical, or gangster. These genres did seem to follow a predictable life cycle. Each had its heyday, and then became worn out and predictable, virtually disappearing. The fact that there are only a few new Westerns or musicals of note since their demise would seem to point to the veracity of the paradigm. Similarly, the "gangsta" movies of the 90s are so vastly different from their originals that they are perhaps treated as separate life forms. What is ignored in this paradigm is the longevity of horror films. Hollywood has been churning these out for over 90 years.

An additional problem manifests itself when we consider the horror genre as a whole, and its polymorphic tendencies. The slasher film is worlds apart from the mad scientist film, which is also entirely different from the vampire film. When the films are viewed as a group, there seems little to round these concepts together under one banner. Instead, if we narrow our focus to the subgenres of horror, we find narrative forms that maintain their existence without succumbing to the death throes of the life cycle paradigm. Films involving vampires have been made nearly consistently since 1931. Perhaps the longevity of the subgenre is due to the immortal nature of the vampire persona, but more likely it points to a flaw in the paradigm. Genres like the Western or musical may seem to die simply because they have not resurrected in a form acceptable to the genre critic. Consider that much of the syntax of the Western may have drifted into the early police drama or cop movies, while the musical, for a time, had its rebirth in the animated films of Disney.

The second organic metaphor stressed by critics is that of biological evolution. Even this model does not accept true variation within the ranks of genre, but embraces predictability. Much of this paradigm encourages a view of films as cycles, each invoking a different aspect of syntax. These cycles therefore account for the variation in genre, but they ultimately repeat. These critics would simply have the genre's syntax shuttle between experimentation and reflexivity, ad infinitum. Altman quotes Feuer's treatment of the backstage musical as evidence for a predictable, and ultimately fixed, view of genre.

> The backstage musical provides a textbook illustration of a genre's development from a period of experimentation in which the conventions are established (1929–33) to a *classical* period during which a balance reigns (1933–53) to a period of reflexivity dominated by parody, contestation and even deconstruction of a genre's native tongue. Indeed, the neat unfolding I have just been enumerating has about it an almost *mathematical* precision, as if one could out of a table of permutations have predicted the emergence of certain new combinations at certain periods in the genre's history [22, emphasis added].

No, this is never the case! If all the factors of audience expectation, studio solvency, and auteurist predisposition could all be accounted for, then perhaps such a prediction might be made. Yet again Feuer's example speaks of a "classical period" that is clearly seen as the purist form for the genre. All other cycles are mere deviations from this "classic moment."

In order for the evolutionary paradigm to work, it must account for the "unexpected mutations" that occur in the scientific model (Altman 22). To quote Richard Dawkins, a zoologist at Oxford and noted evolutionary theorist, "Nothing actually wants to evolve. Evolution is something that happens, willy-nilly" (18). In order for a gene, a basic building block of a living organism, to survive, it must replicate. "One gene may be regarded as a unit that survives through a large number of successive individual bodies" (25). In other words, what Dawkins is pitching is a reevaluation of evolution, from the species level down to the gene level. Genes are the things that want to reproduce, and force organisms toward that end. If we graft genre onto Dawkins' theory of evolution, the result is a system which now examines the smallest working part of the genre: the syntax. By replacing the terms in Dawkins' quote, we get the following view of evolutionary genre: One syntactic element may be regarded as a unit that survives through a large number of successive individual films. Let us again revisit the syntax of THE CROSS as it appears in vampire narratives. Initially the Van Helsing character keeps the vampire at bay through the use of a proffered crucifix. Yet in later films, two crossed objects suffice. Over the course of several films, the syntactic element has reproduced and survived. In even later films the syntax mutates, looking radically different from the original. But, just as modern-day humans look different from chimpanzees through gradual steps of evolution, films of the vampire genre look drastically different when compared side by side.

This idea of syntactic evolution might explain why genres seem to disappear. Some of the syntax of the Western may have drifted into police drama (cop genre). The semantic elements were replaced with modern equivalents (cars for horses, asphalt for dusty road), but the syntax of the duel remains; take the end scene of *Dirty Harry* for example. Another possibility is the mutation of genres into forms not recognized by the original, from the gangster films of the 30s to the gangsta films of the 90s. As Dawkins points out, "An octopus is nothing like a mouse, and both are quite different from an oak tree. Yet in their fundamental chemistry they are rather uniform" (21). Is syntax the fundamental chemistry of genre?

Rather than a *single* "classic period" of balance, I propose thinking of genre as having *several* periods of equilibrium. This balance of experimentation and reflexivity remains in check until an "unexpected mutation" sets it off balance. This could be anything from the collapse of a studio to the removal of a key actor, or even the repression or freedom of ideas under censorship. The audience can also take control of genre mutation. When the genre becomes exhausted, it uses up all its known semantic and syntactic variations until the formula becomes trite and boring. This forces the viewers to seek out new syntactic elements from other genres. This effect is seen in the mutation of the vampire films of the 60s (Hammer Studios), to the vampire pastiches of the 80s (*Fright Night*).

The repetition ingrained in genre has a very practical motive. The studios that invented genres did so because they represented a predictable and marketable commodity. If the audience expects a certain type of movie, the studio will deliver it, even to the point of studios specializing in the "production of certain genres and not others" (Hayward 165). Why vary the formula when it can be counted on to bring in a certain profit? Richard Dawkins would emphasize that nothing wants to evolve. To alter a genre too quickly might turn off the core audience and spell doom for the film, and sometimes the studio. Only minor variations, for the sake of avoiding overt reduplication, are added.

All of this speaks to genre history. By tracing the effects of industry on genre, we may be able to see the evolution of the syntax. Altman views history as vitally important, stating that it "cries out for increased attention by virtue of its ability to scramble generic codes, to blur established generic tableaux and to muddy accepted generic ideas" (12).

Another factor closely aligned to genre history is intertextuality. Films continually refer to each other, drawing from experience, learning from past mistakes. Robert Warshow argues that genre films refer to other genre films and that they create their "own field of reference" (quoted by Cook and Bernink 141). This intertextuality plays on audience expectation. Audiences expect to see a film similar to those that came before, so the producers and artists involved must become knowledgeable of previous films in the genre. "The pleasure of genre film spectatorship," Altman says, "thus derives more from reaffirmation than from novelty" (25). Horror films are unique in that fans have a "cultist knowledge stored up over the decades" (Cook and Bernink 194). Thus, when fans know more of the history of films, they expect more. Producers and auteurs must also be fluent in the genre in order to deliver a film that meets these expectations. Baudry explains that "Some genres films 'fail' because the audience feels that they have not adhered to the generic conventions sufficiently or because they are out of touch with contemporary times" (quoted by Hayward 162). What is a truism for most genres, becomes doubly so with horror. The conventions of this genre are held up to scrutiny by the fans with what compares to religious fervor.

The closest example we have to a true study on genre evolution comes from W. Wright's *Six Guns and Society*. Wright sets up a pair of opposing syntactic elements. In one case the hero protects civilization from the villains outside it. The opposing view makes the society corrupt, with the hero attacking the villains living within its bounds (Hayward 163). The process for the evolution from one extreme to the other is not described, although the change is not as radical as it might seem. The syntax remains the same (the same pattern of confrontation) except the semantic elements have been reversed. This is quite different from the radical departure vampire narratives took in 1987 with the arrival of *The Lost Boys* and *Near Dark*.

When vampire narratives shifted their syntax in the mid 80s, it was more than a simple change of semantics. It was a complete transformation of narrative style. To understand this better, we have to first understand how Andrew Tudor divided the narrative into three types (Cook and Bernink 203). The first is the knowledge narrative, which shows the dangers of scientific knowledge. *Frankenstein* falls neatly into this category. The second is the invasion narrative. Here the unknown invades the known world and wreaks havoc. *Dracula* is an example of this, arriving as he does in England to destroy the character's normalcy. Finally Tudor has the metamorphosis narrative in which the unconscious or the insane emerges within an individual to threaten the known world. The werewolf films epitomize this narrative, detailing the struggle of the lead character to fight against his transformation into a monster. These films can engender a high degree of sympathy for the plight of the monster.

The syntactic evolution in vampire narrative in *The Lost Boys* and *Near Dark* is also a shift in basic narrative structure. The invasion narrative, though still a part of the films, is overshadowed by an emerging metamorphosis narrative. Both of the films' lead characters struggle against vampirism just as Lon Chaney Jr. struggled against the curse of the werewolf. It might seem that the syntax of the werewolf films was borrowed in this new generation of films, though the exact evolution is more complex and will be detailed later.

Furthermore, Tudor goes on to illuminate another shift in narratives that began in the 60s. Earlier films are described as "secure" horror, where there is a clear demarcation between monster and human (Cook and Bernink 204). These films have a redeeming moral and social order that ultimately triumphs at the end (Dracula is destroyed by Van Helsing). However, following a movie like *Psycho*, Tudor argues that there is a shift

In this scene from The Lost Boys *(1987, Warner Bros.), Michael (Jason Patric, not pictured) must overcome his desire to drink blood, even as the rest of the vampire gang taunts him. Left to right: Dwayne, (Billy Wirth), David (Kiefer Sutherland), Paul (Brooke McCarter), Marko (Alex Winter).*

toward 'paranoid' horror that is linked with the metamorphosis narrative. Here the "principal oppositions are internal to the human condition." It may very well be that in order to survive as a genre, vampire narratives adapted to the pressures of the newer "paranoid" horror, aligning themselves with "slasher" horror or films like *The Fly*.

Horror films, and specifically vampire narratives, are aptly suited for a discussion of genre evolution. The vampire genre has had a long life, with only two major slumps, and continues even to today to produce innovative additions to the corpus. A look at the current state of genre criticism has revealed that the question of a fluid, evolving genre has yet to be fully defined and analyzed. The theoretical groundwork has been laid. Let us move onto the films themselves, and see how the transformation from malignant vampire as villain to sympathetic vampire as hero was accomplished.

Semantic-Syntactic Analysis

The semantic-syntactic analysis covers seven areas of interest that evolve through the corpus of vampire films. THE LOOK encompasses the hypnotic stare the vampire uses to control his victims. It primarily deals with the mise-en-scène shot of the vampire staring down an adversary or victim, and also the unspoken communication inherent in the scene. THE BITE explores how the vampire attacks his or her victim, what is seen or unseen in the shot, and how the victim reacts to the attack. The victim's response to becoming a vampire is included under the heading THE INFECTION. This also covers how the vampire deals with the life and conditions of vampirism. The Van Helsing character is dealt with in THE EXPERT, and THE VAMPIRE covers his adversary. Both of these areas discuss the character's appearance, disposition, and mannerisms. The most semantically grounded area is THE CROSS, which accounts for the most prevalent method for repelling a vampire. Finally, how the vampire is ultimately destroyed figures into THE DESTRUCTION. All these aspects are considered via a mise-en-scène analysis, along with available information on the production of the film.

In order to view how the syntax and semantic elements change over time, I have gathered these elements together and charted their progression in Appendix B. Additionally, in order to fully understand the evolution of these elements, the reader should be familiar with the films studied. A synopsis of each film is included in Appendix A.

1

The Malignant Cycle
(1931–1948)

Overview

The films that constitute the malignant cycle, from 1931 to 1948, are highly experimental, with many syntactic and semantic elements explored for the first time. *Dracula* was shot only shortly after the development of talkies and is the first horror film to include sound. Although Lon Chaney's silent films paved the way for horror on film, *Dracula* was to be the bellwether film for the sound age. Many syntactic elements were introduced and subsequently abandoned for years before reemerging in later films. This being said, the films of this cycle do share similar qualities.

The role of the vampire is always one of villainy. Most of the screen time is devoted to the human heroes who do battle with this invading monster. The vampire is always elegant and aristocratic, often dressed in fine clothes. Although, it should be noted that the heroes are also often wealthy in these films, and that for the vampire to travel in their circle, he or she would likewise need to be a moneyed person.

The vampire primarily bites victims in a state of helplessness, either asleep or entranced, and all bites are administered off camera, leaving the audience to infer the attack. The reasons for these omissions are most likely due to censorship and the film code established in Hollywood. Additionally, the victims are primarily female victims (with the notable exception of Dracula biting Renfield). The fangs of the vampire are only inferred from the puncture marks left on the neck, and the bite marks themselves are also merely described. Only in *Son of Dracula* does the audience actually see the two puncture marks.

A new syntax for vampire destruction develops throughout the films of this cycle, one that will become just as common as the stake. Although based on Stoker's novel, and the subsequent stage play by Deane and Balderston, the vampire quickly exhibits an aversion to sunlight. Fans of the novel will remember that Dracula is able to emerge into sunlight,

21

though he is much less powerful. By the end of this cycle of films, a new syntax of destruction by sunlight has entered the genre (as evidenced in *Son of Dracula,* and *Return of the Vampire*).

Finally, a syntax of betrayal pervades the films of this cycle. In each of the four films, the vampire has a servant that betrays him or her. In *Dracula* Renfield tries to convince Seward to send Mina away. Ultimately Dracula breaks his neck for leading Van Helsing and John to Carfax Abbey (although this had nothing to do with Renfield's actions). In *Dracula's Daughter* Sandor wants the Countess to remain a vampire in order to give him eternal life. When he discovers that she plans to give eternal life to another, Dr. Garth, he attempts to kill the doctor, but instead destroys the countess. *Son of Dracula* is evidence to the ultimate betrayal, as Count Alucard is essentially duped by Kay, who then sends her lover, Frank, to destroy him. Tesla abandons Andreas, in *Return of the Vampire,* freeing the servant to attack his former master. In the end he destroys the vampire by dragging him out into the sun, and driving a stake through his heart.

Dracula (1931)

Dracula was the first vampire film to be seen in wide release (see previous notes on *Nosferatu*). All subsequent movies would, to one degree or another, look back upon this film for inspiration. The dominant syntax in Tod Browning's *Dracula* is The Look. The film dedicates twelve shots to Dracula's piercing stare. As Dracula first emerges from his coffin he stares at the camera, as though trying to mesmerize the audience. The camera tracks forward, drawing us forward. His face is highlighted, emphasizing the pale skin and jet black hair. Later, at the Borgo Pass, a befuddled Renfield finds himself face to face with Dracula (disguised as the driver). Here two pinpoints of light illuminate Dracula's eyes as he gazes out toward Renfield, his face filling the screen. In the castle, during dinner, there are three separate scenes where Dracula levels his piercing gaze at Renfield. Here a bar of light is thrown across his face to highlight the eyes. On the ship to London, we once more encounter the pinpoint lights on Dracula's eyes, as he stares down a now rambling and clearly mad Renfield. Before Dracula encounters the lead characters at the theatre, he enthralls a young flower girl. The shot of Dracula's face again shows a bar of light across his eyes.

Once in London, the intensity of Dracula's Look changes. At the theatre Dracula mesmerizes a young servant girl. What is interesting about the composition of this shot is that unlike earlier scenes, where the vampire's hypnotic power is illustrated through a close-up of his face, here Dracula has his back to the camera, and we see only the glazed look of the female usher. After a moment, the film cuts to Dracula's face and the characteristic highlight of his eyes. Another interesting scene comes after Dracula is introduced to Mina, Lucy, Dr. Seward and John. The Count gazes at Lucy after she has returned to watching the ballet. Here the syntax of THE LOOK is not employed to control or dominate, but rather to show Dracula's burning desire. Additionally, instead of highlighting his eyes, three-quarters of Dracula's face is lit.

The rest of the film has Dracula interacting with the other characters, which leaves him less time to sink into his characteristic LOOK. All the following instances occur when Dracula is alone with a single victim. At Seward's Sanatorium, Dracula stands outside, and the camera views him with a long-shot. Renfield seems to be communicating with a taciturn Count. Finally the film gives us the close-up on Dracula's face, again with the highlighted eyes. In his confrontation with Van Helsing, there is no overt lighting of Dracula's face or eyes. Instead, the Count uses his hands to control the scientist and draw him forward. Also, instead of staying silent, Dracula says, "Come here." Van Helsing takes a few halting steps forward, but then backs away, apparently shaking off the vampire's control. The final example of THE LOOK appears when Dracula stands outside Mina's bedroom and wills the maid to remove the wolfsbane. There is a close-up on Dracula's face, but no extra lighting is provided.

Some of the inconsistencies in the lighting of Dracula's face could be explained through the lack of direction. Apparently Tod Browning was an absentee director. David Manners, who played John Harker, recalls that "Tod Browning was always off to the side somewhere," and that for the most part he was directed by the photographer, Karl Freund (Skal 130). Additionally, Browning did not pay close attention to how the film was shot and edited. In one scene, on the balcony, there is an "endless take" of about three minutes where the camera never moves. David J. Skal comments that this was "clearly meant to be broken up with close-ups and reaction shots" (130).

A closer examination of the syntax of THE LOOK reveals that in all but one instance, Dracula is alone with the recipient of his gaze. The semantic elements include the vampire and victim. The face is nearly always shown full frame and the eyes are lit. The syntax implies that some form of unspoken communication is working, perhaps through the eyes, and the victim is forced to comply. The purpose of THE LOOK seems to be the hypnosis and control of the victim.

The appearance of THE VAMPIRE is that of the dignified aristocrat.

Although a cape is mentioned in Stoker's novel, it figures prominently with Bela Lugosi's Dracula. In many scenes, Dracula uses the cape to envelop a victim or to shield his face from a proffered cross. The famous accent that was to become associated with Dracula was more a result of Lugosi's inadequacy with English than an intentional effect. Lugosi had to learn his lines phonetically, and this accounted for some of the odd pauses he inserts into his lines.

Count Dracula's face is deathly pale with full dark lips. This may be an extension of the stage play where Lugosi wore green makeup to accent the deathly pallor of his character. Skal states that Lugosi "clashed with the Universal make up man, Jack Pierce, over the character's appearance [...] insisting on doing his makeup himself" (132). Skal implies that it was Lugosi who refused to wear the fangs, a clear part in the script. Yet Browning and the studio may have also contributed to the lack of this highly identifiable vampire trait. Skal regards Browning as "lazy," saying that he "sabotaged" the script's visual potential. Budget may have also played a factor. The original script had a scene on the boat to England that called for a large close-up of Dracula, fangs bared. However Skal (quoting Lugosi) says, "the studios were hell-bent on saving money" (131). The boat footage itself was reused from an earlier silent film (*The Storm Breaker*), which accounts for the jerky, speeded up appearance of the sailors. Another scene, in the script but cut from the film, involved the Count's attack of the flower girl. Here the script called for Dracula to part his lips and reveal fangs. Finally, the scene in Lucy's bedroom may have been affected by censorship. The Hayes Code required films to conform in many ways to a predetermined moral code. The scene with Lucy was toned down from the original script that called for Dracula to show canine-like teeth. All these factors conspire to eliminate a physical factor of the vampire that the audience surely knew was there. The bite marks are described as two holes. The novel itself describes the fangs. The overall effect of the absence of fangs was to make THE VAMPIRE appear more human and less supernatural.

Once the victim is under Dracula's thrall, the vampire moves in for THE BITE. It should be strongly noted that Dracula is never seen biting anyone. All the bites are inferred by the position of his body and the subsequent dialogue regarding bite marks on the neck. These marks are also never shown. No doubt a great deal of these missing moments are a result of the censorship of the film. The first BITE occurs when Renfield succumbs to the drugged wine. The three vampire brides approach the prone figure, only to be swept away by Dracula. The Count leans over Renfield, hands held out like claws. The scene ends as Dracula descends slowly toward the body. This is the only male character that Dracula attacks in the film. The next BITE scene occurs immediately after Dracula arrives in London with the flower girl. Here Dracula employs THE LOOK to paralyze his victim. He then grasps her shoulders and the two drift off camera before the bite is actually delivered.

The remaining BITE scenes involve the other major characters, Lucy and Mina. In both instances Dracula enters the bedroom through an opened window in the form of a bat and returns to human form via a cutaway to the sleeping victim. With Lucy, Dracula approaches gradually until almost face to face with the sleeping woman. At this point the scene fades, implying a bite. Later, when he approaches Mina, the film cuts to a subjective camera, from Mina's point of view, with Lugosi's face dominating the frame. This scene also fades before the bite is accomplished. The final BITE inflicted by Dracula happens outside the home. Dracula draws Mina outside, opens his cape, and turns to envelop her. The cape blocks the viewer from seeing this bite.

The syntax of THE BITE in *Dracula* involves the semantic elements of

This publicity still from Dracula *(1931, Universal) is as close as Dracula (Bela Lugosi) comes to biting Mina (Helen Chandler).*

vampire and victim. The staging of each scene has the victim either sleeping or hypnotized, thus the semantic elements of a bedroom or the glazed look of a trance is required. In four out of the five scenes, the victim is sleeping (Renfield is drugged, lying on the floor). These bites always occur in private, and often in the bedroom, considered a very private area.

THE INFECTION differs for Lucy and Mina. Lucy seems to die after one bite. She then returns later as the woman in white (described in a newspaper article). Yet Mina requires a series of bites to transform her into a vampire. Once bitten by Dracula, she seems to spend the rest of the film in a kind of trance. On the patio, Mina exhibits a trance-like state. She stares at John's neck longingly. After receiving instructions from a circling bat (assumed to be Dracula), she asks John to hide Van Helsing's cross. She then attempts to mimic Dracula's LOOK and fixes John in her gaze. He is befuddled, questioning her behavior. Mina leans forward, toward John and the camera. Finally the two move off camera. The bite is ultimately stopped by the intervention of Van Helsing and his crucifix. Later, Mina explains that, in addition to biting her, Dracula made her drink his blood. After Dracula has the wolfsbane removed from her room, Mina comes to him and follows him to Carfax Abbey. The connection between Dracula and his victim is made overt when Van Helsing stakes Dracula. Mina clutches her chest, and then seems to have broken free from the trance. She tells John, "I heard you calling, but couldn't say anything." This implies that, once bitten, the vampire exerts a kind of mental control over his victim. This syntax is mimicked in the character of Renfield, who seems to respond to Dracula telepathically. Interestingly, the film never deals with the flower girl who was bitten early on. Did she return as Lucy did? Additionally Lucy's sub-plot is never fully developed. Skal notes that this storyline was "simply dropped in mid-film and never resolved" (139).

The implied syntax of THE INFECTION is that the victim falls under the control of the vampire. A trance-like state (or maniacal in the case of Renfield) falls over the victim's face after being bitten. Even though the victim may not want to follow Dracula's command, she is helpless to resist.

THE EXPERT in *Dracula* is of course Van Helsing. Here the doctor is portrayed as a scientist. In his first appearance in the film, he is analyzing a vial of blood in a test tube. He has white hair and thick round glasses. Upon testing the blood he concludes that the culprit is the undead or nosferatu. When Seward objects to such a creature being real, Van Helsing responds by saying, "The superstition of yesterday can become the scientific reality of today." Van Helsing takes on the role of scientific expert, legitimizing the supernatural myth with scientific reality. Van Helsing's most defining moment comes in his individual confrontation with the Count.

Dracula's mind control seems to have only a brief effect on the expert, who then responds with his tool of control, the cross.

THE CROSS is not the weapon of choice for Van Helsing, who prefers wolfsbane (oddly substituted for garlic). A crucifix first appears in the opening scene in Transylvania. The innkeeper's wife gives Renfield a small rosary to protect him. Later, at the dinner table inside Dracula's castle, Renfield has need of it. He cuts his finger on a paperclip, and Dracula is drawn toward the blood. In a close-up of Renfield's hand, the crucifix falls into the shot. Instantly Dracula pivots away and throws his arm up to cover his face. In the confrontation between the vampire and Van Helsing, Dracula exhibits a similar action. Van Helsing casually holds the cross in front of his chest. Dracula now uses his cape to block his face. He spins around and flees from the room. Soon after, Van Helsing uses the same crucifix (it appears to be the same prop used by Renfield) to prevent Mina from biting John. The reaction to this cross, however, is not shown on screen. Rather Van Helsing rushes onto the patio and the audience hears a scream from Mina off camera. John takes the cross away, and Helen Chandler, the actress who played Mina, seems to forget that it is still in the scene. John, holding the crucifix, tries to calm her. When Chandler finally notices that John is still holding the cross, she turns away from it, though not as violently as did Dracula.

The syntax of THE CROSS in the film *Dracula* involves the semantic elements of a small crucifix, an expert, and a vampire. There seems no need for a dramatic gesture in presenting the cross. Even with Renfield, the rosary simply falls into the shot. The vampire's response is the same: hide the face and move away. The hiding of the face might be linked to the vampire's ability to control via his eyes.

At the end of the film, Van Helsing finally destroys Dracula. The syntax of THE DESTRUCTION involves the EXPERT (here Van Helsing) destroying the vampire asleep in his coffin. In the actual scene, Van Helsing and John find Dracula asleep after the sun had risen. Van Helsing creates a stake by ripping apart the coffin lid. He then positions the makeshift stake above the body of Dracula, and holds a crowbar up to deliver the fatal blow. The actual deed is not shown. Only the sound of the blow is heard through the cavernous crypt.

The effects of sunlight are hinted at throughout the film. When Renfield arrives in Transylvania, the film cuts to a shot of the sun setting. The innkeeper says, "Look! The sun. When it is gone, they leave their coffins." Van Helsing confirms that the vampire's power "lasts only from sunset to sunrise." In addition, there are two scenes (the same shot repeated twice to save money) where Dracula emerges from his coffin just as the sun sets.

These semantic elements of the sun setting and the vampire's coffin fore-shadow a new method of destruction, which will eventually equal the stake.

Dracula's Daughter

Universal faced a unique problem when making the next movie in the Dracula series (a problem that would later plague Hammer). According to Skal, Bela Lugosi "had reached the point of actually hating the part" (132). Added to this was the acknowledged fact that Lugosi had a drug addiction, which made him an unreliable actor. This left Universal with no star to play Dracula. How could they create a Dracula movie with no lead character? The solution Universal pursued was to loosely adapt a novella by Bram Stoker called "Dracula's Guest."

As a whole, this film relies heavily on the psychological aspects of vampirism. The vampire, Countess Marya Zaleska, struggles with her condition, creating the first sympathetic vampire in film. After burning Dracula's body, she says, "Free, free forever [...] free to live as a woman. Free to take my place in the bright world of the living, instead of among the shadows of the dead." The theme of freedom, a release from her condition, dominates the film. On the next night, Marya says, "The spell is broken. I can live a normal life now, think normal things, even play normal music again." However the notes she plays on the piano become frantic. Her servant, Sandor, takes her burgeoning hope and twists it to darkness. When Marya asks what he sees in her eyes, he responds with one word: "Death."

Later, at the dinner party, Marya meets the psychiatrist Geoffrey Garth. He considers vampirism a mental disease. "Like any disease of the mind," Garth states, "it can be cured. All we have to discover is what brought about the obsession in order to affect mental release." Marya repeats the last word, "release," soon to become a motto for her long sought freedom.

The Countess attempts to test her will power by having Sandor bring her a young model. She says she will test the "strength of a human mind against the powers of darkness." What's interesting here is the use of the word human. Clearly, this film regards vampirism as less supernatural and more of a mental affliction. Aligned with this viewpoint, Dracula's daughter has no special abilities like her father. Her only ability of note is THE LOOK she employs to subdue her victims, and even here she requires a ring.

After Marya succumbs to her desire for blood, she confides once more in Dr. Garth. "It came over me again, that awful power and command, wordless, insistent, and I had to obey." She hints that somehow Dracula is controlling her from the grave. The curse of vampirism is stronger than her human will.

The syntax of THE INFECTION in *Dracula's Daughter* shows a vampire who is at odds with her condition. She continually yo-yos from the optimism that she will overcome her condition to a fervent descent into bloodlust. The only other victim to survive (for a short time) is Lili, a girl plagued with amnesia, whose eyes are glazed over in a trance. When the doctors finally bring her around, Lili is able to get out a few scattered words before dying.

The appearance of THE VAMPIRE starts off as mysterious, in the same fashion as Dracula, but she quickly blends with the other characters in the film. Her entrance into the film is strikingly composed through the use of a black cloak and hood, with her eyes as the only feature visible. Yet after the initial scene, the Countess changes wardrobes several times. Her clothes begin black, and over the course of the film change to grey. Compare these to Janet's white dress and stole. The outfits of the two women may be symbolic of the opposition of good and evil as they vie for the same prize: Doctor Geoffrey Garth.

Another unique aspect of this film is that it has not one, but two EXPERTS. Van Helsing carries over from *Dracula* and he introduces the audience to Dr. Garth, a noted psychiatrist. Their first conversation, in the doctor's study, echoes the science over superstition motif in *Dracula*. In fact, Van Helsing repeats a line that is only slightly altered from the first film: "Who can define the boundary line between the superstition of yesterday and the scientific fact of tomorrow." If Van Helsing is meant to represent the open mindedness of science, Dr. Garth represents the cold hard logic of the modern mind. He states quite plainly, "There's no room for superstition." His office is filled with test tubes and scientific equipment, despite being a psychiatrist. In the end, when the Countess offers him the immortality of vampirism, he says simply, "I don't believe in your spells and your magic." The boldness of his statement effectively states that since he refuses to believe in vampires, they just don't exist.

The syntax of THE EXPERT again involves the semantic element of a man of learning. Van Helsing is a professor, and Garth is a doctor. Instead of knowing the ins and outs of vampire superstition, Garth seeks to defeat the vampire by disavowing its existence, thus robbing it of power.

Compare Garth's steadfast belief in science to the mesmerism of Marya. She calls her ability "something older and more powerful" than his hypnosis. Dracula's daughter also employs THE LOOK, yet seems to require a ring of polished silver to accomplish the deed. This semantic element could be related to the cliché of the swinging pocket watch in the traditional stage hypnotist. In the first scene, inside Whitby jail, the film shows a close-up of Marya's hand, the ring gleaming with light. A moment later, we see a close-up of the vampire's eyes. The connection between mesmerism and her gaze is clear. The victim, Alfred, is so entranced by her mesmerism that when the sergeant returns with the Scotland Yard inspector, he does not notice them. When the sergeant slaps the officer on the back, Alfred falls to the ground.

Later, on the street, the Countess holds her ring up next to her eyes, and the combination enthralls a young man. The camera slowly loses focus on her face, which may be the victim's point of view. Marya uses her ring and stare combination again on Lili. The young girl begins to fall into the trance, yet shakes it off. She resists the Countess, saying she doesn't want to pose anymore.

THE LOOK diminishes in intensity over the course of the film. At the start, her trance is so powerful that the officer seems dead. Yet she fails to hypnotize Lili, and has to ask permission to use her powers on Dr. Garth. It seems that as she wavers in her conviction as a vampire, so too her powers weaken. This reflects Dr. Garth's refusal to believe in the supernatural: "I don't believe in your spells."

The syntax of THE LOOK is similar to *Dracula*. The vampire is alone with her victim. The semantic element of the highlighted eyes is replaced with the ring. The purpose is also to control and subdue her victims.

Also like *Dracula*, THE BITE involves several implied bites, with unseen fangs, and mentioned (but not seen) marks on the neck. There are only two explicit bites in the film, the Countess's first male victim and Lili. Although the vampire is alone with each victim, Lili breaks the hypnotic trance, and screams when bit.

THE CROSS is used only once, during the cremation of Dracula's body. Just as in the former film, the syntax holds true in *Dracula's Daughter*. Marya averts her head as she grasps the makeshift cross, two sticks tied together. An interesting extension to the syntax involves the servant, Sandor, who also turns away from the cross.

Countess Marya Zaleska is destroyed using a similar syntax as *Dracula* with some semantic changes. In *Dracula's Daughter* a wooden arrow replaces the stake. The most significant change is the character that accomplishes the task. In *Dracula's Daughter* the servant, Sandor, shoots Marya, rather than one of the experts. The final DESTRUCTION may have been an accident, as he may have been aiming for Dr. Garth.

A few more hints of the dangers of sunlight emerge in this film. Van Helsing tells Dr. Garth that vampires must return to their graves by sunlight or die. This fact is acted out when the Countess and Sandor flee to London before dawn. After Marya bites the young man, she returns home, saying, "Hurry, hurry. It's almost daylight." The audience never sees what will happen if the vampire stays out when the sun rises. That is left for the next movie to explore.

Son of Dracula

Critics have often discounted or ignored *Son of Dracula*. The film is often absent from the vampire corpus, and Lon Chaney Jr.'s portrayal of Dracula is called into question. Leonard Wolf, a Dracula scholar, calls Lon Chaney Jr.'s performance wooden and indifferent, stating that the actor is "the worst possible choice to play Dracula" (200). The use of Lon Chaney Jr. may have been due to economics. Chaney was an inexpensive actor to cast. Additionally, his previous role in *Wolfman* would forever typecast him as a sympathetic character, and this sympathy carries over into his performance as Alucard. Add this to a script that is stronger on character and dialogue than on actual incident, and the film gives the impression that not a lot is happening. This being said, *Son of Dracula* did much for the genre, introducing many elements that would be repeated in films to come.

One significant error in chronology needs to be cleared before *Son of Dracula* can be properly studied. In many sources, *Return of the Vampire* and *Son of Dracula* are listed as being released in 1944. This could account for the dismissal of *Son of Dracula* as a minor note in the genre. *Return of the Vampire* has Bela Lugosi as the vampire, a werewolf henchman, and a dramatic death sequence involving sunlight. However, close attention to the release dates shows that *Son of Dracula* was released on November fifth, 1943, while *Return of the Vampire* greeted audiences on January first of the next year. There is a strong possibility that these films did influence one another. Universal had knowledge of Columbia's encroachment on their Dracula property, and this may have caused them to rush *Son of Dracula* to the screen.

Son of Dracula employs the fewest scenes of mesmerism of all the films in this cycle. Only when Count Alucard convinces the Justice of the Peace to marry Kay and himself does he use his hypnotic abilities. Yet this scene shows only the reaction shot of the Justice of the Peace, and not a close-up of the vampire's eyes. The remaining scenes where the Count employs THE LOOK are simply a few shots of Alucard gazing defiantly at the camera. The most notable is after Frank shoots Kay through the Count's body.

THE CROSS repeats the syntax established in *Dracula*. Professor Laszlo, in the Van Helsing role, holds a cross up, after Count Alucard had seized Dr. Brewster by the neck. The vampire's face twitches with anger and fright, and he slowly backs away. Instead of hiding his face, he keeps his eyes fixed on the simple cross, cupped casually in Professor Laszlo's hand. The Count finally backs into the door, and makes his escape by transforming into mist. There is another scene where the original syntax of the vampire hiding his face is repeated, but the cross is replaced by a shadow. Moonlight shines across a grave marker, and the shadow of the cross is enough to make Count Alucard back away. Here he makes his escape by transforming into a bat.

THE BITE is an incident that the audience must assume for fact because the scene is never witnessed, nor even implied in the film. Only three such attacks occur in the film: first Colonel Caldwell; then the boy, Tommy; and finally Katherine Caldwell. The last bite is up for debate, with some critics claiming it was her morbidity and fear of death that caused the transformation. Even Dr. Laszlo reminds Dr. Brewster that "the girl was morbid." However, there is no need to assume that Count Alucard did not bite her. In the film, Frank shoots Kay, but a short time later, she seems to be fine. Additionally, Kay herself states that she achieved immortality through Count Alucard. The only bite the audience does see involves Kay in the form of a bat. The scene is shot in silhouette, as the bat drinks from Frank's neck.

In *Son of Dracula* we see a new twist on the syntax of THE INFECTION. Here the victim of vampirism embraces her state. In fact Kay has planned for this, longing for her and Frank to spend eternity together. Unlike other victims, she only portrays the trance-like state after her initial transformation, when she sits up in bed after her fatal gunshot. Later, Kay seems to have preserved her personality and is under no control from Count Alucard. Some of the old syntax remains with Tommy. He arrives unconscious and rambles about a foreign man and mist (very similar to Lili in *Dracula's Daughter*).

Son of Dracula begins to show an evolving syntax of THE EXPERT tracking down the vampire. In this film there are again two experts, though both make significant screen appearances, unlike *Dracula's Daughter*, where Van Helsing was only a carryover from the first film. Also, a new role for the Expert emerges, that of tracking down the vampire though any means necessary. Dr. Brewster takes on this active role, breaking open suitcases, trespassing, and basically being nosey. In many ways he is forced to assume such questionable acts because Count Alucard knows the law and uses it to his advantage. After Dr. Brewster pokes around the cellar, Count Alucard states that *he* is now the master, and Dr. Brewster owes him an explanation. Later, Alucard repeats that he is the owner of the house. "I am master," Alucard says. "Anyone who enters here without my permission will be considered a trespasser."

Dr. Brewster establishes his legitimacy as an EXPERT by reading Bram

Count Alucard (Lon Chaney, Jr.) is never shown biting Kay (Louise Allbritton), despite the appearance of this publicity still from Son of Dracula *(1943, Universal).*

Stoker's *Dracula* and by contacting Laszlo, the Hungarian professor. The professor, constituting the other half of THE EXPERT, comes complete with graying hair, spectacles, and a Hungarian accent. The old syntax of debate over superstition and science is performed in the familiar setting of the study. This debate quickly turns to Professor Laszlo's explanation of the vampire as a sort of plague. On speaking of his homeland, the Carpathian hills, Laszlo says, "What was once a happy productive region is now a barren waste, villages depopulated, the land abandoned." The idea that America offers virgin territory is repeated three times, two of them by Count Alucard, who says this new land has "a young and virile race." This is perhaps the closest to the plague aspect put forth in *Nosferatu* and Stoker's novel.

THE VAMPIRE presented by Lon Chaney, Jr. shows marked differences from Lugosi and Holden's efforts. Here the vampire is marked by anger and physicality. He holds true to the aristocratic roots, maintaining a cape and his title, but Count Alucard irritates easily. In his first speaking lines, the count forcibly demands entrance, even though there has been a death in the family. Unlike previous vampires, who seem to attack a victim only

Unlike previous vampires, Count Alucard (Lon Chaney, Jr.) doesn't mind getting his hands dirty. In this scene from Son of Dracula *(1943, Universal), he grabs Frank (Robert Paige) by the neck while Kay (Louise Allbritton) tries to restrain him.*

when rendered helpless, Count Alucard does not shy away from getting his hands dirty. He tosses Frank through a set of doors, and nearly strangles Dr. Brewster. In the final scene of destruction, he attempts to strangle Frank twice, even hurling him against the burning coffin.

THE DESTRUCTION of the vampire is accomplished by burning his grave before sunrise. Frank discovers the coffin and sets it alight with dried moss. When Count Alucard arrives, he yells at Frank, "Put it out!" After several hopeless attempts to extinguish the fire, Alucard grabs Frank by the throat, about to choke the life out of him. Then he mysteriously looks away. The film cuts to a shot of the sun rising. Alucard's eyes glaze over, he stiffens, and falls into a puddle of water. Shafts of light stream down, bathing the figure in sunlight. A close-up of Alucard's hand shows the skin fade and vanish, leaving only bone and the ring on his finger. Next to *Nosferatu*, this is the first death by sunlight, and the first to show the disintegration of flesh. Fire is closely tied to this process, as Frank goes on to burn Kay's coffin and body.

Son of Dracula borrows the syntax of a romance film in many of its key scenes. When Alucard initially faces Kay, preparing to bite her, the film places them in a two-shot, with both characters facing each other. Instead of controlling his victim, Alucard speaks to her of eternal love: "Ours will be a different life, without material needs, a life that will last though eternity." Kay responds by fluttering her eyelids, and tilting her head back, as though awaiting a kiss from a lover. This scene is repeated again with Kay and Frank in the jail cell. The same two-shot is employed, now with Kay assuming the role of Count Alucard. She tells Frank, "We will spend eternity together." This romanticism is underscored by J. Salter's score, which becomes tender near the end of the film. The syntax of romance is fully embraced in the next series of films in the 60s and 70s.

Return of the Vampire

This film sees the return of Bela Lugosi as Armand Tesla, in a role very close to his performance in *Dracula*. Columbia made this picture distinctively different from *Dracula* in order to avoid copyright issues with Universal. The story, although noticeably altered from the Stoker novel or stage play, contains many of the same elements. A young female is attacked in her bedroom. The vampire has a servant, like Renfield, who ultimately betrays his master. Finally the expert, Lady Jane Ainsley, researches the lore of the vampire.

The action begins in medias res, even before the opening credits, with the vampire biting a young girl. This scene follows the syntax of other BITE scenes. The vampire advances on a victim, and Armand Tesla raises his cape before the audience can see the deed. One difference in this bite scene from previous films is in the reaction of the victim. She displays visible signs of fear, screaming. A similar scene plays out when Tesla bites Nicki as a child; only here the shadow of his outstretched cape is seen devouring the girl before she screams. After Tesla reemerges from destruction, he takes another anonymous female victim in a short recap of the opening scene.

The Bite is also played out with Nicki and John. The vampire victim, Nicki, remains trance-like, under Tesla's control, as she stares longingly at John's neck. Just before the bite, the camera pans quickly to the window, showing Tesla's face framed by the curtains. The scene is meant to make the viewer believe that Nicki bites John, but in fact it is a ruse set up by Tesla, as further punishment for Lady Jane.

This last scene shows how controlling The Infection becomes in *Return of the Vampire.* As before, the victims of the vampire stare blankly, in a trance. The first girl, Norcutt, repeats a scene similar to Lili in *Dracula's Daughter,* revealing a few details, then dying. Unlike previous films, an extreme close-up reveals the two pin-prick wounds of the vampire's fangs. Doctor Saunders reveals that "once attacked, a victim is completely dominated" by the vampire. This is true for Nicki, who when bitten as a child, is still under Tesla's control as an adult. Three separate times in the film, as Nicki lies sleeping, Telsa calls her to action. The vampire accomplishes the telepathy via a voice-over. Nicki leaves her bed and walks in a vacant-eyed trance.

The Look of the vampire is used more to establish control than to render helplessness. When Nicki comes to him the first time, Tesla commands her: "Look at me!" This is accompanied by an extreme close-up of Tesla's eyes, lit from below. When put up against the romantic syntax of *Son of Dracula,* this film reverts to the traditional syntax of shot/countershot between Tesla and Nicki. Nicki is entranced and mute through the extent of Tesla's speech. "You are mine, mine forever," says Tesla. He relates the same tale of immortal life as Alucard did in *Son of Dracula,* but now it holds none of the romance as it did with Lon Chaney Jr. It functions as more of a command. "You will go with me to my native country, where no deaths can claim you, or tear us apart. Your mind is no longer your own." A second extreme close-up of Tesla's eyes follows, after which, Nicki faints.

Tesla's Look is also used to establish control over Andreas, his werewolf servant. After Tesla's first destruction, Andreas was set free. When he again meets the stare of Tesla, his will crumbles. Andreas tries to fight back, saying "You have no power over me." He credits Lady Jane for cleansing him of the vampire's evil spell. Tesla counters: "Look at me, Andreas!" Another extreme close-up of the vampire's eyes is all that is needed to reestablish control. Andreas transforms back in to wolf-man, and Tesla's groveling servant.

THE VAMPIRE remains a mystery at the start of the film. His face is hidden from view, until he is killed and returns. No doubt this was done deliberately. This was the first time Lugosi played a true vampire since Dracula in 1931. The first thing the audience sees of Tesla is a close-up of his hand as it opens the lid of the coffin. A ring, with a tragedy mask, adorns his finger. This is possibly a concession by Columbia, as other Draculas have the crest on their rings. In the opening shots, only the vampire's black cape and high collar are seen. When he confronts Andreas for the first time, the audience finally sees Tesla's face. Lugosi appears much as he did in *Dracula,* only this time he is perhaps more cordial in social gatherings. He kisses the lady's hands, and even offers Lady Jane an arm.

Like the previous two films, *Return of the Vampire* has two experts. First is Doctor Walter Saunders, whose notes open the film, via a voice-over. He is the traditional professor, with graying hair and a pencil mustache. The second expert is a woman, a first in the film genre. Dr. Lady Jane Ainsley establishes credibility by reading Tesla's book *The Supernatural and Its Manifestations.* Much as in previous films, both experts are immediately tied to science. They first appear in a laboratory, with Lady Jane examining a slide of blood under a microscope. Additionally the debate over superstition and science is taken up, first in the hospital, but then in the familiar setting of the study. After Doctor Saunders dies, this debate is continued, to some extent, with Sir Fredrick, Chief Commissioner for Scotland Yard. This film also contains an important confrontation between the vampire and the expert. Tesla mocks the doctor, Lady Jane, by saying, "With all your scientific knowledge, you have achieved nothing." Yet she surprises him by revealing a cross.

The crosses in *Return of the Vampire,* both the pendant hung above a sleeping John and the cross embedded onto the organ, glow with light. When Lady Jane pulls away the sheet music to reveal the cross, Tesla responds with a raised cape. The light of the cross reflects onto his cape. He backs away, finally disappearing in an explosion of mist. Andreas also discovers a crucifix in the dirt floor of the demolished church. This cross serves a dual purpose. Not only does it force Tesla away from the sleeping Nicki, but it also breaks the vampire's control over his servant. As Andreas stares at the crucifix, he hears Lady Jane speaking in voice-over, reminding him of his goodness. He transforms from a werewolf back into a man.

Return of the Vampire holds the unique distinction of having the vam-

Andreas (Matt Willis, top) fulfills one of the recurring syntactic elements of the malignant cycle. The servant betrays his master, Armand Tesla (Bela Lugosi), which leads to the vampire's destruction in Return of the Vampire *(1944, Columbia).*

pire die at the start of the film, only to rise again. The first DESTRUCTION has the two experts drive a metal spike into the vampire's chest. The scene is witnessed on camera for the first time. Doctor Saunders does the deed with the butt end of a hatchet. Unfortunately the destruction is not permanent. After a German air raid disrupts the cemetery, Tesla's body is revealed. Two rescue workers pull the spike out, and hear a groan from the body. Tesla is later seen emerging from the ground. A medium-shot shows his hand push through a mound of dirt.

Andreas destroys the vampire at the end of the film. He drags the unconscious body out into the daylight. There seem to be no adverse effects on the vampire until he wakes up. Then Tesla uses his hands and cape to block the sunlight. There is a cut to a shot of the sun, full in the sky. Andreas finally destroys the vampire using the same method as Doctor

Saunders. He pounds a metal spike into the heart using a brick. Only now, instead of aging as he did in the cemetery, Tesla's flesh melts away in the sunlight. The syntax of this DESTRUCTION apparently requires a combination of the two elements: sunlight and a metal spike. However, combined with *Son of Dracula*'s disintegration, a new syntax of destruction by sunlight has emerged, to be used effectively by Hammer in *Horror of Dracula*.

The End of the Universal Horror Cycle

A number of factors contrived to end the Universal Horror cycle; nearly all had to do with economics. Universal was considered one of "The Little Three" because, unlike the smaller studios of the time, it was able to have its films run in first-run theaters owned by the "Big Five": Warner Brothers, RKO, Twentieth Century-Fox, Paramount and MGM. On May 3rd, 1948, an antitrust suit succeeded against the studios, and Universal had no guarantee to first-run theaters. This year also marks the last horror film to feature its feature characters: Dracula, Frankenstein, and the Wolfman. *Abbott and Costello Meet Frankenstein* was hardly a horror film, going for gags more than scares. After this, Universal would switch its output to the emerging science fiction genre. Horror films would not return en masse until 1957.

El Vampiro [The Vampire]

The first serious vampire film to come out of Mexico is a transitional film. Historically, it fits with the next cycle of films, which begin in 1958. The syntax of the film, however, shares much in common with the films of the malignant cycle, and I have placed it here for analysis. As an entry into the genre, *El Vampiro* should not be ignored. It contains several firsts, most notably the first fangs on screen since *Nosferatu*.

THE LOOK, although present, is not used for control. Rather the vampire stares at his potential victim from afar. Señor Duval stands in the courtyard of the opening shot. His eyes are framed in an extreme close-up. They are lit by a swath of light like Lugosi, and just before the attack, the lighting rotates, altering the shadows on his face. In another scene, both vampires, Eloise and Duval, stare off into space and speak to each other via voice-over. Eloise gazes into the courtyard, awaiting Duval. She begins to speak, but when the film cuts to Duval in his carriage, her voice continues. Duval also gazes blankly forward. His voice-over responds to Eloise. This is similar to Lugosi's telepathic voice-over used in *Return of the Vampire*, although here it is between two vampires, rather than vampire and victim.

THE INFECTION is hardly a viable syntax in *El Vampiro*. The maid, Marilyn, explains that the vampire needs only to bite a victim twice to initiate the transformation, though this is never shown on film. Eloise, the victim bitten in the opening credits, appears as a full fledged vampire by the time Martha arrives. The only consistent syntax involves the victims fainting immediately after a bite attack by the vampire.

El Vampiro also has the weakest EXPERT of all the films in this cycle. Dr. Henry is tied more closely to the syntax of a romantic hero than the vampire expert. He legitimizes himself by reading a handwritten book on the death of Lavud, Duval's brother. Yet Dr. Henry has help in hunting the vampires. Aunt Mary knocks this book off the shelf, and it is she who ultimately destroys the two vampires. Additionally, all the information on vampires arrives via Marilyn, the maid. Still, Henry is a doctor, and he and Marilyn have a debate over the existence of vampires. Henry's most dramatic moment uses none of the semantic elements associated with the vampire film. Instead he and Duval sword fight, Henry using a torch. This is a syntax more closely related to adventure films than horror.

THE VAMPIRE as evoked by Germán Robles is the epitome of the malignant cycle. He has a pale face, framed by a high collared black cape. He even wears a medallion similar to Lugosi's Dracula. *El Vampiro* adds Eloise to this evolving syntax. She is dressed in a flowing black gown with a long mantilla and low-cut blouse. Both of these vampires are highly dignified. When Martha faints from Eloise's poison, they hardly seem to notice. This continues the tradition of the vampire appearing suave in social gatherings, but passionate and determined when faced with a victim.

Aunt Mary is the key propagator of crosses in the film. She is continually seen toting an enormous crucifix. She weaves a cross out of straw and leaves it on Martha's pillow. Duval, when he sees this, grimaces and hides his face behind his cape. Only when Martha accidentally sweeps the cross off the bed with her arm is the vampire free to attack. In one other scene, Anselmo enters wearing a cross. Eloise and Duval avert their heads while still maintaining their dignity.

Aunt Mary is the one who finally destroys both vampires. She strangles Eloise in the mines. The two women struggle until Eloise succumbs. Duval, meanwhile, shields his face when he hears a cock crow, and quickly retires to his coffin. Mary finds him and uses the broken leg of a chair as a wooden stake. She pushes up the coffin lid and jams the stake down. The film shows the stake enter the vampire's chest. Instantly Martha, who was asleep, awakes. This is similar to Mina's waking from her trance at the end of *Dracula*. Eloise begins to age, her flesh withering, finally fading into bone.

Even the movie poster for El Vampiro *(1958, Cinematográfica ABSA) shows the bloody bite marks left by Count Duval (Germán Robles) on the victim's neck.*

What sets *El Vampiro* apart from previous films is that it finally crosses the line of implying THE BITE to actually showing it. In the opening title sequence, Duval attacks a clearly hysterical woman. He leans over her and collapses onto her neck. The woman faints. Duval draws the cape over his bite. After a moment, the film cuts to Duval's back. The vampire stands and leaves the woman draped over the bed. The camera zooms onto her neck. The audience sees two fresh bloody marks on her neck. In comparison to the hinted at violence of the previous films, this scene is truly brutal. Yet, *El Vampiro* is not sated with one such attack. The film has four. As the vampire is traveling in his coach, he stops to assault a young boy. He closes the distance by transforming into a bat. After returning to human form, Duval wastes no time. He grasps the boy and bites the neck. The boy gasps, and falls to the ground. Duval envelops his victim in his cape. The entire attack lasts perhaps thirty seconds.

Duval's attack on Martha is a cinema first. The vampire opens his mouth to reveal two fangs. He raises his cape, not to block the action, but as a flourish. The film switches to a medium-shot of Duval near Martha's neck, his fangs clearly visible in the shot. He bites the girl, wrapping the cape around her neck. During the entire attack, Martha sleeps, oblivious. Duval leaves and the camera zooms in on her bite marks. The second attempted attack on Martha plays more like a physical assault. Martha is awake, and struggles violently. She screams, and the next time she appears, the vampire is carrying her limp body. The final bite seems more opportunistic than the others. Eloise sneaks up behind Ambrose. There is little subtly to her attack as she grabs him and bites his neck. When Eloise releases her victim, he crumples to the floor.

The syntax of THE BITE has expanded in this film. Here there are fangs, and the vampire moves quickly to bite the victim. Although eventually blocked by the cape, the initial attack is visible on screen. The whole act is swift and brief, the vampire leaving only moments later. The camera zooms in to show the fresh bite marks on the victim's neck. On the whole, *El Vampiro* shows a much more violent form of vampirism, one to be mimicked by Christopher Lee only a year later.

2

THE EROTIC CYCLE
(1957–1985)

Overview

The erotic film cycle began May 8, 1957, with the American rele[se] of *Horror of Dracula*. Released one month later in its native country of England, Hammer Studios' second foray into horror was an unprecedented success. Pam Cook and Mieke Bernink, editors of *The Cinema Book*, estimate that *Horror of Dracula* and *The Curse of Frankenstein* grossed more than four million dollars combined (87). Three events conspired to bring the vampire back to the screen with such tremendous force.

Florence Stoker's prolonged struggle for complete ownership of *Dracula* led to Universal Studios obtaining exclusive rights to the character and storyline. Only Columbia's *Return of the Vampire* came close to violating that copyright. After Universal ceased production of its horror films, it maintained rights over the franchise. In 1957, Universal sponsored Hammer studios to make a new version of Dracula. Universal "expressly forbade" any imitation of the Lugosi character or set designs (87). This let Hammer studios freely reinvent the story as they saw fit.

David Pirie, an expert on Hammer horror, explains that Hammer's policy was to make films that capitalized on "subjects and characters that were pre-sold to the public either through radio and television or via myth and legend" (quoted by Cook and Bernink 85). In 1951, a relaxation of British film censorship and the arrival of the new X-certificate rating helped a struggling Hammer reach new audiences. The 1955 release of *The Quartermass Xperiment* took full advantage of the new adult X-certificate with the spelling of its title. The combination of science fiction and horror was a commercial success, breaking box office records. In 1956, the Production Code of the Motion Picture Association of America was revised and relaxed, thus opening the door to a wider release of Hammer films across the Atlantic. Hammer took an extreme risk when it devoted everything to the production of *The Curse of Frankenstein*. The studio knew that in order to survive, it had to "shake off their B-feature reputation" (86). They took the bold step, completely changing their output, shelving ten films already slated for production.

The last piece of the puzzle was the return of color to film. Sir James Carreras, then the head of Hammer, realized that "there had never been a *Frankenstein* or *Dracula* in colour [*sic*]" (87). With vivid Technicolor, Hammer's take on Dracula was strikingly different from its Universal progenitor.

Highly sensual scenes of vampirism, especially THE BITE, characterize the films of the erotic cycle. The interaction of the vampire and his female victims appears somewhere between violent assault and sexual intercourse. Such movie titles like *Sex and the Vampire* (1970), *Lust for a Vampire* (1970), and *J   ʿ ʿ.n Vampires* (1970), exemplify the shift in the narrative. The vampire often vacillates between extreme physical action and tender or erotic moments.

Matching the vampire's changing mood, these films show victims in one of two categories: those victims that the vampire treats with relative kindness, and those with which the vampire disposes of without thought. The first type of victim often reacts to the bite with a mix of fear and erotic expectation. Victims seem almost willing to accept the bite of the vampire, and the filming of such scenes underscores these romantic qualities, such as the love scene between Frank Langella's Dracula and Lucy. The victims in the second category are often dealt with in a physically brutal manner, having their throats crushed or being thrown aside. Additionally, films of this cycle often have more than one active vampire. The lesser vampires—vampire brides or recently transformed vampires—lack the complex dynamic of the main vampire. They show no mercy, using whatever means necessary to obtain blood from a victim.

This film cycle sees the rise of THE EXPERT from a mere tool of exposition to an active screen character. Initiated through the excellent performances of Peter Cushing, the new vampire expert becomes a staple of the vampire narrative. THE EXPERT now tracks down the vampire, confronting the creature whenever possible. This vampire hunter comes prepared for battle with stakes, a mallet, and a cross. The expert alone accomplishes the final destruction of the vampire. This destruction typically includes the expert driving a stake through the vampire's heart using three strikes from a mallet.

The vampire maintains an aristocratic heritage, characteristically cold and distant, however more humanistic qualities seep in over time. A new syntax, borrowed from the Universal Mummy films, begins to emerge. The motivation for the vampire's continual pursuit of a certain victim centers on the search for a lost love, reincarnated in the film's heroine. This syntax developed first with Barnabas Collins in Dan Curtis's television series *Dark Shadows,* which also is the first to show the vampire as the heroic lead. This development of the vampire as the hero is the focus of the final film cycle, the sympathetic cycle.

Horror of Dracula

Horror of Dracula is the first film to show blood on screen. The first scene, after the opening credits, exploits the new semantic element of color. As the camera zooms in on a coffin, bright red blood dribbles over the nameplate of Dracula.

The Horror of Dracula shows homage to Lugosi in the syntax of THE LOOK. The film has a medium-shot of Dracula as he stands on Lucy's patio. A band of light highlights his eyes. Although this scene is the only one of

At 6' 4", Christopher Lee made an imposing Dracula in Horror of Dracula *(1958, Hammer).*

this type in the film, it effectively links Christopher Lee's Dracula with Lugosi. THE LOOK is not used again in the film, Lee's vampire preferring to deal erotically with his victims or violently with his foes.

The appearance of THE VAMPIRE continues the semantic elements from previous films. Dracula wears a black cape with high collar and a ring on his finger. He first appears at the top of a flight of stairs, in silhouette, accompanied by a surge in James Bernard's score. He is exceptionally polite to Jonathan, but in a later scene Dracula appears utterly transformed. His eyes are bloodshot. He bares a set of fangs, and fresh blood has run down the sides of his mouth. His appearance seems more like a ravenous animal than the suave aristocrat of the previous scene. He leaps over a table, brutally tossing his vampire bride to one side, leaving Lugosi's Dracula looking sluggish and passive in comparison. There has been some comparison of Lee's Dracula with Germán Robles's Senor Duval in *El Vampiro*. There are certainly parallels in their performances. Duval viciously attacked his victims, moving with furious passion, and he too bared his fangs. The website *Vampyres Online* claims that Christopher Lee credited Robles's performance with "being the inspiration behind his version." I cannot, however, find confirmation of this in other literature.

Dracula is not the only vampire in the film. His bride appears strikingly different from Countess Zaleska in *Dracula's Daughter*. She is dressed in a low cut pastel dress. She also portrays a duality on screen. When she meets Jonathan, she pleads with him, using her female wiles to get close. She then turns the tables, biting Jonathan on the neck, ushering in perhaps the most copied scene of any vampire film. The syntax of THE VAMPIRE in *Horror of Dracula* expands on the duality established in earlier films. Here the demarcation of the social vampire from the predatory vampire has a new semantic element: fangs. When the vampire is social, he or she appears as a normal human. Yet when preparing for an attack, the vampire bares fangs, and shows blood trickling down the chin.

The syntax for this scene shows the female vampire using her perceived vulnerability to lower the defenses of the male victim. The scene shows a medium-shot of the two in an embrace. Only then does the vampire show her true identity and attack. This is the moment of transformation for the vampire bride. The film shows her bite Jonathan in a close-up. She notices his neck as the musical score swells, then clamps her fangs onto her victim. Later, Jonathan's neck shows two puncture marks with trails of Technicolor blood running out.

Two of the film's most passionate bite attacks come when Dracula attacks Lucy and Mina. Lucy seems to have been waiting for him. She listens at the door to make sure no one is near, and then opens the French doors to the patio. She even removes her cross, lying on the bed and looking toward the patio expectantly. Just before the scene cuts, Lucy reaches up to feel her neck. Later, Dracula appears at the French doors. He circles her bed, keeping his eyes fixed on Lucy. Finally, as he sinks down for the bite, Lucy's expression changes to fear. Dracula raises his cape to block the bite from the camera.

There is one implied bite for Mina when she arrives at the mortician's office. Later, back at the Holmwood house, Dracula follows Mina into the bedroom, and reaches behind to close the door. The film employs a shot/reaction-shot as Mina sits on the bed and Dracula smiles, showing his fangs. He grasps her face and leans in close. Rather than going straight for the neck, Dracula makes as though to kiss her, moving passionately over her forehead, eyes, lips. When he finally moves back to the neck, Dracula pushes Mina back onto the bed. Later, Mina is found passed out on the bed; a close-up shows two rills of blood on her neck. The syntax of the scene is very close to sexual intercourse or rape. A similar syntax was implied in *El Vampiro*, when Duval attacks Martha.

Van Helsing explains how the vampire's INFECTION functions. He says, "Victims consciously detest being dominated by vampirism, but are unable to relinquish the practice ... similar to addiction to drugs." Lucy displays the complex duality of desire and loathing in the scene in her bedroom. She longs for Dracula to return, yet when he leans in to bite her, her longing turns to fear. The next night, after having the maid remove the garlic, Lucy vacillates between fear and expectation. Mina displays a similar reaction before she is bitten. Here, THE INFECTION uses the syntax of addiction. The previous syntax of control by the vampire is combined with a drug addict's need for a fix. This enables the victims to display desire for the vampire's bite, without truly wanting it.

Horror of Dracula is important as much for its revitalization of THE EXPERT as its updating THE VAMPIRE. Peter Cushing plays Van Helsing as a vampire hunter, taking the destruction of the creature as his personal task. Both he and his colleague come prepared, having a bundle of wooden stakes and a mallet. The experts, either Van Helsing or Jonathan, destroy all the vampires in the film. Van Helsing is a middle-aged man dressed in a suit and hat. He is very polite, bowing to Arthur and kissing Mina's hand. Yet when need arises, he can be extraordinarily agile, springing over a banister to chase Dracula, or leaping up onto the draperies. As in previous films, Van Helsing gains his knowledge through books. He learns of Dracula through Jonathan's journal, and later he compares this to his own notes recorded on a phonograph. The addition of this device is an element borrowed from Stoker's original novel.

Peter Cushing continued to play Van Helsing in many more Dracula movies. His EXPERT did more than study and expound on the theories of vampirism. He actively fought Dracula. Each of the Hammer films contains a confrontation between THE EXPERT and THE VAMPIRE. In the final confrontation of *Horror of Dracula,* Van Helsing seems nearly beaten, and Dracula takes a moment to experience a moment of satisfaction. Van Helsing leaps up onto a table, and pulls the draperies down. Sunlight floods into the room, catching Dracula's leg. Dracula screams as his foot shrivels to bone. His eyes have gone to their bloodshot red. Soon his hand and finally his whole body dissolves, turning to ash. After Dracula's DESTRUCTION, the burn on Mina's hand fades away. As the ashy remains of Dracula blow away, only his ring is left.

The other vampires are disposed of using the syntax from previous films. Jonathan uses a wooden stake and mallet to do the deed. In *Horror of Dracula* the coffins are stone with open tops. He places the stake over the heart. A shadow on the wall shows him raising the mallet. Perhaps this is to suggest that, as in previous films, the actual blow will not be shown. There is the sound of the strike accompanied by the scream of the vampire bride. The film then switches to Jonathan delivering the second blow, and a third strike brings a death wail from the female vampire. Jonathan is overwhelmed by the task, leaning heavily on the coffin. The vampire bride has aged, the actress replaced by an older woman with pale skin. This reversion to a human form is repeated with the destruction of Lucy.

Van Helsing also uses a bundle of stakes and mallet. He places the stake over Lucy's heart, raises the mallet, and strikes. Here the film changes to a close-up of the stake piercing Lucy's chest. Lucy wakes and screams. A close-up shows her face twisted into an ugly visage of pain. With the second strike, blood erupts from Lucy's chest, and only with the third does she close her eyes and rest. When Van Helsing shows the body to Arthur, Lucy has returned to a natural state. She appears beautiful, the burn mark gone from her forehead, and the shot is accompanied by a swell from the romantic musical score.

The syntax of DESTRUCTION hints at a further development of the vampire's INFECTION. In each case, the vampire reverts to its true, human form. In the case of Lucy, she becomes beautiful, because she was only recently infected. The vampire's bride, on the other hand, grows old, transforming to her true age. Dracula, who has existed for many centuries, decomposes to dust.

A new syntax is introduced with the use of THE CROSS. When a true crucifix is unavailable, Van Helsing uses two candlestick holders to form a cross. This he presents forcefully toward Dracula, who is driven back into the sunlight. The syntax seems to imply that someone must physically present this makeshift cross in order to be effective. Dracula, over the course of the film, passed by many cross-shaped items (window panes, doors, etc.) without any ill effects.

Another new syntax, borrowed from Stoker's novel, is the use of an actual cross to damage and identify a prospective vampire. In the novel, Van Helsing uses a holy wafer for this purpose, but *Horror of Dracula* has Van Helsing use a cross. At the crypt, Lucy bears down on Arthur ready to attack. Van Helsing repels her by holding a cross between the vampire

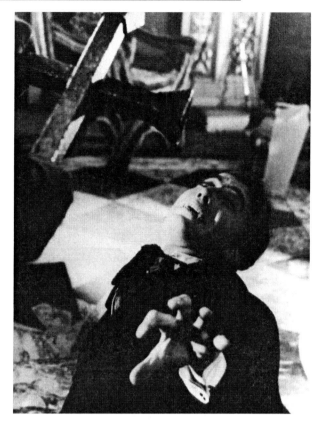

In a pinch, Van Helsing (Peter Cushing) uses two crossed candlesticks to form a cross, which repels Dracula (Christopher Lee) as effectively as a crucifix in Horror of Dracula *(1958, Hammer).*

and her victim. Lucy grimaces and stares at the cross. She is driven back, followed by Van Helsing. When she can go no further, he holds the cross at arm's length, placing it to her forehead. There is a sizzling sound and Lucy screams. When Van Helsing removes the cross, a burn mark remains on her forehead. A less adversarial scene is played out with Mina. Arthur insists that she wear a cross, and he drops it into her hand. She gasps and brings the clutched cross to her breast. Mina finally collapses. When Van Helsing removes the cross form Mina's hand, a close-up shows a burn mark in the shape of the cross, etched into the center of her palm.

Horror of Dracula introduces many new semantic elements, the cross that sears the vampire's flesh, the expert's stakes and mallet, the vampire's fangs and blood, and of course color. However, these elements are used to enhance the syntactic elements already present in the vampire narrative. The syntax of EXPERT and VAMPIRE as adversaries is intensified, with Van Helsing destroying all the vampires. Furthermore, the act of vampirism becomes more overtly sexual. Although these bite scenes are aggressively erotic, this opens the door to a more romantic vampire.

Dark Shadows

The television soap opera *Dark Shadows* represents the origin of the vampire as hero. This drastic transformation of the vampire narrative was the result of a series of mistakes that ultimately resonated with the audience.

By the spring of 1967, ABC was in third place in the ratings, and put pressure on Dan Curtis, creator of the series *Dark Shadows*. In a drastic bid to raise the show's ratings, Curtis added a vampire to his soap opera. In Kathryn Leigh Scott's book, *The Dark Shadows Companion,* she calls the addition a "desperate measure called for by desperate times" (117). In Curtis's own words, the show had to "go all the way with the supernatural stuff." The thought was that the vampire would only serve for two weeks, just enough to raise the ratings. If that didn't happen, at least they would go down in flames.

On Thursday, April 17, 1967, a small-time drifter by the name of Willie Loomis searches for treasure in the Collins mausoleum. He finds a coffin bound in chains, and uses his tools to wrench open the lid. His eyes widen in terror as a hand rises to grip his throat. The vampire Barnabas makes his first appearance in *Dark Shadows.*

The casting of this vampire was anything but ordinary. Jonathan Frid moved to California hoping to start a position as a drama professor. His agent persuaded him to try out, pointing out that the job was only intended to last for two weeks. Dan Curtis, who was in Europe, was sent three photos of prospective actors, intending to send back the one he wanted cast in the role of Barnabas. Curtis sent back Frid's photo, but when he returned on the day of shooting Barnabas's first scene, he told the producer that he had sent back the wrong photo. By then it was too late to change the actor.

The casting of THE EXPERT was also a fortunate mistake. The intention was to have a Dr. Julian Hoffman track down and combat the vampire, but a typo rendered the doctor a woman: Julia. By casting the vampire hunter as a woman, new avenues for narrative development opened up. Grayson Hall was determined to develop her role, and tried to find a reason for her character to be obsessed with a vampire. She decided to have her character fall in love with Barnabas. Grayson recalls that she never told

Dan Curtis of her decision, but "the audience picked up on it and wrote in their approval" (123).

In fact, a torrent of fan mail was the key reason for the shift of the vampire from villain to hero. The ratings soared, and fan mail for Frid surpassed Lugosi and Lee, with some 1,500 letters a day. Grayson, too, was besieged by mail from people who identified with her predicament. Scott sums this up as a love triangle that could never be resolved. "The impossibility of [Julia's] love for Barnabas, and Barnabas' [sic] hopeless pining after Josette, created one of the program's major plotlines, a triangle which would continue to the end of the series" (123). Teenagers identified with the vampire's isolation and inability to fit into the modern world. The vampire was becoming the center of the storyline.

The syntax of THE VAMPIRE in *Dark Shadows* portrays some of characteristics of previous incarnations. He transforms into a bat, and has no reflection, yet there are no crosses used against him. Also, THE LOOK seems to hold no supernatural power. There are close-up shots of Barnabas as he surveys a potential victim, yet these lack the intensity of Lugosi or Lee. Additionally, Barnabas is never destroyed in the series. A stake appears to be the method mentioned (it is even tried once, but on a doppelganger of the vampire). Only with his first appearance in episode 211 is there a hint of how to immobilize the vampire. Willie finds Barnabas sealed in his coffin, bound tightly in chains. The chains have held him hostage for nearly two hundred years, and he awakes to a world unfamiliar to him.

Although Barnabas is not actually shown biting anyone in the series (the scenes end by fading to black), there are several scenes in which the vampire fulfills the syntax. The first attack appears in episode 225/226 and 227 (due to release dates changing, some episodes have two numbers, thus 225 and 226 are the same episode). Barnabas discovers a young waitress, Maggie Evans, who bears a striking resemblance to his long lost love, Josette du Prés. This return, or reincarnation, of a lost love is a syntax borrowed from Universal's Mummy series, where the mummy would find the female lead to be the spitting image of his older, now dead, lover. Barnabas arranges for her father, Sam, to be away, and enters the bedroom through a pair of French doors (very similar to Lee's entrance in *Horror of Dracula*). There is a close-up of Barnabas as he stares malevolently toward Maggie sleeping in bed. Her fingers first clutch the covers, then move up to feel her neck. Another close-up of the vampire reveals his fangs as he opens his mouth to deliver the bite.

Another, more explicit bite appears in episode 350. Barnabas has aged to nearly two hundred years, and is desperate for blood. Carolyn Collins searches the basement, and has discovered Barnabas's coffin. An elderly version of the vampire appears and quickly closes the distance. She comments on how old he seems. Barnabas responds by grabbing her, and then lightly brushing the hair away from her neck. The shot tightens from medium to close-up as Barnabas tilts his head and reveals his fangs. Carolyn's scream continues as the scene fades to black.

The victims of the vampire display lethargy and lack of strength. Willie, the first to suffer THE INFECTION, is so tired during the day that he must sleep, virtually fainting on the bed. After Maggie's first bite, she can barely stand up, dropping a cup of coffee in the café. Victims also display a shift in personality. Willie turns from a juvenile delinquent into a timid and meek servant of Barnabas. Maggie comes to believe she is Josette so fully that she even answers to the name. Eventually her personality deteriorates, and she adopts a childlike state. After a single bite, Carolyn expresses a desire to do anything for Barnabas, stating, "I never want to fail him."

Dark Shadows borrows from the already existing syntax of the soap opera, which relies on unfulfilled romance, and the roles of THE VAMPIRE and THE EXPERT are altered drastically because of this. Julia Hoffman is the vampire EXPERT. She is an older woman and is initially introduced as Maggie's doctor at Windcliff Sanitarium. She also sets up a laboratory that has more in common with Dr. Frankenstein than a psychiatrist. She qualifies herself by studying many books on the Collins family history. In episode 288, she finds that the vampire casts no reflection, and in 289 she opens the coffin to reveal a sleeping, and unaware, Barnabas.

The confrontation between the two occurs in episode 290. Victoria's voice-over at the start of the episode states, "Deep within the night, opposing forces stalk each other. Forces so opposite, no peace is possible. And their meeting, when it comes, will shatter the ancient truce between the living and the dead." The meeting of Dr. Hoffman and Barnabas flips the usual syntax on its head. Instead of confronting the vampire with a crucifix, Julia offers an exchange of information. She lures the vampire to her room, placing pillows under the sheets to simulate her body. She then surprises Barnabas, and welcomes him. He responds by attempting to choke her. She offers to help him, saying, "You don't have to live this life."

Her research has focused on the boundary between life and death. She sees Barnabas as the missing link, and offers a cure for vampirism. Dr. Hoffman describes the vampire's condition in purely scientific terms, with few supernatural qualities. She explains that the vampire has an imbalance in the blood that causes more cells to be destroyed than created.

Throughout the series, Julia goes to great lengths to protect Barnabas. She hypnotizes Maggie, wiping out the memory of her kidnapping,

Barnabas (Jonathan Frid) in Dark Shadows *(1967, Dan Curtis Productions), dresses Maggie Evans (Kathryn Leigh Scott) in Josette's dress, trying to recreate his lost love.*

and even helps Barnabas poison Dr. Woodward, who threatens to expose the vampire. Dr. Hoffman finally gives the ultimate sacrifice. When her cure takes a wrong turn, aging Barnabas two hundred years, she proposes he bite her as a way of saving himself.

The syntax of THE EXPERT in *Dark Shadows* has the expert work alongside the vampire. The teamwork seems to be based on a common goal, the research and cure of vampirism, but it has a deeper cause. Dr. Hoffman's obsession with Barnabas is founded on infatuation. Much of this is due to the casting of a female expert. The syntax of romance between expert and vampire is taken up again much later with the television series *Buffy the Vampire Slayer*.

The most dramatic and long lasting change of the vampire narrative lies in the syntax of THE VAMPIRE. Even before letters poured in to Frid, prompting a continuation of his character, Barnabas was written as a guilt ridden and melancholic character. Immediately after being released from his coffin, in episode 212, he confronts Josette's painting and says, "I'm free now, and alive [...]. I've returned to live the life I never had." This is an echo of Marya Zaleska's speech in the opening frames of *Dracula's Daughter*. When he meets Maggie for the first time in episode 221, he comments on how lonely the night can be: "One gets used to loneliness. It's part of an existence." The existence of this vampire is not one of bloodlust or merciless control of his victims. Barnabas is plagued by guilt over the death of his lover, Josette. She fell off a cliff trying to escape from him after he had transformed into a vampire. Barnabas blames himself for Josette's death, and longs to bring her back. He offers several of his victims Josette's music box, and attempts to mesmerize them into believing they are Josette.

His guilt over Josette softens his resolve. In episode 287, he invades Victoria's bedroom, and even leans over her, ready to bite. He halts, and retreats. A painting of Josette hangs on the wall, and he looks to this. This scene repeats in 289. Here Barnabas is determined to bite Victoria, but she turns her head in sleep, and faces him. He reaches forward and touches her face, then slowly backs away. Circling around the bed he opens the music box, and begins the melody. Finally in episode 349, the audience hears his interior monologue via a voiceover. This time he is desperate for blood to reverse his two hundred years of aging. He approaches Victoria in her bed once more, and stares down on her. He thinks, "She's so lovely, so innocent. I can't do it. I can't."

THE VAMPIRE of *Dark Shadows* bears physical resemblance to his predecessors. He wears a more modern version of the cape, a dark gray overcoat with a high collar. He dons a ring with a black onyx stone. When preparing to bite a victim, Barnabas displays fangs. Yet the heart of a ruthless predator does not beat within him. Instead, this vampire pines for his lost love. He struggles with his condition, the curse of vampirism. In other words, the vampire is rendered more human, with compassion sometimes overruling passion.

Not long after *Dark Shadows,* Dracula leapt off the page of Stoker's novel and became a real person.

The Historical Dracula

Two authors, Raymond T. McNally and Radu Florescu, made history when they established a connection between the literary character of Bram Stoker's Dracula and the fifteenth century Romanian prince Vlad the Impaler. In 1967, McNally was one of the first people to discover and explore Castle Dracula. The research he and Florescu did on the historical Dracula led to the book *In Search of Dracula: A True History of Dracula,* published in 1972. Some reviewers noted the lack of footnotes, and suggested that Florescu had invented the details of the prince's life. The two countered the very next year with the publication of *Dracula: A Biography of Vlad the Impaler, 1431–76.* This more scholarly book led to further research on the Romanian prince.

The concept of Dracula as a historical figure influenced several films, most notably the 1974 release of *Dracula* by Dan Curtis. James Hart also wanted to ground his leading character in history when he wrote *Bram Stoker's Dracula.* Finally, actor Christopher Lee had grown dissatisfied with the portrayals of Dracula in the Hammer films. In 1975 he narrated and starred in a Swedish documentary about Vlad the Impaler, titled *Vem var Dracula?* (released as *In Search of Dracula* in the United States).

The work on the historical Dracula undoubtedly influenced science fiction writer Fredrick Thomas Saberhagen. In the mid–1970s he began dabbling with the theme of Dracula, casting him as the hero rather than the villain. In the first volume of his series, *The Dracula Tapes* (1975), he has Dracula tell his side of the story. The count takes the readers step by step through the story of Bram Stoker's novel, revealing how Dracula's intentions were misunderstood. He tried to save Lucy Westenra from Van Helsing's ignorance of blood types when making transfusions. The vampire also admits to falling in love with Mina Murray. Saberhagen's novel received mixed reviews, but garnered a dedicated audience. Furthermore, the fact that Dracula told his tale via tape recorder leaves some speculation as to the influence on Anne Rice, whose vampire Louis tells his story of being a vampire to a reporter playing a tape recorder.

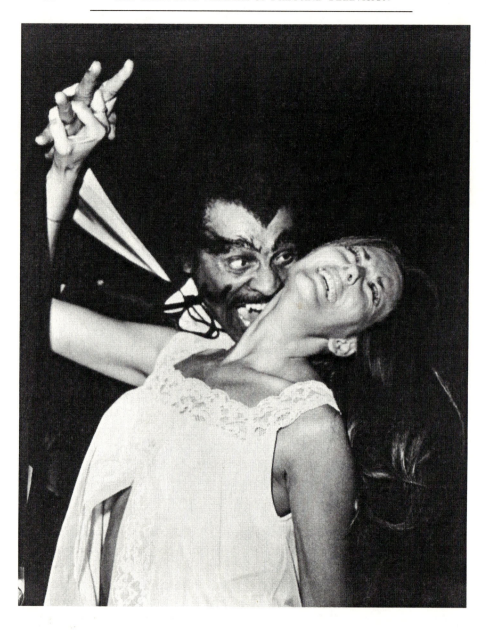

As in this scene from Blacula *(1972, American International), when Mamuwalde attacks a victim (unidentified actress), he transforms into Blacula (William Marshall).*

Blacula

Quite possibly the title of this film predisposes modern viewers to expect a comedy or a camp portrayal of the vampire. Nothing is farther from the truth. *Blacula* is a well-executed vampire narrative that continues the romantic syntax set forth in *Dark Shadows*.

On the surface, William Marshall plays a vampire similar to Lee's Dracula. He adopts two forms, one social and one predatory. Physically, he is dressed in a black cape with high collar, and has a mustache. The social vampire calls himself Mamuwalde, and is the epitome of nobility. He is not smug or condescending like the portrayal of Dracula in the opening scene. Instead the prince is courteous and polite, offering to kiss Michelle's hand. Mamuwalde also assumes the syntax of the romantic hero. After his first meeting with Tina on the street, he paces next to his coffin. Romantic music accompanies this scene as thoughts of her dominate his mind. Later, he meets Tina at her apartment, telling her that she is his lost love "recreated." He will not force himself upon her, saying, "You must come to me freely with love, or not at all. I will not take you by force."

This is the same sentiment expressed by Barnabas when he considers biting Victoria.

The vampire and potential victim fulfill the romantic syntax by embracing in a kiss, and ultimately having sex. At first Tina expresses doubt, sending Mamuwalde away. He says, "I live again, to lose you twice." She catches him before he leaves, and they kiss. Later they appear in bed after lovemaking. Mamuwalde will not force vampirism upon her. He wants her to choose, telling her that "All time belongs to us."

The curse placed upon Mamuwalde through Dracula's bite creates a bloodthirsty monster within the

Mamuwalde (William Marshall) is the suave prince who woos his love in Blacula *(1972, American International).*

prince. Dracula says, "A hunger, a wild gnawing, animal hunger will grow in you, a hunger for human blood." When Blacula first rises from his coffin, he sees the blood on Billy's arm. He staggers forward, his face contorted into an expression of excitement. His physical appearance transforms. His eyebrows become overgrown, and hair sprouts from his cheeks. A widow's peak fills out his forehead. He bares two fangs, long enough to be visible even with his mouth closed. His eyes leak with red blood, and after he attacks his victims, his lips are also red with blood. This version of the prince has none of the subtly of Mamuwalde. He solves problems physically, beating his adversaries into submission. He often chokes his enemies, crushing their throats. One victim is lifted above his head and tossed down a flight of stairs.

The syntax of THE VAMPIRE is more than the simple duality of a Jekyll and Hyde, thanks in large part to a superb performance by William Marshall. Mamuwalde fights to overcome the ravenous hunger of his condition. He is torn in two directions, one commanded by Dracula's curse, the other directed by his love for Tina. The duality of Marshall's vampire is expressed more fully in the sequel, when he embraces his vampire form, telling the heroes to call him Blacula instead of Mamuwalde.

THE LOOK is an underused syntax in *Blacula*. After rising from his grave, and disposing of the antique dealers Billy and Bobby, the vampire dons his cape. The film shows him staring out toward the audience in a medium-shot that tightens to a close-up. A voice-over repeats Dracula's line: "I curse you with my name. You shall be Blacula." Here the syntax of THE LOOK is merely employing the semantic elements of a close-up and the vampire staring for the purpose of highlighting interior monologue. Later in the film Blacula stands on the roof and looks toward the bedroom of his victim. Tina sits up as a whistling sound plays over the scene. She responds to commands given telepathically. Tina then walks through the streets in a trance-like state as romantic music plays. This scene plays more closely to the syntax as set forth by previous films.

The vampire employs THE BITE quite often throughout the film. Blacula's first attack comes when he is released from his coffin. The victims, Bobby and Billy, stand in stunned silence as the vampire approaches. He lunges for Billy's bandaged arm, sinking in his fangs. Afterwards, he lifts his head, and a close-up shows his face with an expression of ecstasy. Bobby struggles to get away, but the vampire grabs him by the collar and hoists him up. The victim faints. Blacula growls, panting heavily as he pulls the head to one side, exposing the neck. He delivers a bite, then moves away. Another close-up reveals two bloody bite marks on his neck. These wounds are described later at the funeral home as being two to three inches deep with flesh torn out in big chunks.

When Blacula encounters the cabbie, Juanita Jones, she behaves with little overt fear, backpedaling only after calling him "boy." The vampire gradually transforms from Mamuwalde to Blacula, growing hair, and his eyes widening at the prospect of fresh blood. Finally he grabs the victim's head and moves close as though to kiss her. He jerks the head to one side, exposing the neck. He growls again and bites the victim. The attack on Nancy, the photo girl, is swift and violent. She opens the curtains to the dark room to find Blacula with arms raised like claws. He sweeps toward the girl, who panics and attempts to flee. He grips her head, fixing one hand over her mouth, and bites her exposed neck. She continues to struggle even as the shot fades out.

An attack similar to the vampire bride from *Horror of Dracula* occurs when Nancy later collapses on the porch of her house. Officer Barnes sees this and rushes to her aid. She is weak, and cannot stand on her own. He picks her up to carry her back inside. Suddenly she appears revitalized. A close-up shows her baring fangs and biting his neck. Juanita's attack on Sam, the morgue attendant, is another rapid assault. She opens the door and charges down the hallway. Her arms are raised like claws. She grips Sam and pushes him off screen.

Blacula's final bite of Tina is done out of desperation rather than bloodlust. She is shot by a police officer, and falls to the floor. He says, "Forgive me. Now this is the only way." He leans over her and reveals her neck. The scene is underscored by romantic music. As he bites her, Tina's eyes flutter and she finally faints. This response is different from the other attacks in the film. The victim does not struggle or scream. Only after the scene is finished does the audience see Mamuwalde transformed into Blacula. Thus the syntax of THE BITE is twofold: either the need to sate his ravenous hunger, or a romantic union. He forces himself on his victims, who struggle and scream. But when faced with his lost love, Tina, Mamuwalde bites only when necessary, to preserve her life rather than destroy it.

THE INFECTION of *Blacula* spreads quickly. Dr. Thomas speaks as if it were a plague: "Vampires multiply geometrically." After being bitten, a victim is completely drained of blood, the face appearing ashen. Each victim has two puncture wounds on the neck, shown in a close-up. Most victims "revive" as vampires soon after death. Bobby moves his hand while in the funeral home, and Nancy transforms into a vampire only moments after being bitten. These lesser vampires are motivated solely by hunger, leaping on new victims without pause. Their faces appear deathly pale, with a green or white hue, and their hair becomes shaggy and overgrown. Each one bares long fangs jutting out of the mouth.

Doctor Gordon Thomas is the film's EXPERT. He is an older man, who periodically dons glasses. As a member of the Scientific Investigation Division, he has ties to the police department, and he has his own laboratory complete with test tubes and microscopes. Like the experts before him, Dr. Thomas gains knowledge through books, and he explains the affects of vampirism in Lt. Peters's office, instead of the typical study. He actively seeks the vampire, and doesn't shy away from confrontation. At the nightclub, both Mamuwalde and Dr. Thomas exchange jabs in a game of subtle wordplay. Dr. Thomas attempts to put the vampire on the defensive, but Mamuwalde responds with aplomb, countering each comment with a smile. Dr. Thomas physically disposes of all the lesser vampires at the warehouse. He hurls lit lamps, igniting the creatures. Another vampire jumps him from above, but Dr. Thomas turns the tables, leaping on the vampire with a stake made from a broken shovel handle. This EXPERT is knowledgeable and takes actions into his own hands.

Only Dr. Thomas uses a CROSS in the film. When Juanita springs up to attack Lt. Peters in the morgue, Dr. Thomas presents the cross. The vampire cowers before it, screaming and attempting to block it with her hands. He uses the cross to back her up against a window. When the light from the sun strikes her, she screams again and falls to the floor, dead.

Dr. Thomas personally destroys another vampire when he digs up Billy in his coffin. As soon as he opens the lid, the green-faced creature leaps toward him. Dr. Thomas pulls a prepared stake from his coat pocket and jams it into the vampire's chest. He then uses the shovel to drive the stake home, striking it three times. The scene includes a close-up of the shovelhead striking the stake, but no blood accompanies it. At the end of the film, Dr. Thomas and Lt. Peters prepare to destroy Blacula. Lt. Peters has a stake formed from another broken shovel handle. As Dr. Thomas opens the lid to the coffin, Lt. Peters drives home the stake. Unfortunately the vampire is not Blacula, but the recently transformed Tina. She appears as the others, with wild hair and fangs. After sitting up and screaming, she finally collapses in the coffin. Within moments she has reverted to her human form.

When Blacula sees his destroyed bride, he approaches the coffin. He says, "What is left for this cursed creature? His only reason for living has been taken away." He kisses her hand and stands. Dismissing Dr. Thomas, he climbs to the top of the chemical plant, up into the sunlight. Several cut-away shots show the sun blazing above. He struggles to reach the surface,

Opposite: *Despite the scene on the movie poster, Blacula (William Marshall) destroys himself through exposure to sunlight.*

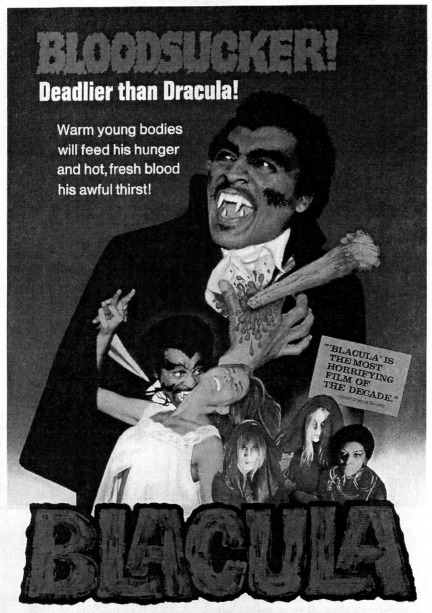

finally holding a hand up to block the light. As he collapses to the ground, he covers his face with his cape. By the time Dr. Thomas removes the cape, Blacula's face appears shriveled and decayed. Maggots crawl out of his eye sockets and mouth, while his skin smokes in the sunlight. Finally the flesh fades to bone.

The syntax of THE DESTRUCTION is similar to previous films. The expert disposes of the vampires using a stake driven through the heart. Only the end scene shows the shift in the vampire's character. Rather than being destroyed by another, Blacula sacrifices himself. He abhors his condition, and without Tina, has no reason to continue existing. This connection between vampire and victim is revisited within the original Dracula text by Dan Curtis.

Dracula (1974)

Much praise has been lauded over Dan Curtis's version of Dracula, most of it for the wrong reason. Many critics favor this version of Dracula for its faithfulness to the original Stoker novel. The creation of the script, by Richard Matheson, does attempt to bypass both the stage play by Hamilton Deane and John L. Balderston, which it does successfully, and *Horror of Dracula*, which it does not.

The very first appearance of Jack Palance could very well have been Christopher Lee. He is draped in a long black cape, and moves with the characteristic swiftness of Lee's portrayal in *Horror of Dracula*. The abruptness with which Palance delivers his lines also echoes Lee's civility, and both performances show that the social aspect of the vampire is merely a façade. Finally, the destruction of Dracula, far from being accurate to Stoker's novel, steals the scene from *Horror of Dracula* in which Van Helsing yet again tears down the curtains to reveal the sun.

Dan Curtis's *Dracula* does tie its plot more closely to Stoker's novel; however, it does so selectively. Matheson's script eliminates several characters, Quincey, Seward, and Renfield, and as a consequence brushes aside certain storylines, notably the sanitarium. Also the script adds the element of a lost love in the form of Lucy Westenra. Although credited to Matheson, this element is pure Dan Curtis. The syntax was already established in *Dark Shadows,* and the dress worn by the past incarnation of Lucy bears more than a passing resemblance to the dress worn by Josette. Additionally, all the scenes where Dracula remembers his lost love are underscored by tinkling romantic music akin to Josette's music box.

The script was strongly influenced by *In Search of Dracula: A True History of Dracula and Vampire Legends* published in 1972 by Raymond T.

McNally and Radu Florescu. This book proposed a link between the fictional character Dracula and the actual historical figure of Vlad Tepes. The film picks up this detail by having a painting of Dracula titled "Vlad Tepes: Prince of Wallachia: 1475." In the portrait Dracula is seen riding a horse into battle. The woman pictured next to him is the woman he lost, only to be recreated in Lucy. At the end of the film, Dan Curtis pays homage to the historical antecedent of Vlad the Impaler. As the camera zooms in on the painting, sounds of clanking armor and soldiers' voices can be heard. The soldiers are calling out "Dracula," over and over. Finally captions roll onto the screen explicitly relating Dracula to the historical figure Vlad.

The appearance of THE VAMPIRE in *Dracula* shifts only a little from previous versions. He wears a long dark cape through most of the film, but in some of the opening scenes, Dracula is dressed in various period suits. Jack Palance also attempts a slight Hungarian accent. Two fangs are present when the vampire attacks his victims.

The demeanor of this Dracula is one of superiority, taking the manner of Lee's Dracula and elevating it. Dracula is abrupt, cutting off Jonathan in mid sentence. Although superficially polite, the vampire is only being civil. He greets Jonathan warmly, but when done speaking, walks away, ignoring any further comment by his guest. Jonathan is even left to close the door himself. When the young solicitor mentions photos of the properties, Dracula must see them immediately, interrupting the dinner he has laid out for his guest.

The personality of Dracula also takes a turn to the sentimental when he sees the photo of Lucy. A gentle romantic music enters the film each time he sees her. The fact that Dracula believes her to be the reincarnation of his lost love is related through the painting and several flashbacks showing the young prince with the girl. Yet when Dracula is denied his prize, his inner fury arises. After discovering that Lucy has been destroyed, he hurls the lid of her coffin aside. He then overturns Lucy's coffin and proceeds to upend everything in the mausoleum.

This Dracula is extremely physical, easily flinging people aside when in his way. As the brides attack Jonathan, he tosses them away, baring his fangs. Later, at the hotel, he chokes one hotel clerk, throws another out a window, and finally hurls a third down a flight a stairs. The vampire is shown to be quite strong. He bends the bars at the zoo to release a wolf, and easily splinters locked doors.

The syntax of this VAMPIRE revolves around physicality and romance. He is exceedingly tender with Lucy, often drifting into sentimental daydreams at the thought of her. Yet when denied his desire, he will go to any

Dracula (Jack Palance) upturns a table onto Arthur (Simon Ward, left) and Van Hels-ing (Nigel Davenport) rather than cower before a crucifix in Dracula *(1974, Universal). The portrait of Vlad Tepes can be seen in the background.*

length to seek his revenge. A similar syntax is expressed in *Blacula.* When he is forced to transform Tina into a vampire, he wantonly destroys all the police in the chemical plant as revenge. Yet in *Blacula,* when Mamuwalde finds his true love destroyed, he opts for sacrifice, while Palance's Dracula first tries revenge, and then self-preservation.

Dracula uses THE LOOK only once to control his victim. Standing outside Lucy's bedroom, the film shows a shot/counter-shot of the room and his face. Each time the camera zooms in, ending in an extreme close-up of the vampire's eyes. Dracula's staring face is superimposed on the sleeping Lucy. Finally she wakes, exhibiting glazed eyes, and sleepwalks toward the waiting count.

There are several other occurrences in which the camera settles on the vampire's face for a close-up. In each of these, Dracula contemplates his lost love, accompanied by the tinkling tones of a music box. The first comes after first seeing a photo of Lucy. Dracula stares into space, and is so lost in thought that he hardly hears Jonathan speaking his name. When he next sees the photo, his face again softens, and the film blurs into a flashback. Thus the syntax of THE LOOK is twofold, one of romantic contemplation, the other mental control of his victim.

The scenes portraying the vampire's BITE are equally split between eroticism and physical attack. The vampire brides are not subtle in their attacks. In their first attack on Jonathan, one bride rushes toward him, arms upraised like claws. The other two follow suit, piling on top of their helpless victim. These vampires also hiss and growl as they attack, appearing more like animals than sentient creatures. Jonathan's later attack on Van Helsing and Arthur, brief though it is, mimics the brides actions. Lucy offers the only subtle attack when she approaches Arthur. She draws her former lover close, kissing him at first. When Arthur embraces her, rejoicing at their reunion, she turns on him. In a close-up, she bares her fangs and moves to bite his neck. This scene is almost identical to the one where the vampire bride bites Jonathan in *Horror of Dracula*.

Dracula, on the other hand, is filled with passion and tenderness when he bites Lucy. The scenes have the characteristic romantic music, as Dracula tenderly holds Lucy's head. They fervently kiss, Dracula exploring all of Lucy's face. Again this echoes the scene from *Horror of Dracula* when

Dracula (Jack Palance) draws Lucy (Fiona Lewis) close to bite her in this scene from Dracula *(1974, Universal).*

Dracula kisses Mina. Finally, Palance offers a pained look when he is finally forced to bite his lost love. A close-up reveals Lucy in a state of arousal, gently moaning as the scene slowly fades. When her body is discovered later, she maintains her glazed look, and blood is splattered on her neck. The second bite of Lucy is not seen on screen. Arthur and Van Helsing discover her body by a tree, her legs askew as though she had been a victim of rape. Blood is again present on her neck, though this time tears have run down her face. It should be noted that the position of her body, at death, is similar to the flashback death scene of Dracula's original lover.

The syntax of THE BITE takes two forms. For the vampire brides or other created vampires it functions as a vicious attack, its only purpose to gain blood. For Dracula, the bite is used as a way to unite himself with his victim. The process is overtly sexual and tied to the romantic yearning to recreate a lost love.

THE INFECTION of the victims follows the usual pattern of Stoker's novel. Lucy is weak and bedridden, wearing a bandage around her neck. After a victim dies from the vampire's attack, he or she rises as a vampire. Dan Curtis's *Dracula* explores the connection that victim and vampire share. Mina drinks Dracula's blood, and thereafter can sense his thoughts. This connection works both ways, allowing Dracula to spy on the movements of Van Helsing and Arthur.

THE EXPERT, offered by Van Helsing, follows the syntax of previous films. He is an older man, and a doctor who has some previous knowledge of vampires. He debates the vampire's existence with Arthur in the setting of the study. Arthur asks him, "How can you, a man of science, believe in such things?" Unlike Van Sloan's expert, Nigel Davenport pursues his quarry more actively. He comes prepared with stakes, a mallet, and a cross.

THE CROSS is used extensively in the film, as a set dressing, a way to identify a vampire, and to keep the creature at bay. The captain of the Demeter, lashed to the wheel, is seen clutching a cross. A cross of garlic flowers is also visible hanging from the French doors to Lucy's bedroom. Later, the cross is used more actively to ward off the vampire. After Lucy's failed attempt to bite Arthur, she charges at Van Helsing. He produces a large silver cross, which flashes in the light. Lucy halts and covers her eyes. Unable to bear the cross, she flees from the room. Dracula is not as severely affected. When Jonathan presents the cross, the vampire grimaces and averts his eyes. He then paces the room, seeking a way around the loathsome object. Dracula finally overturns a table, knocking the cross out of Jonathan's hands. The cross also functions as a method to identify a victim of vampirism. In a scene where Mina lies in bed, the maid leans in, dangling a blurred cross in the foreground. The focus quickly shifts to the cross and Mina snatches it. The sound of sizzling accompanies visible smoke wafting from Mina's hand. She tosses the cross away, showing red and blistered skin. When she sees her wound, Mina breaks out into a heart-wrenching scream.

THE DESTRUCTION of the vampires in *Dracula* takes on two forms. For the vampire brides and Lucy, staking is used. For the more dramatic climax, a combination of sunlight and a pierced heart finally do away with Dracula.

Van Helsing personally destroys Lucy. He arrives at the coffin, which in this scene has no lid. The film switches to a

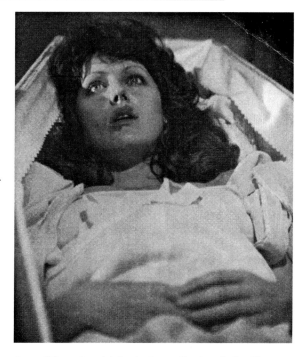

Lucy (Fiona Lewis) lies in her coffin, just before Van Helsing destroys her with a stake in the 1974 Dracula.

subjective camera from Lucy's point of view. From a low angle the camera views an enormous stake placed upon the heart. Van Helsing raises his mallet and strikes. Lucy utters a scream as Van Helsing continues, delivering three strikes. Afterward, Lucy quiets and lays dead. The destruction of the brides is seen in montage, with striking sounds and screaming. Arthur pushes the vampire Jonathan into a pit lined with stalagmites. A medium-shot shows him impaled through the heart and blood splattered onto his shirt.

Dracula is disposed of in a scene both reminiscent of *Horror of Dracula* and *Return of the Vampire*. As the vampire chokes Arthur, Van Helsing rips down the curtains, revealing daylight. Dracula turns to face the window, and the film cuts to the sun, zooming in until it is full frame. Dracula staggers away, but is confronted by sunlight everywhere he goes. (This syntax of a vampire trapped by light is repeated later in the film *Fright Night*.) Finally Dracula collapses against an upturned table. Van Helsing takes a spear and thrusts it through the vampire's heart. Dracula cries out in pain. Through a series of shot/counter-shots between Dracula and Van

Helsing, the expert drives the spear deeper with two more thrusts, finally piercing the table. At this point, Dracula's face relaxes and his head drops.

The syntax of this scene suggests that the main vampire now requires something extra to accomplish his final destruction. Much as Peter Cushing required a cross coupled with sunlight to destroy the vampire in *Horror of Dracula*, so Davenport's Van Helsing uses a stake and sunlight. Much of this has to do with the emergence of multiple vampires in the film. When the lesser vampires are dealt with in typical fashion, something more dramatic must be done with the lead villain. This is simply an extension of narrative structure, but it also hints at the exhaustion of semantic devices used in the vampire narrative. As the audience sees certain forms of destruction, it wants something different and more exciting the next go around. This is precisely the problem that faced Hammer studios, spelling the end to their series of vampire films.

The emergence of multiple vampires in film would soon lead to an entire community of vampires. Up to this point, vampires have lived aloof, separate from the world. When they do interact it is to prey upon humans, either for food or to create minions. Soon one author would change all of this.

Lestat and the Vampire Family

In 1976, Anne Rice published *Interview with the Vampire*, the first book in what would become *The Vampire Chronicles*. Although started as a short story as early as 1969, the full concept that would lead to a vampire family did not become a novel until 1973. In the novel, vampires are no longer solitary creatures. The syntax of the lone vampire, enduring the centuries, is replaced by Lestat and the family of companions he creates with Louis and the child Claudia. Here the reader discovers vampires interacting with other vampires as equals. This is a far cry from the Christopher Lee Dracula and his vampire brides, or Blacula and the spawn of vampires he created. Here the vampires form familial bonds, even living together as a group in the Theater of the Vampire.

Ironically *Interview with a Vampire* was optioned in 1976 by Paramount Pictures, but would not see theaters until 1994, with Geffen Pictures. Because of this, many of the themes put forth in Rice's book appeared in other films long before her novel reached the screen. Most notably, the concept of the vampires forming families was taken up in the film *Near Dark,* in 1987.

Rice returned to the theme of vampires with the release of *The Vampire Lestat* in 1985 and *The Queen of the Damned* in 1988. Her novels coincided with the growing gothic culture, and had a built-in audience of followers. The Gothics saw themselves as the new Romantics, and would dress and act very much like the androgynous characters of her novels. *Interview with the Vampire* has become the second best-selling vampire book of all time, just behind *Dracula,* and its popularity led to the creation of a role-playing game, *Vampire: The Masquerade.*

New Hollywood and The Emergence of Paranoid Horror

After 1948 and the anti-trust suit which began dismantling studio ownership of theaters, many studios were bought up by large conglomerates. Hammer studios, perhaps one of the last to function in the "Classic Hollywood" style, saw the end to its horror cycle with the 1973 release of *Satanic Rites for Dracula.* Several factors contributed to Hammer's demise. First was the inventiveness that each film had to go through to both revive Dracula from his destruction in the previous film, and to find a new, climactic way to dispose of the vampire in the new film. In *Dracula Prince of Darkness* (1965), for example, it took nearly half the film before Dracula reappeared. Additionally, Hammer worked hard to differentiate their product from television. In the opening of the 1969 *Taste the Blood of Dracula,* the studio uses Roy Kinnear, a well known television comedian, to confront the horrific visage of Dracula (Cook and Bernink 87). Finally the vampire films of Hammer could hardly compete with films like *The Exorcist* or *The Omen,* both of which functioned in the New Hollywood ideal of "event" cinema.

Pauline Kael, a prominent film columnist, summed up the methodology of New Hollywood succinctly: "The real power in the new conglomerate Hollywood rested with the advertising and marketing people 'who not only determine which movies get financed but which movies are going to sell'" (quoted by Cook and Bernink 98). The blockbusters of the 1970s shifted how Hollywood created films. J. Hoberman, in his article "Ten years that shook the world" cites the fact that "Hollywood's ten top-grossing films have all been released since 1975" (quoted by Cook and Bernink 102). Event movies, such as *Airport* and *Earthquake,* were concerned with having a large opening day. The idea of making a picture that earned a modest profit was eclipsed by the tremendous profit potential of these "film events."

Older "Classic Hollywood" created films that concentrated on telling a story, focusing on dramatic conflict and narrative progression. New Hollywood was concerned with "high concept," aptly described by Steven Spielberg: "If a person can tell me the idea in 25 words or less it's going to make a pretty good movie" (quoted by Cook and Bernink 103). This notion of idea over narrative meant that an audience could be pre-sold, and that advertising could saturate audiences on television. The fact that *Jaws* was released on 464 screens and was the highest grossing movie to date proved the point. Only films that could be successfully pitched and advertised interested the studios of the New Hollywood era. This, along with a shift in the horror genre, spelled doom for the traditional vampire film.

The introduction of *Psycho* (1960) to the horror landscape ushered in a progression of "paranoid" horror that centered on the duality of consciousness and unconsciousness, sanity and insanity. Cook and Bernink cite a new era in horror where "the earlier sense of a world whose moral and social order is worth defending has disappeared" (204). This "paranoid" horror had the *unknown* emerge from within society, rather than invade from outside. This led inexorably to the development of "slasher" horror films such as *Halloween, Friday the 13th,* and *Nightmare on Elm Street* that would dominate the 1980s.

The vampire narrative, if it was to compete with these new forces, needed to adapt. The remaining two films of the erotic cycle each exhibit one or more of these new elements. The 1979 *Dracula* was an "event" film, which linked the revived stage play with cinema. *Fright Night,* on the other hand, adapted to the new "paranoid" horror by casting a teenager in the lead, and advertising the film to fit the dominant "slasher" genre.

Dracula (1979)

John Badham's *Dracula* began as an extremely successful revival of the stage play. The play, essentially based on the Hamilton Deane and John L. Balderston original, centered on Frank Langella's romantic portrayal of Dracula.

THE VAMPIRE as played by Langella is very different from previous and later efforts. In terms of the film itself, Dracula is at odds with the other portrayals of the vampire. The vampire brides, Mina and Lucy, exhibit all the expected semantic elements. Both bare fangs when attacking their victims. Both appear pale, though Mina is chalky white, with sunken eyes and flaking skin. Both vampires develop solid black eyes when angered or are about to attack. Dracula, by comparison, appears as a normal human in every way. He never shows fangs, even when biting his victims. In fact Langella had some very specific ideas about how the role was to be played. He fought with Universal, refusing to wear fangs or to have any blood on him at all. The Count wears a long black cape with a high collar, and a bright white shirt that opens to reveal his chest.

Langella's performance lacks the savagery of other vampires from this film cycle. His movements are purposeful, with no unnecessary gestures. When he holds Lucy's back and takes her hand to dance, the motions are effortless and precise. He is sensual when biting his victims, especially with his chosen lover, Lucy. Both the actor and director, John Badham, saw this scene as a sort of "vampire wedding." It is clear, from the scene, that the two are joining in a sort of vampire lovemaking.

Langella's vampire is hardly physical. Though he exhibits great strength, ripping the bars from a window, he does this gracefully. Only in the final scene of his destruction does he move with furious passion, attempting to preserve himself and dislodge the hook embedded in his back. Thus the syntax for THE VAMPIRE is twofold, one for the main vampire, and one for the brides. The main vampire is a lover, a "Gothic hero" in the words of Langella from "The Revamping of Dracula" behind the scenes documentary.

Dracula employs a semantic change in THE LOOK. Although Dracula controls his victims, accompanied by a close-up of his face, Langella adds a deft wave of his hand, which he thought would mimic the two-fingered claw of a bat. When Mina is put under his spell, the camera focuses on the vampire's hand rather than eyes. The traditional syntax reasserts itself when Dracula faces Van Helsing. Dracula raises his hand and commands the expert to come to him. Van Helsing's eyes flicker and he complies, stepping forward. The film switches to an extreme close-up of the vampire's eyes as he commands his victim to obey. Langella's *Dracula* is the first to show true semantic replacement. The syntax of control is still present, but a close-up of the vampire's hand sometimes replaces the close-up of the eyes.

The very first BITE in the film comes when Dracula, in the form of a bat, bites a helpless and panicking Renfield. The next occurrence happens in Mina's bedroom. Although steeped in eroticism, this bite scene leaves more to the imagination than would be expected for a modern audience. It plays more like a scene from a film in the malignant cycle. Dracula enters through French doors and pauses to stare at his victim. Mina relaxes into her bed and unbuttons her blouse. His shadow falls over her face as the scene ends. The lack of a more explicit bite might be attributed to Langella's unwillingness to show fangs or blood. He stresses a romantic Dracula, and thus would have downplayed any scenes where he bites his victims.

The bites attempted by the vampire brides fit the established syntax more completely. When Mina faces her father, she pleads with him, thus lowering his guard. She approaches him and prepares to deliver a bite to the neck, but is halted by the sudden appearance of Dr. Seward. Later, when

Lucy does bite Jonathan, she mimics the scene from *Horror of Dracula*. Lucy plays on Jonathan's love for her. She kisses him, gently holding his head. She pushes him down onto the bed. In a close-up of her face and his neck, she transforms. Fangs appear in her mouth, and her eyes darken to black. With a sigh of glee she bites his neck. He struggles, only to be released by the appearance of a cross, presented by Van Helsing.

When Dracula bites Lucy, the scene is laid out more along the syntax of romance and sex. The film shows the characters in a two-shot, facing each other and holding hands. Dracula removes Lucy's robe and his own cape. He picks her up and carries her to bed, their eyes always fixed on each other. Laying her on the covers, he says, "I need your blood." He doesn't force himself, but rather asks permission, in much the same way as Blacula does with Tina. Next Dracula says, "I need ..." and begins kissing her midsection. They kiss passionately and Lucy starts to moan softly. A fire burns in the background. All the elements of a romantic love scene are present. At this point, the vampire actually delivers the bite, and the film chooses this moment to shift into what director Badham calls the "vampire wedding." A red laser and smoke effect encircles the lovers. The same director who shot all the opening credits of the James Bond films, Morris Binder, assisted the scene. As the vampire and lover float in the red smoke, images of candles and a bat are superimposed. John Williams's score finally spikes as the camera pulls back, and the scene ends.

Although far different from any other bite scene, the "vampire wedding" is the culmination of previous efforts. The introduction of the romantic syntax from *Dark Shadows* and the eroticism of *Horror of Dracula* are fully realized in the embrace between Lucy and Dracula. The entire scene is set up in such a way that the viewer hardly notices the actual bite. There are no fangs or blood. Instead all attention is focused on the romantic tension between the two characters.

THE INFECTION is also tinged by the romantic syntax. Although Mina wasted away, finally suffocating in bed after a bite from Dracula, Lucy functions more like a woman kept from her true love than one infected and controlled by a vampire. Each time before meeting Dracula, she removes the cross from her neck. She takes a carriage toward Dracula's home, only to be stopped by Van Helsing, Jonathan, and Dr. Seward. When confronted about her ties to Dracula, she calls him "the saddest, the kindest of all." When she bolts from the carriage, it takes all three men to subdue her. Even in the sanitarium cell, she does what she can to illicit information for Dracula. Finally, at the end of the film, as romantic music plays, she gives a half smile of satisfaction as Dracula's cape drifts away on the wind. Her look suggests that she will meet him again.

Here, the syntax of THE INFECTION shows a lover entranced by the vampire. She is not Dracula's lost love, as in *Blacula* or the 1974 *Dracula*, but someone who has willingly fallen for the vampire. The syntax is split, however, appearing differently for Mina. She is a typical victim, wasting away and transforming into a bloodthirsty vampire.

THE EXPERT, as played by Laurence Olivier, exhibits all the semantic elements associated with the role: he is a professor, and an older man; he also comes prepared with a stake and various crosses. He studies up on the vampire by reading a book containing a picture of a vampire bat. But this Van Helsing is less physical than previous vampire hunters. Much of this has to do with the age and health of the actor. On set, Olivier had a disease that caused him to bleed at the slightest action. Even gripping a prop too tightly would cause his fingers to bleed. Additionally, he could not run or perform the same strenuous stunts that Peter Cushing did as his Van Helsing. Therefore, although the character actively seeks out the vampire, his motions are not exaggerated, like the experts before him.

THE CROSS is used extensively, but inconsistently, in the film. Various syntaxes compete with each other, none showing dominance. At first, Dr. Seward uses a cross against a transformed Mina. The implement seems to have no effect as the vampire continues to attempt a bite. Finally he presses the cross against her forehead. The skin sizzles and smokes. Mina screams and attempts to flee. There is another instance of semantic change when Van Helsing presents garlic to Dracula. The vampire follows the syntax of being presented with a cross. He covers his face with his cape and moves away. Later in the scene, when Dracula is about to bite the professor, Van Helsing presents a true cross. Dracula backs away, and is driven against a wall. He says the word "sacrilege," then flees the scene.

When Jonathan attempts to present a cross in the Carfax crypt, it seems to have no effect on the vampire. Instead of averting his eyes, Dracula grabs the cross, which immediately bursts into flames. Dracula then tosses the cross aside as though it were meaningless. Finally, Van Helsing presents a cross to Lucy. Rather than avert her eyes, she watches the cross, whimpering. The film uses subjective camera from Van Helsing's point of view. Lucy finally faints, ending the scene according to the syntax. Then she revives, this time with a normal skin tone. She grabs the cross with no ill effects and kisses it. It seems as though the makers of *Dracula* weren't sure themselves how the rules of this syntax should play out. They explored all the options, settling on none.

With only two vampires destroyed, only the methods of stake and sunlight are utilized. Mina is impaled with a long wooden stake. She screams in pain and looks at her father, Van Helsing, as though confused.

In this scene from the 1979 film Dracula, *released by Universal, Dracula (Frank Langella) fears the cross, and backs away from Van Helsing (Laurence Olivier).*

She finally passes out, leaning on his shoulder. To complete THE DESTRUCTION, Van Helsing cuts out Mina's heart. When Dracula attacks Jonathan in the form of a bat, sunlight causes him to burst into flame. This hints at what will happen when Dracula, in human form, is introduced to sunlight. The film doesn't deliver on this promise. When Dracula is hoisted up into the rigging of the ship, he flails madly against the sunlight, growling like an animal. The film switches to several shots of the sun, each closer than the last. The final shot appears to be from the surface of the sun itself. Dracula ages on screen, first appearing with gray hair, then white. His skin flakes away, burning. Finally he slumps over, appearing to be dead. Badham leaves his destruction open for debate. In the final frames of the film, Dracula's cape drifts away on the wind. The smile from Lucy hints that this may not be the end for him. The attempt was to end the film romantically, holding out hope that the two lovers, Dracula and Lucy, might be reunited some time in the future.

Although possessing a tremendous budget and the full backing of Universal, *Dracula* was hampered at the box office by the release of another film, *Love at First Bite*. Coming out before the more serious film, the comedy stole some of the film's energy. However, these were not the only vampire narratives to appear this year. Another film took the public by storm, not in theaters, but on the small screen.

Salem's Lot

The adaptation of Stephen King's second novel was originally destined for the silver screen. *Night of the Living Dead*'s George Romero was approached to direct. The announcement of two other vampire movies, John Badham's *Dracula* and Werner Herzog's *Nosferatu: Phantom der Nacht*, caused Warner Brothers to scrap a theatrical release and turn instead to television. Romero left the project feeling hampered by the limitations of television.

Salem's Lot holds a unique place in the study of vampire narratives. Although coming after such films as *Horror of Dracula* and Dan Curtis's *Dracula*, it harkens back toward the malignant cycle of films, where the vampire is little more than a creature spreading evil. A great deal of this viewpoint comes from the original writing by King.

The character of Kurt Barlow, as he appears in the mini-series, seems to be lifted wholly from the 1922 film *Nosferatu*. Physically he bears little resemblance to the other vampires of the *Salem's Lot* mini-series or the erotic cycle. His skin is pale to the point of being blue, and his mouth is full of sharp teeth. He has a bald head and sports pointed ears, just like Max Schreck's portrayal of Count Orlok, from *Nosferatu*. Although approving of the overall adaptation, Stephen King took issue with this depiction of Barlow. In the novel, the vampire speaks, taunting the heroes through his wit. Director Tobe Hooper's Barlow never says a word and seems to appear in scenes suddenly like a malevolent boogeyman. He is not romantic or even the least bit erotic. Some of this change may have been linked to the remake of *Nosferatu* earlier that year. Additionally, the Gothic movement was growing more popular in the late 70s, and the bald-headed, pointy-eared Max Schreck had become their icon.

Another drastic change from King's original text occurs with Paul Monash's treatment of Susan Norton. Having been bitten by Barlow, she became a vampire herself. In the original novel, Ben Mears finds her sleeping body and is forced to dispose of it with a stake before dealing with Barlow. The same scene plays out in the mini-series, but after the destruction of Barlow and in a fictional town in Mexico. Monash has Susan track down Mears because of her love for him. She appears completely human, lacking the pale skin of the other vampires in the film. She lies seductively in a silk dress, her eyes closed to hide her bright vampire irises. She offers Mears the chance to be together with him forever, always young. She draws him in for a kiss, turning his head to expose the neck—a syntax very similar to the bride biting Jonathan in *Horror of Dracula*. The addition of this scene, and this form of vampire, is an acknowledgement of the current state of the genre. All the films from *Horror of Dracula* to Dan Curtis's *Dracula* have had vampires that share an erotic or romantic connection with the victim. Susan Norton fulfills this role.

Nearly all of the screen time in *Salem's Lot* is devoted to the victims turned into vampires. As vampires make more vampires, these creatures soon overrun the town. Bearing some resemblance to the created vampires from *Blacula*, these lesser vampires all have pale skin and yellow eyes that seem almost to glow in the night. They use slow, exaggerated, movements—walking or crawling toward their victims. The transformed boy, Ralphie Glick, floats gently through the air toward his brother. These vampires are also capable of quick movements, such as when Danny Glick jumps up to bite Mike Ryerson in the cemetery. Overall the lesser vampires appear animalistic, growling and hissing as they attack their prey.

The syntax of THE VAMPIRE is as disjointed as it was in John Badham's *Dracula*. Barlow appears as little more than a boogeyman, a monstrous creature that leaps out of the shadows to attack its victims. The lesser vampires put their victims into a trance, stalking them slowly. Only Susan Norton follows the syntax established in previous films, seducing her victim.

One of the strongest syntactic elements of *Salem's Lot* is THE LOOK. Although no special lighting or close-ups highlight the face, the vampire's glowing yellow eyes command the viewer's attention. When Ralphie Glick scratches on the window outside the bedroom, Danny walks forward in a trance. Even the expert, Berk, seems entranced by Mike Ryerson. As Mike rocks in the rocking chair, Berk sways gently, mimicking the motion. Both the vampires and experts draw attention to THE LOOK of the vampire. Mike Ryerson commands Berk to look at him. Berk is only able to break the trance by looking away from the vampire. Several times throughout the mini-series, Ben Mears warns people not to look at the vampire's eyes, forcibly pushing Mark Petrie away when he catches a glance of Barlow's eyes. Even Mike Ryerson, as he describes being bitten, repeats the words, "Eyes ... eyes." When asked about whose eyes he saw, he simply responds: "Bright and scary."

The victims who stare into the vampire's eyes cannot recall the specifics of the attack. It is as if the vampire becomes akin to a snake hypnotizing its prey. The victims remember only vague details, believing the incident to be a dream. When Mike stumbles in to meet Mears and Berk at a local bar, he looks pale and feels sick. Although he has puncture wounds from Danny Glick, he can't remember being bitten. He says only, "Don't remember ... I dreamed." When pressed for details, he points at something off screen and says, "I remember ... dream ... somebody out there ... then I let 'em in."

When a victim finally dies, they rise as a vampire within hours. They seem to retain none of their former personality. Mike Ryerson, and Marjorie Glick growl and hiss as they lust for blood. The syntax for THE INFECTION in *Salem's Lot* has the victims becoming weak, tired, and pale from loss of blood. A final bite, and subsequent draining of blood, is required for their death and transformation. Afterward, the victim looses all humanity. Again, Susan is the exception, retaining her love for Ben.

The vampire's BITE often occurs in a bedroom. Ralphie first comes to his brother in their bedroom, and later attacks when Danny is in his hospital bed. Once transformed, Danny attempts to attack Mark in his bedroom. Although Mike Ryerson is first bitten in the cemetery atop Danny Glick's coffin, his final bite occurs in the spare bedroom of Jason Berk. Finally, Barlow attacks Ned Tebbets in jail as he lies in bed.

In nearly all the bite scenes, the vampire approaches the victim, who is in an entranced state. The vampire tilts the head to reveal the neck, and open the mouth wide, revealing two fangs. Only with Barlow does the syntax change. He suddenly pops up into the frame with a close-up of his ghastly face. With Ted frozen with fear, Barlow drapes his cape over the victim to hide the act of biting.

Again there is a disconnection between the syntax of the main vampire, Barlow, and the lesser, created, vampires. In *Blacula,* the difference between THE BITE syntax of the main vampire and the lesser vampires had to do with romance. Tina afforded different treatment simply because of his feelings for her. Barlow seems to have no feelings. His different treatment, in appearance and syntax, has more to do with the usage of two different types of vampires. Barlow looks and acts more like a vampire from the malignant cycle. The lesser vampires follow a similar syntax as other films from the erotic cycle.

Salem's Lot has the most experts of any other vampire film. Some of this has to do with King's writing style, and his use of a group of individuals thrown into crisis. However careful analysis shows that there may be only two experts active at any given time. The opening scene, with Mark Petrie and Ben Mears holding the glowing bottle of holy water, clearly shows who we should consider the experts by the end of the film. But what of Jason Berk? He knows to use a cross against the vampires, and confronts Mike Ryerson. He is an older man and spends time studying library books on vampires. Yet his time in the film is limited. Berk has a heart attack and is rendered incapacitated. It is at this point that Ben Mears steps into the role of expert. He convinces Susan to hang hawthorn around her home, and Dr. Norton to investigate the body of Marjorie Glick. Thus there are two functioning older experts, Berk and Ben. Each actively seeks them out in an attempt to destroy the creatures. As Berk fails, Mears steps up to take his place.

The inclusion of Mark Petrie is unique to the genre. He is a boy, but his room is filled with scientific equipment and chemicals, horror masks, posters, and toys. He fits the syntax of THE EXPERT in every way except his age. There have been multiple experts since *Dracula's Daughter,* but the experts have always been older. Yet Mark's role cannot be overlooked. He is the first character to encounter a vampire and survive. When Danny comes to his window, he seems to fall under the same trance as Ralphie or Mike. At the last moment, Mark takes a cross from his model graveyard and holds it up. He brings a pair of stakes up to the Marsten House in an attempt to dispose of Barlow. Were it not for the intervention of Barlow's servant, Mr. Straker, Mark might have succeeded.

The syntax of THE EXPERT in *Salem's Lot* shows varying degrees of experience. Mark has all the knowledge needed, but not the strength. Jason Berk quickly learns about vampires, but is too old to effectively continue. Ben Mears, cast in the syntax of hero, must take on the role of expert to win the day. Along with Mark, they destroy Barlow and end the threat.

THE CROSS is effectively wielded by one of the three experts in the film. When Mark Petrie holds his model cross to Danny Glick, he does so at arm's length. There is a spike in the musical score as the young vampire jerks back. Danny gasps and covers his face with his arms. Mark commands him to, "Go away!" Jason Berk also uses a cross to drive Mike Ryerson away. He breaks the vampire's trance by looking down at his cross. When he holds it up, Mike backs toward the window. Mike, a somewhat older man than Danny, does not hide his face from the cross. Instead he is defiant, hissing as he moves away. Berk finally pushes the cross forward and Mike falls backward out the window.

Father Callahan, being a priest, should be able to effectively wield a cross. In the scene where he faces Barlow, Straker speaks for the vampire. "You can do nothing against the master," he says. He offers a deal to Father Callahan, asking him to throw away his cross: "Your faith against his faith." Callahan has been established as a drunk, with more faith in the bottle than the Holy Ghost. When the priest attempts to hold the cross up and drive the vampire back, Barlow casually grabs the cross and tosses it aside. The instrument of faith is next seen bent and useless on the floor.

Compare this scene with that of Ben Mears fending off Marjorie Glick. Instead of coming prepared with a cross, Mears fashions one out of two tongue depressors and some tape. He blesses the cross and then begins to say the Lord's Prayer. When Marjorie Glick awakes as a vampire, Mears defends himself by holding up the cross. The vampire hisses and claws at the air, but backs away. When Mears places the makeshift cross on Marjorie's forehead, it burns her skin, emitting smoke and a sizzling sound. After the cross is removed, a burnt impression is left on the skin. In a very unusual scene, Marjorie screams and vanishes. Two medical trays fall to the ground as if knocked over. Whether she transforms into mist or is destroyed is left in question.

Ben Mears (David Soul, right) and Mark Petrie (Lance Kerwin) sneak into the root cellar and prepare to destroy the vampire Barlow in Salem's Lot *(1979, Warner Bros.).*

The syntax of THE CROSS establishes that the person using a cross must have faith for it to work. When used effectively, the vampire is driven away. However, there is some consideration of the vampire's maturity. Danny must hide his face, while Mike and Marjorie merely back away, seemingly defiant. The question of whether Barlow could overcome any cross, or just those wielded by the unfaithful, is unanswered.

The only certain DESTRUCTION appears with Barlow. Ben Mears and Mark Petrie drag his coffin out into the basement. Ben opens the lid and shoves a stake in the heart. Barlow hisses and growls, attempting to stop Ben. Using a hammer, Ben pounds the stake farther in. Finally the vampire stops struggling. The next shot shows the skin melted away and naked bone. Susan is killed in much the same way, although she doesn't struggle as violently. The syntax of fire is hinted at as Ben and Mark set fire to the Marsten house. The screams of the vampires trapped inside are heard as the house goes up in flames.

One unique aspect of *Salem's Lot* is the inclusion of Mr. Straker as Barlow's servant. Unlike previous films like *Dracula's Daughter* or *Return of the Vampire*, the servant becomes a more major character than the main vampire. This may be due to the casting of prominent actor James Mason in the role. He is even given many of Barlow's lines from the novel. His destruction calls into question the servant's humanity. Ben fires five bullets into Straker, and only after the fourth does he begin to weaken. Straker is also exceedingly strong, picking up Dr. Norton and impaling the man on a wall full of taxidermy animals.

Salem's Lot, though only appearing on television, had a major impact on viewers and future vampire films. It would take six years before the next major vampire event, but the next film not only paid homage to many scenes from the mini-series, but even shot on the same set as the Marsten House.

Fright Night

John Badham's *Dracula* combined the syntactic elements of the vampire narrative with romance. *Fright Night* added the syntax of the teen "slasher" film to the mix, creating a true genre pastiche. The film has many elements to associate it with the teen horror movies of the time. The opening scene has teenagers making out on the floor next to a bed. In fact a teenager, rather than the mature heroes of previous vampire films, plays the lead role. The girlfriend is virginal, and ends up in a lover's tiff with the hero. There are even some token scenes at the local high school. Most importantly, the adults of the film do not believe the hero and are noticeably absent or ineffective throughout the film.

The theatrical trailer refers to the vampire as "something not human, something horrifying, something unspeakably evil." The scenes from the trailer show the vampire briefly, and only transformed in his hideous, monster make up. The trailer refers to the vampire as "it," never using the word "vampire." The movie poster reduces the traditional figure of the vampire to a tiny silhouette in the window of a house. Ominous clouds dominate the sky, forming grotesque fanged creatures more akin to demons than vampires. The advertising makes the film seem more like a haunted house movie or a creature feature than a vampire film.

When the film opens, it immediately goes about acknowledging the fact that the older vampire films are not at all scary. A washed up actor, Peter Vincent, hosts a late-night horror show that plays, among other things, Hammer films. Peter Vincent is an obvious parody of Peter Cushing. As if to emphasize the point that vampires are passé, the character is fired from his job because, "nobody wants to see vampire killers anymore, or vampires either. Apparently all they want are demented madmen, running around in ski masks, hacking up young virgins." This critique of modern horror, delivered by Roddy McDowell, who plays Peter Vincent, sums up the problem with the vampire narrative. It has become out of touch with modern audiences. It needs to evolve to survive. By combining it with the already popular syntax of the teen "slasher" film, the vampire narrative is able to make a comeback. In fact *Fright Night* spawned a sequel as well as a multitude of vampire films in the late 1980s and early 1990s. These newer films would follow in its footsteps, casting teenagers as the lead characters, and create the sympathetic film cycle. *Fright Night,* however, still belongs to the erotic cycle as it continues to maintain ties to the romantic syntax so popular through the 1970s.

There are two experts in the film, neither of whom is able to defeat the vampire at the start of the film. Peter Vincent contains all the semantic elements of THE EXPERT. He is an older man and is first seen with a box full of stakes, mallets, and crosses. His clothes echo those of Van Helsing from the Hammer films. Yet he is only an actor and too timid to ever fully take on a vampire. He seems to represent the washed up expert. Charley Brewster (whose last name may have been inspired by the expert in *Son of Dracula*) is full of vigor, preferring to charge headlong into battle with the vampire. He is young and naïve, often unable to defend himself against his more experienced adversary, Jerry Dandridge.

Freed from the study or library, the debate between supernatural forces and science takes a shift in *Fright Night.* "Paranoid" horror centers on the difference between sanity and insanity, and this is the focus of debate in the film. No one believes Charley when he says that a vampire is living next door to him. Peter Vincent thinks he is insane, and Ed comments, "There are no such things as vampires, fruitcake."

Living next to Dandridge, Charley confronts him several times. In many of these confrontations, subtle verbal threats are passed back and forth between the inexperienced Charley and the vampire. Instead of reading up on vampire lore and myth, Charley pays his friend, Ed, for the information. Finally, he enlists the help of the more experienced Peter Vincent. Together, these experts finally confront and defeat the vampires. Peter Vincent runs Ed through with a stake, and they both break the windows to ultimately destroy Dandridge.

The syntax of THE EXPERT, really does not differ much from previous films. Except for the semantic change of older man to younger teen, many of the same functions apply. They are the ones who utilize the cross and stake to track down and destroy the vampires. They engage in an ongoing debate about whether the vampires are in fact real.

THE VAMPIRE, Jerry Dandridge, dresses in modern clothes, yet maintains many of the elements of previous vampires. He wears a gray trench coat with the label turned up like the collar of a cape. Underneath he has a white shirt, unbuttoned to show off his chest, like Langella's shirt. Dandridge even wears a silver crest ring. He has the other physical characteristics of vampires: fangs that appear when needed, dark hair, a deep growling voice when attacking, and dark "wolf" eyes. Jerry takes the duality of the vampire to an entirely new level. Although Blacula physically transformed from the noble and polite Mamuwalde to a bloodthirsty vampire, the effects were superficial. Advancements in make up allowed *Fright Night* to extend these transformations to the horrific.

Charley Brewster (William Ragsdale), though passionate about destroying vampires, is woefully unprepared. This publicity still from Fright Night *(1985, Columbia) shows him with a sharpened stake and hammer.*

When Dandridge becomes angry, such as receiving a pencil thrust through the hand, he transforms into something more demon than human. His fingers lengthen and grow long sharp fingernails shaped like claws. His voice deepens to a low animal growl. His mouth has three sets of oversized fangs more akin to wolf's teeth than vampire fangs. The skin becomes mottled, and pointed ears jut up through wild hair. Finally the eyes are a deep red, using contacts meant to simulate wolf eyes. In this state, the vampire is often filled with anger and frustration.

When he transforms back to a more human form, a calm intellect pervades the vampire. His actions are simple without unnecessary use of force. He flicks open a nailed window with only two fingers. Dandridge is also quite sensible. After being damaged by Charley, he has the opportunity to destroy him, but is stopped by the cries of his mother from the other room. A vampire from a previous film might not have given a second though to killing both characters, but Dandridge is a modern vampire. He knows the police will have questions. The vampire even evokes some sympathy in his first physical confrontation with Charley. He holds the teen by the throat up against a wall, saying, "You deserve to die boy. Of course, I could give you something I don't have ... a choice." He wants Charley to forget about him and what he'd seen. In previous films, such kind treatment was reserved for the vampire's lover. The fact that Dandridge could, at first, kill Charley but chooses not to hints at the developing sympathy of the vampire character.

Ultimately the syntax of The Vampire plays out as a dual character, one who is predatory or a kind lover. Dandridge sees a re-creation of his lost love in Amy. His treatment of her is far gentler than the bouncers at the club. These he tosses around, slashing one by the throat.

The Look is reserved for Amy, the lost love of the vampire. He stares at her in the dance club, zigzagging back and forth through the crowd like an animal stalking its prey. The vampire finally pops up in front of his lover, and takes her onto the dance floor. Amy's eyes are glazed over in a trance. On the dance floor, she exhibits an uncharacteristic sensuality, and the two share a sexually charged dance.

Initially Charley sees Dandridge Bite a prostitute through his bedroom window, although the scene is only implied and ends before the attack can actually be delivered. Romantic music plays as Dandridge undresses the woman. He raises his head, baring a single pair of fangs, but stops when he sees Charley watching. His delicacy extends to other victims. When the vampire traps Evil Ed in an alley, he presents vampirism to the young teen. It is clear that this is an offer Evil cannot refuse, but instead of attacking, Dandridge holds out a hand toward his victim. He says, "They won't pick on you anymore. [...] All you have to do is take my hand." His hand has transformed to long fingers with claw-like nails. When Evil accepts, Dandridge enfolds his victim in the trench coat. Later, two puncture marks are visible on Evil's neck, implying a bite.

Only when Dandridge is alone with Amy does the film actually show a full BITE scene. The scene has many semantic elements borrowed from romance films. A fire burns in the background, and Amy sits on a fur rug. She is dressed in a long flowing dress, while the vampire removes his shirt, baring his chest. Romantic music accompanies the scene. The two kiss, and Amy unfastens her dress, baring her neck and chest. At this point, Dandridge finally bares a double set of fangs and opens his mouth wide. In a close-up showing the vampire's face and the victim's neck and shoulders, Dandridge lowers for the bite, along with a strong crunching sound. Amy gasps as the vampire holds the bite for the remainder of the scene. Rills of red blood trickle down her back as Amy softly moans. The syntax of this scene is quite similar to Dracula and Lucy's "vampire wedding" in the 1979 *Dracula*.

Both of the lesser vampires, Evil and Amy, are much more physical when they attack. Evil charges Peter Vincent, a mess of fangs jutting out of his mouth. Amy uses sympathy to lower Charley's defenses. She turns

After being bitten by Dandridge, Amy's (Amanda Bearse) entire demeanor changes in Fright Night *(1985, Columbia).*

her back on him and cries, saying, "You promised you wouldn't let him get me." As Charley reaches to comfort her, Amy raises her head revealing an exaggerated smile full of sharp teeth. She spins on her former boyfriend, arms raised like claws, and charges.

As in former films, the syntax for THE BITE is different for various vampires. The master or main vampire treats his lover, and some other victims, tenderly. Whereas the lesser vampires are always physical, often charging their victims.

THE INFECTION in *Fright Night* has the victims convert to vampirism quickly. Evil completely accepts vampirism, relishing his new power. Amy, too, seems to have forgotten about her feelings for Charley. Her hair grows and she adopts a more sexual demeanor. She is connected to Dandridge and is under his control. He commands her to awake and kill Charley and Peter Vincent.

The inconsistencies of THE CROSS syntax in Langella's *Dracula* are resolved in *Fright Night*. Early on, Evil states that in order for a cross to work on a vampire, the user must have faith. Dandridge repeats this axiom when Peter Vincent presents his cross. Instead of cowering before the instrument, as expected by the syntax, the vampire laughs. He then grips the cross in one hand, crushing it. He says to Peter, "You have to have faith for this to work on me." As if to test this point, Charley holds up his cross, this time backing it with his faith. The vampire fixes his eyes on the cross, and moans, backing away. Later, Peter Vincent attempts to use the cross against Dandridge again. Initially it seems to have failed, as before. The vampire starts to hide behind his arm, but then realizing who it is, laughs at Peter Vincent. The now bolstered vampire killer redoubles his effort, and Dandridge cringes, hiding behind his arm.

THE CROSS also reveals a difference in strength in the various vampires. The lesser vampires, Evil and Amy, cower easily before Peter Vincent's cross. When Evil attacks the actor in his apartment, Peter Vincent places a cross on the creature's forehead. Instantly smoke issues from Evil's skin, along with a sizzling sound. Peter Vincent removes the cross to reveal a burnt X mark on the vampire's forehead. Evil grabs his head, whimpers, and collapses. Peter Vincent then drives the vampire out of the apartment using the cross.

Just as there are two physical forms to the vampire, there are two levels of strength for the vampire. More effort is needed to gain results on a more experienced vampire. This could explain some of the inconsistencies of THE CROSS syntax in Langella's *Dracula*.

THE DESTRUCTION of Dandridge in *Fright Night* has echoes from John Badham's *Dracula* as well as Dan Curtis's *Dracula*. When sunlight first

In this scene from Fright Night *(1985, Columbia), Peter Vincent (Roddy McDowall, left) touches the cross to Evil's (Stephen Geoffreys) forehead, accompanied by smoke and a sizzling sound.*

strikes the vampire, transformed into a bat, he is attempting to bite the throat of Peter Vincent. This scene follows the same syntax of the bite attack of Jonathan in the 1979 *Dracula*. In that scene, Van Helsing knocks a support beam loose to let the daylight into the mine. When a beam of light strikes the bat, it bursts into flames. In *Fright Night*, light streams in through a broken stained-glass window. Peter Vincent lifts the attacking bat up into the light, and it begins to smoke and light on fire. Later, in the basement, Charley breaks the blacked-out windows, sending shafts of daylight into the room. Dandridge stands in the center of the room as more shafts of light fence him in. He panics, groaning and growling. This is similar to Jack Palance's performance during his destruction scene. Unlike previous films, Dandridge will not enter the sunlight. Charley finally removes a plank, striking the vampire full in the chest with sunlight. Dandridge is flung backward as green flame explodes from his body. His flesh tears, slipping away from bone. The skeleton underneath is that of a giant demonic bat. There is a final explosion of fire and the skeleton vanishes.

There are two scenes in which vampires are attacked with stakes. With Evil, the attack appears to be successful. Peter Vincent, attempting to escape the vampire, knocks over a table. Evil, transformed into a wolf, charges down the hall in slow-motion. The expert raises a broken table leg, impaling the wolf, and sending it over the balcony. The wolf moans on the floor below, gradually transforming back into Evil's human form. The vampire tries to pull the stake out, but does not have the strength. After Peter Vincent is sure that the creature is dead, he removes the stake.

A similar syntax occurs when Peter Vincent encounters Dandridge in his coffin. The expert hammers a stake into the vampire's heart. Suddenly Dandridge stands up in his coffin. He grips the stake and strains, finally removing the instrument. What would seem to be a new syntax has in fact been used before, back with *Return of the Vampire*. What finally happens to Evil's body remains a mystery. In the final scene, a flash of eyes appear from the dark, accompanied by a voice-over by Evil. This fits in well with the syntax of teen "slasher" movies, where the killer never dies with the first attack, often surviving to return in a sequel.

Although *Fright Night* did have a sequel, it was without the character of Evil. The appearance and demeanor of his character, however, carried over into the next two films. Evil, dressed in street clothes, and fueled with an adolescent's desire for a good time was soon to become the staple for a new cycle of vampire films.

3

THE SYMPATHETIC CYCLE
(1987–)

Overview

At first glance, the vampire films of the 80s and 90s seem to go in every conceivable direction, totally unraveling the syntax established by previous corpus. These films move away from the aristocratic realm, and place the vampire within the context of everyday life. The vampires of the sympathetic film cycle, spanning from 1987 to present day, come from every walk of life. As the role of the vampire expands, so does the traditional vampire narrative.

Some of the confusion about the films of this period comes from too narrow a view of the vampire narrative. In order to revive, vampires needed to adapt to the prevailing audience taste. Horror franchises like *Halloween* (1978), *Friday the 13th* (1980), or *Nightmare on Elm Street* (1985) all involved teenagers struggling against seemingly unstoppable psychotic killers. Parental involvement was reduced to a minimum. *Fright Night* proved that vampires could still scare, and led to the production of *Near Dark*, and *The Lost Boys*.

Many of the films of this cycle are genre pastiches, combining the vampire narrative with other successful genres. *The Lost Boys* combines elements of a teen gang, while *Near Dark* adds syntactic elements from the Western. *Buffy the Vampire Slayer* stars a teenager in high school, adding the syntax of the teen drama. These films did not cross over into other genres, but rather incorporated syntactic and semantic elements from other genres, meshing them with the vampire narrative.

The most important shift in these films comes with the vampire assuming hero status. In all the films of this cycle, the vampire has sympathetic qualities, dominating the screen time in the film. This sympathetic vampire takes two different tracks. In one instance, a victim is infected and becomes a vampire. The victim must then fight against the condition of vampirism, and this struggle becomes the focus of the film. In *The Lost Boys*, and *Near Dark*, Michael, and Caleb each resist the bloodlust, desperately fighting to regain their mortality. In *Buffy the Vampire Slayer*, and *Blade*, an already existing vampire seeks to throw off his condition, and redeem himself for his past bloodletting. The other track sees the vampirism as a curse, and the vampire as the victim. The title character of *Bram Stoker's Dracula* centers on the character's unwillingness to condemn his true love to the curse of vampirism. It takes the romantic syntax of John Badham's *Dracula* farther, establishing the vampire as the sympathetic villain. At the end of the film, the audience understands why he must be destroyed, but it is only Mina who can do the deed. Dracula's lover must end his eternal suffering. In *Interview with the Vampire* Louis spends much of the film avoiding the necessity of killing involved with vampirism. He clings to his human morals. Additionally, Claudia is portrayed as a mature woman trapped in the body of a child through the curse of vampirism.

Many of the supernatural qualities of vampirism are dropped from the vampire narrative. The expert takes a diminished role, and the hypnotic LOOK and religious aspect of THE CROSS are virtually abandoned. The vampires of these films begin to borrow more from action films, choosing physical combat over THE BITE. The vampire becomes much more physical, transforming into an animalistic state when attacking victims. The transformation usually involves altered eyes that appear like those of a wolf or bat, long fingers with claw-like nails, fangs, and a raised forehead. The predatory vampire shows a physical representation of the animal lust within.

The Lost Boys

Although campy and riddled with bright colors and rock music, Schumacher's *The Lost Boys* picks up on the teen movie trend set forth in *Fright Night*. As originally scripted, *The Lost Boys* started as a very different movie from the one audiences saw in 1987. Playing off the popularity of *Goonies*, the original screenplay, penned by Janice Fischer and James Jeremias, had all the characters as fifth and sixth grade children. The Frog Brothers were eight-year-old Cub Scouts, and Star was a boy. When Schumacher came on board the project, he loved the title, but scrapped the concept. Instead, he cast the characters as teenagers, and changed the male character of Star to a female love interest. Much of the new tone that Schumacher was after, the sexy and hip vampires, is due to the efforts of screenwriter Jeffery Boam.

The Lost Boys fulfills many of the requirements for the teen movie. Nearly all the major characters are teenagers, and these characters dominate the film. The adults—mom, grandpa, and the head vampire Max—are hardly seen in the film. Additionally, the film was targeted at the hip status of vampirism. The film tagline runs: "Sleep all day. Party all night. Never grow old. Never die. It's fun to be a vampire." The film seems to equate being a vampire to the ultimate in cool, a rock star lifestyle.

This film has seven fully functioning vampires, all sharing screen time. When David and the other vampires first appear on screen, the syntax mimics that of a teen gang movie. The four vampires stroll along a merry-go-round, only to mix it up with a rival gang leader. These vampires are decked out with long hair, earrings, biker jackets, and they ride motorcycles. David even has a cigarette tucked behind one ear. Although a lesser vampire, David assumes the lead role as villain. His personality is also that of the teen gang leader. He plays cruel jokes on Michael, almost leading him off a cliff, or making Michael believe he's eating maggots. Though after these pranks, David does appear somewhat guilty, apologizing to Michael.

When David, or the others of his vampire gang prepare to attack, they undergo physical transformation. Their skin becomes pale, and they sprout double fangs. Their forehead and brow protrudes to affect a slightly demonic look. Red and black eyes and long sharp fingernails complete the transformation. Even the head vampire, Max, changes into this predatory form at the end of the film, though through most of the film he appears as a benign video shop owner.

The syntax of THE VAMPIRE is more straightforward for the gang members. Although they have a separate physical form, used for attacking or when angered, their personality does not shift, nor does the treatment of victims differ. Max, hardly seen in his vampire role, does portray the duality of past vampires. As he woos Lucy, the mom, he is kind and romantic, yet when he transforms at the end, he is uncompromising and vicious.

THE INFECTION is the dominant syntax of the film. The hero, Michael, is predisposed to join the vampires and their gang. At the start of the film he rides a motorcycle up to his grandfather's house, and later on he purchases a leather jacket. These semantic elements link him to David's gang of vampires, who all wear leather jackets and ride motorcycles. Michael's infection does not involve a bite from a vampire. Instead, the hero succumbs through peer pressure by drinking a bottle of wine, which is actually vampire blood. During this scene, the other gang members chant Michael's name. Later the pressure to conform is portrayed in the cliché of jumping off a bridge. The entire syntax of this infection is similar to an initiation into a gang. During the attack on the "surf nazi" beach party, David says, "Initiation's over, Michael. Time to join the club." In order to fully "join the club," and move from half-vampire to full vampire Michael must kill a victim. Two others, Star and Laddie, also fall under the label of half-vampires.

Unlike the infected victims of previous films, Michael struggles against the effects of the vampire's bloodlust. When he goes to drink milk, a sudden pain strikes his stomach. Michael collapses to the floor as the sound of a beating heart plays over the scene. Michael is next seen only as a silhouette, climbing the stairs toward his little brother, Sam. Later, Michael tries to sleep, but again the beating heart dominates the soundtrack. When faced with the bloodbath at the "surf nazi" beach party, Michael can hardly control himself. The camera switches back to him, fully transformed with pale skin, raised forehead, and fangs. The camera zooms in on his face as he struggles with his hunger. Sweat beads on his face, and finally Michael falls back.

Later, Star relates the difficulty of vampirism: "For me it gets harder and harder to resist. I'm weak." The vampire's INFECTION picks up the syntax of a drug addition, and adds the peer pressure of the gang initiation. The film also explicitly separates the half-vampires from the full vampires. Star and Laddie sleep in a bed, while David and the others sleep in a cave.

The film also clearly separates victims-as-food-source, from victims-as-potential-converts. The first two BITE scenes are implied, and targeted toward characters that have annoyed David. First to be attacked is the guard who made the gang leave the boardwalk. The film uses a subjective camera from the point of view of the vampires, flying over the victim. A screeching noise, sounding a little like the cries of a bat, accompanies the vampire's flight. The victim attempts to flee, only to be dragged up into the air with a scream. Through the entire scene, the vampire gang is never seen. Later the rival gang leader and his girlfriend are attacked in their car. The vampires rip the roof from the car, again unseen. Subjective camera is used to see the panic of the victims as they are hauled up into the sky. Finally, at the "surf nazi" beach party, David is seen actually biting a victim. He sinks his teeth into a surfer's head, accompanied by a geyser of blood. All the attacks in this scene occur in a rapid series of cuts. One victim shows a gaping neck wound. All these victims are clearly not going to rise as vampires. They are never seen again in the film.

Only when Max attempts to bite Lucy does the standard syntax of the vampire BITE establish itself. The head vampire, transformed into his predatory form, extends his hand to the victim. The offer is not entirely free to resist. Max has Sam in a grip and intends to break his neck if she won't comply. Lucy takes his hand and is drawn into the vampire's embrace. A close-up of the vampire and the victim's neck is used for the actual bite.

Max opens his mouth wide, revealing fangs, and prepares to sink them into Lucy's neck. The implication is that Lucy will become infected and rise as a vampire.

The syntax of THE BITE shows a clear distinction between attacking for food and for initiation. The extremely swift and physical attacks of the gang signal either revenge killing, or bloodlust. The syntax of Max's bite is slower and more fluid. He completely controls the situation.

THE LOOK as a syntactic element has diminished through the last few films, and has little function in *The Lost Boys*. There are two scenes that contain either the syntax or the semantic elements for THE LOOK. When David offers Michael Chinese food, he demonstrates the syntax of controlling the victim through hypnotic powers. Few of the semantic elements of THE LOOK are used. A medium-shot of David shows him hand over the rice. As Michael eats it, David chuckles. He suggests that Michael is actually eating maggots. A close-up reveals insects crawling instead of rice. Another scene involves some of the semantic elements, without the control of the victim through hypnotic powers. When Michael stalks up the stairs toward Sam, the semantic elements of vampire and victim are established. A series of rapid cuts alternate between the dog, Nanook, and Michael. With each shot, the camera tightens on Michael, until achieving an extreme close-up of his eyes.

The Lost Boys has the youngest experts in film. The Frog brothers, perhaps fourteen, fulfill the syntax of THE EXPERT. They work in a comic book store, and already know much about the vampire lore. Another preteen, Sam, also assumes the role of EXPERT He accepts the vampire comic books, and is seen reading them. Throughout the picture, the three consult often about the state of vampirism. These experts test Max to see if he is a vampire. They use the tools of the trade: stakes, and holy water. These experts destroy all of the lesser vampires. Though clearly not the lead role Peter Cushing explored in the Hammer films, these experts do contribute to the destruction of the vampires.

There is only one authentic use of THE CROSS syntax in *The Lost Boys,* and this is an homage to *Salem's Lot*. In the scene, Sam is trying to call his mother while his brother, Michael, floats outside the window. Sam raises his fingers to create a cross. The effect is meant to reference a similar scene in *Salem's Lot* when Mark Petrie uses a cross to ward off Danny Glick although the ultimate effect in *The Lost Boys* is more comedic than serious.

THE CROSS sees a major semantic alteration to the syntax. Instead of using crosses on the vampires, the experts utilize holy water. The effects follow the same syntax of THE CROSS as seen in previous films. Instead of touching the vampire with the cross and having the skin sizzle and smoke, holy water is now splashed on for the same effect. The original syntax saw the expert forcefully present the cross to a vampire. Now, the experts hold up a squirt gun, and spray holy water onto the vampires. When the Frog brothers splash water onto one vampire, he grips his face in pain. The skin instantly smokes, and later the skin is pitted and burned.

Holy water is also used to destroy a vampire. The Frog brothers, along with the dog, Nanook, knock a vampire into a tub of holy water. The vampire flails and screams as smoke billows from the tub. The vampire seems to die, following the "false death" syntax of teen horror films. When the vampire revives, the water in the tub boils. The vampire dips beneath the boiling holy water and emerges as a skeleton.

The destruction of the other vampires is accomplished by thrusting a stake through the heart. One gang member receives a stake while hanging upside down in his cave, which serves as the vampire's coffin. Edgar Frog jams the stake through the sleeping vampire, piercing all the way through the chest. A gooey blood gushes out of the chest. The vampire falls to the ground, flailing and screaming. Sam kills another vampire using a bow and arrow. This vampire also exhibits a "false death," before jumping up to attack the expert. Sam shoots again, this time piercing the heart. The vampire flies backward, crashing into a stereo system. Electricity courses through the creature, and the limbs explode in bursts of blood.

David is also destroyed with a stake of sorts in another reference to *Salem's Lot.* In the miniseries, Straker lifts up Dr. Norton and pushes him onto a wall full of

David (Kiefer Sutherland) recoils when sunlight strikes his hand, an implied form of destruction, in The Lost Boys *(1987, Warner Bros.).*

mounted animal horns. In *The Lost Boys*, Michael tosses David onto a pair of antelope horns from Grandpa's taxidermy workshop. Smoke drifts from the wound as the vampire cries in pain. A light shines on the body, illuminating the creature as it relaxes and finally dies. Later, David returns to normal, losing the predatory look of the vampire. The hopes for a sequel required that David somehow survive. This is the reason he does not disintegrate like the other vampires. David was to return in the film *Lost Girls*.

Finally, the master vampire, Max, is also destroyed with a massive stake shot out from Grandpa's jeep. A massive stake pierces through the vampire, who flies backward and explodes with fire. This scene echoes the destruction of Jerry Dandridge in *Fright Night*.

The syntax of The Destruction remains true in its treatment of infected victims. Michael, Star, and Laddie all return to normal after the main vampire is destroyed. Thus the return to the status quo happens through the destruction of the abnormal creatures, the vampires. In the next film, the return to normalcy is accomplished through a somewhat more forced solution.

Near Dark

As with *The Lost Boys*, the vampire's infection is the most important syntax throughout *Near Dark* although some syntactic elements are downplayed or utterly dropped in the film. The reason for this lies in the history of the film. Originally, director Kathryn Bigelow wanted to film a Western. When she wasn't able to secure any financing, she pitched a vampire Western, and *Near Dark* was born.

Many of the traditional semantic and syntactic elements of the vampire genre are deliberately removed from the film. According to *The 80's Movie Rewind*, Bigelow's concept was to strip away the "gothic underpinning that surrounded vampires, like holy water, bats, and then merging that with the classic elements of a Western or road movie." The syntax of The Look is absent in the film. The vampires never exert any kind of mental control, nor is the close-up of their face used as they stare down a victim. Crosses do not appear anywhere in the film, either as scenery or tools to injure the vampires. The syntax of The Expert is relegated to a minor role. Loy Colton, a veterinarian, searches for the vampires in much the same way that the experts of past films hunted vampires. Also, Loy ultimately saves Caleb and Mae, curing them of their infection through a blood transfusion.

Like *Fright Night* and *The Lost Boys*, *Near Dark* is a mixture of genres. It has the romantic syntax established during the erotic cycle, but also the added element of the Western. The setting of the film is Oklahoma, and the hero, Caleb, wears a cowboy hat, and a single spur. In the final confrontation, Caleb rides down the street on his horse with a lasso at his side. The town is deserted, with all the businesses dark. A close-up of horse's hooves shows a tumbleweed blow along the street by the wind. Later, Severen stands on one end of the street and throws Caleb to the foreground, an arrangement similar to the western showdown. Severen even uses his six-shooter to fire a shot into the head of an unwary truck driver. This is deliberate. Bigelow wanted the vampires to be "modern gunslingers" (*The 80's Movie Rewind*).

In Near Dark *(1987, F/M Entertainment), Jesse (Lance Henricksen) wears a towel over his head to protect himself from sunlight.*

THE VAMPIRE in *Near Dark* is modeled off of a family, with each character serving a different role. Jesse Hooker acts as the father, and Diamondback as the mother. These positions are not based on genetic ties, rather on the character's leadership roles and apparent age relative to the others. Severen and Mae play the roles of older brother and sister. The vampire child is Homer although his personality seems to be of an old man. This is a syntax borrowed from Anne Rice's novel, *The Interview with the Vampire*. All of the vampires dress in scruffy street clothes. When avoiding sunlight, the vampires cover themselves in thick blankets and wear goggles.

The syntax for THE BITE reverses the arrangement of vampire and lover. When Mae encounters Caleb, he is the one who pursues her. She has an opportunity to attack when he draws her close with a lasso. They kiss, and then fall into an embrace. In a close-up of her face and his neck, she is prepared to bite. She hesitates, and then pulls away. Instead of wooing and biting her lover, she resists the temptation. Still, Caleb presses the physical relationship. He insists on a kiss. Mae obliges, moving toward his neck. This time, in another close-up, she does bite his neck. At first he appears aroused until hearing a small puncture sound. Then he jerks away. Blood appears on her lips, though she never shows fangs. A bloody puncture wound is visible on his neck.

Severen also physically bites a customer in the bar. He applies pressure to the victim's head, finally twisting it and snapping the neck. A close-up shows the vampire lean in for a bite on the victim's neck. The scene is too dark to show fangs. After the bite, the vampire burps, and wipes blood from his mouth.

Many of the other BITE scenes do not involve the vampire's implied fangs. At the bar, Jesse and Diamondback attack a waitress. Jesse initiates the scene, following the syntax of THE BITE. He pulls the victim into an embrace on his lap. The film cuts to Diamondback flipping open a butterfly knife. She pulls back the victim's head, exposing the neck. The throat is slit off camera. Jesse uses a glass mug to catch the blood, and then pushes the victim to the floor. Severen also uses a cutting device to extract blood. When attacking the bartender, he slashes at the throat with his spur. A bloody gash appears on the skin before the victim slumps to the floor.

A new syntax is added to THE BITE in *Near Dark,* also borrowed from Rice's novel. When Caleb is unable to feed, Mae gives him blood. She bites her own wrist, and offers it to a kneeling Caleb. In a close-up shot, he grabs her arm and greedily drinks. The sound of heart beating overlays the scene. As Caleb drinks more, the heartbeat accelerates. Mae tries to remove her arm, but Caleb grips it tighter. She finally forces her arm away. This is a direct reference to Rice's novel and her syntax for vampire infection (See *Interview with the Vampire* movie analysis). In preparation for this film, Bigelow read Stoker's *Dracula* and Rice's *Interview with the Vampire.* Instead of using the wrist bite for infection, Bigelow chooses to show how a vampire who is unwilling to kill can survive. Mae must help him survive by giving him some of her own blood. This process is not without risk.

This scene is repeated after Caleb fails to attack the trucker. Mae lifts the victim's neck and bites. In the next shot, Caleb is kneeling and drinking from Mae's wrist, the victim dead on the ground. This time she must yank her arm away from Caleb. She stumbles and falls to the ground. Caleb is also on the ground, grinning. She tells him that if he drinks too much it will kill her. As a response, Caleb continues to smile, a gleam in his eye.

His ignorance to Mae's condition underlies the nature of the vampire INFECTION. *Near Dark* portrays vampirism as a drug addiction, with instant effect. Immediately after being nipped by Mae, Caleb begins to suffer the effects of vampirism. The emerging daylight causes him to stagger. The film includes a medium-shot of the sun rising in the sky. Caleb begins to smoke and his skin blackens.

The link to drug addiction is made explicitly clear when Caleb enters the bus station. At this point, Caleb has gone without blood for too long. He is pale and sweating. Pains wrack his stomach, and he doubles over in agony. He tries to eat a candy bar, but spits it out. An undercover cop even thinks that he is a drug addict, asking him what he's on. While interrogating Caleb, he reaches up with a bandaged hand. Immediately, Caleb is drawn to the sight of blood.

Just as in *Lost Boys* the syntax of initiation occurs with Caleb's relationship to the other vampires. Mae takes on the duty of teaching Caleb how to live as a vampire. The others speak of her "carrying" Caleb. Later, the initiation is linked to the romantic syntax established between Mae and Caleb. For Mae the beauty of the night is everything, but "the night has its price." She tells Caleb, "You have to learn to kill." Mae brushes aside the nastier aspects of killing humans, saying, "Don't think of it as killing. Don't think at all."

The syntax of THE INFECTION has the victim transform into a vampire in a matter of minutes. The new vampire is addicted to blood, and must have a "fix" every few days. Initiation into this cycle of addiction is also part of the syntax, causing the vampires to band together in family units. The infection is ultimately cured through a total transfusion of blood. This element, Bigelow says, was inspired from Stoker's original novel, *Dracula*.

These vampires are destroyed only through sunlight. Bullets cause pain, but are ultimately ineffective. When Homer leaps from the car into the morning light, his face begins to billow smoke. Flames burst from his head. Finally the vampire falls to his knees, screaming, and explodes in a burst of fire. Jesse and Diamondback also succumb to sunlight. Jesse's hand turns charcoal black in the light, quickly sprouting flame. Black smoke swirls from the car. The doors fly from the body of the car as the vehicle explodes in flames. Fire is strongly associated with THE DESTRUCTION syntax. Rather than sunlight, the explosion of a gasoline truck destroys Severen. The syntax of this scene is remarkably similar to *The Terminator*, which would be explained by the presence of writer/director Kathryn Bigelow. She was eventually married to James Cameron, director of *The Terminator*.

Near Dark is the continuation of the syntax of a hero struggling with the vampire's infection. Caleb, like Michael, fights against the urge to kill and drink blood. Bigelow wanted to explore the idea of "redeemable vampires who give up the ability to live forever" (*The 80's Movie Rewind*). She also wanted to inject an "erotic charge" into the vampire narrative, "sexualizing the violence." This idea of mixing romance, sex, and a struggle to over-come the condition of vampirism would be picked up and fully explored by the next film.

Bram Stoker's Dracula

Because *Bram Stoker's Dracula* attempts to stay close to the text of Stoker's novel, many of the developments of the sympathetic film cycle are lost. The vampire is elevated, once again, to aristocracy. The mesh of gen-res (beyond what Stoker originally infused into the novel) is not present. At first glance, the film appears to be a straightforward Dracula narrative, which might fit better in the erotic film cycle.

A closer look at the syntax of THE VAMPIRE reveals that the creature, as played by Gary Oldman, has a sympathetic side. Langella started the shift in his stage performance, and subsequent film role as the notorious count. Although his film centered on the vampire even more than the other characters, the connection with the audience is not a personal one. The first scene in the 1979 *Dracula* shows the vampire already transformed into a half-wolf state. A hairy clawed hand reaches up out of a crate of earth. The syntax of this scene establishes that Dracula is an animal and a vil-lain. However sensual he later becomes with Lucy, the initial appearance is malevolent, a creature that destroys sailors and wrecks ships. Even at the end, as Dracula withers under a barrage of sunlight, he is transformed into a hideously aged creature. The seared flesh on his face is not the death deserving of a hero, but rather the film's villain. Compare these with the opening and closing scenes of *Bram Stoker's Dracula*.

An extensive prologue is added to Francis Ford Coppola's film, show-ing the vampire in his mortal form. Curtis's 1974 *Dracula* included some flashbacks, but not to the same extent. In *Bram Stoker's Dracula*, the prince is a young, valiant warrior. His love for Elisabeta is evident through on-screen displays of affection. The film shows him as not only the central character of the narrative, but also a sympathetic one. He sobs over the letter left by his deceased lover, and quickly turns to rage when the church condemns her as a suicide.

THE DESTRUCTION of Dracula, although following the novel, takes a turn after Quincey drives his knife into the vampire's chest. Mina drags Dracula back into the castle, to the very spot where he renounced God and embraced eternal life through blood. The film opts out of using sun-light to destroy the vampire. The syntax of that destruction requires the vampire's skin to melt, revealing bone, and would show the vampire as a creature or demon, not a person worthy of sympathy. Instead, Mina kisses

Dracula (Gary Oldman) appears as Prince Vlad when he meets Mina (Winona Ryder) in London in Bram Stoker's Dracula *(1992, Columbia).*

the creature, pale, withered, and deformed as he is. A shaft of light illuminates the vampire's face, transforming it first to the prince from the prologue, then to the human form seen in London. Mina then says, "Our love is stronger than death." Dracula responds by saying, "Give me peace." Mina jams the knife all the way through Dracula's chest. The pale color fades from Dracula's face just before he rolls his eyes up to die. The vampire does not disintegrate or burst into flame, but simply perishes. Mina completes the task by using the knife to slice off his head. The final frames of the film show a painting on the ceiling of the prince and his lover, Elisabeta, hand in hand. This vampire ends as a mortal, not a demonic creature, dying in virtually the same spot as Elisabeta from the prologue.

Bram Stoker's Dracula shows THE VAMPIRE as a dual creature, one social and one predatory. Although Dracula assumes various forms in the film, they fall into these two categories. The social vampire starts as an old man in his castle. He has pale, wrinkled skin with long white hair. He wears a red robe with a train that drags behind him for some fifteen feet. He speaks quietly and is exceptionally polite to Jonathan Harker. The only hint at his true nature comes when Jonathan chuckles at one of Dracula's comments. In one swift motion, the vampire brandishes a sword, pointing it at the solicitor. Dracula later produces hairy palms and long pointed fingers, more aspects of his underlying animalistic nature. In nearly all his encounters with Mina (the woman who bares a striking resemblance to Elisabeta) prince Vlad acts every bit the gentleman. He is younger and dressed in various sumptuous suits or jackets. His skin, though pale, has more color than in his castle.

When attacking a victim, Dracula assumes an animalistic form. In his courtyard assault of Lucy, he grows black matted fur and his face twists to a shape midway between an ape and a wolf. He sports a mouth lined with sharp teeth, his gums oozing blood. Later in the film, when confronted by Van Helsing and the other characters, Dracula transforms into a gigantic bat. He loses all hair, and his arms fold up like wings. Many times, while biting a victim, Dracula assumes certain aspects of these two animals. His skin turns pale and his nose flattens to become almost bat-like. As he opens his mouth to deliver a bite, fangs grow out of his teeth, and his eyes turn blood red.

Dracula understands the duality of THE VAMPIRE, and shuns the predatory side of his condition. When Mina finds him transformed into a wolf, copulating with Lucy, Dracula says, "No, do not see me." He causes her to forget the scene. Later, in London, Dracula is prepared to bite Mina. The scene shows all the semantic and syntactic elements of THE BITE. Mina has been pressed back, her neck exposed. Dracula leans back and a close-up

Dracula (Gary Oldman) becomes more animalistic when he prepares to bite Mina (Winona Ryder) in Bram Stoker's Dracula *(1992, Columbia), but he cannot go through with the act.*

shows him with red eyes and fangs. He sinks down toward his victim's neck, and growls like an animal. Then Dracula stops himself. He sees Mina's face, and strokes her cheek. Quivering, he backs off, twisting away from Mina. Dracula even raises his hand to hold off the temptation. Both of these scenes show the disgust with his animal side. This scene may have been influenced by Anne Rice's novel, *Interview with the Vampire*. The difference between Dracula and the novel's hero, Louis, is that Louis struggles with taking any human life. For Dracula, only the one he loves deserves such restraint. The bloodlust is perfectly acceptable for other victims, like Lucy.

During Mina and Jonathan's wedding, the film inter-cuts the scene of Dracula consummating his relationship with Lucy. Dracula is angry that he has lost Mina, and seeks to take his revenge out on Lucy. The only time Dracula transforms into a full animal, a wolf, occurs during this scene. The wolf leaps up onto Lucy's bed, devouring her throat as Dracula gives in fully to his animal desires. As he bites her neck, the film cuts to a two-shot of Mina and Jonathan kissing. Thus the vampire's bite and the kiss are explicitly linked.

Dracula is ashamed and remorseful over his condition. When he finally has Mina alone, he cannot bring himself to transform her into a vampire. Dracula describes what he is, and what he has done. He says, "I am nothing. Lifeless. Soulless." He cannot even face Mina when he says this. Later, as Mina is about to drink the vampire's blood, Dracula forces her to stop. He will not curse her with his condition, saying, "I love you too much to condemn you." It is only through Mina's insistence that she becomes a vampire.

The syntax of this vampire fits within the sympathetic film cycle. Dracula struggles with his condition. When faced with his lost love, he chooses not to transform her, unlike Dandridge in *Fright Night*, or Dracula in Dan Curtis's *Dracula*. In the annotated screenplay, edited by Diana Landau, Gary Oldman says he "tried to show the good and bad paralleling one another" (162). Associate producer Susie Landau says the character of Dracula is "totally isolated and lonely." She felt that Oldman captured that feeling of "tremendous weariness." Even though *Bram Stoker's Dracula* attempts to bring the text directly onto screen, it cannot escape the transformations to the vampire narrative, and the current state of the genre. Screenwriter James V. Hart, in adding the reincarnated love of Mina, added a level of sympathy to Dracula not seen before in film.

In contrast, the other vampires of the film openly embrace their condition. Van Helsing comments that Lucy is not a random victim, but a "wanton follower" of the vampire. Lucy and the other brides use their sexual allure to ensnare their victims. In bed, Lucy attempts to lure Quincey in for a bite, shifting her legs and stretching out her arms. Later, after her death, she plays on Arthur's sympathy, enticing him toward an embrace. The vampire brides of Dracula's castle actively pursue Jonathan, literally raping him in a chiffon-lined bed. The syntax of these vampires is typical of lesser vampires. They seek blood at any cost.

Dracula uses THE LOOK to establish control over his victim, but with new semantic elements. The shadow of the vampire envelops the crowded parlor where Mina stands. His shadowy hand strokes her neck, and a voice-over speaks in Romanian. Mina's eyes are fixed, seemingly staring at nothing. The film cuts to a close-up of Dracula's face emerging from the shadows. His eyes are clouded over, and his face is lit from below. Later, the vampire's face appears super-imposed onto a raging thunderstorm. First only an extreme close-up of Dracula's eyes appears over Mina and Lucy. A spike in Wojciech Kilar's score highlights the scene. The two women appear frightened by the storm. Later, Dracula's entire face stares down from the sky, and the women giggle and run wildly in the rain. The vampire chuckles, and the camera sways from side to side.

When Mina and Dracula meet in London to drink absinthe, the film employs a microscopic view of their eyes. First the film shows a shot of Dracula's eye so large that it fills the frame. The film switches to a shot of the bubbling liquor, which might also be a yellow tinted view of blood cells. Finally, the scene is bookended by another extreme close-up of a single eye, this time Mina's. The syntax of control plays out when Mina begins to describe Dracula's castle and homeland as though she had lived there. She creates a psychic connection with Dracula's past love, Elisabeta.

Again, *Bram Stoker's Dracula* incorporates new or forgotten semantic elements into the syntax THE BITE. The sexual aspect of the bite is exaggerated as both the brides and Dracula lick the wound after biting the victim. When the brides attack Jonathan, purring as their bodies rub up against his, they first kiss the victim's chest and wrists before baring fangs and biting. Later, Jonathan's body is covered with bloody bite marks. Dracula's attack on Lucy begins with him physically copulating with her on top of a stone bench. In an extreme close-up of the vampire's face, Dracula growls and bites Lucy's throat. The victim appears aroused by the attack. Dracula's later attack on Mina shows a more romantic eroticism. The vampire kisses Mina's neck first before biting with a crunching sound. Romantic music swells in the background. When he pulls away from her throat, the vampire wraps his arms around her in a rapturous embrace. Dracula employs a semantic element borrowed from the film *Nosferatu* in one of his attacks on Lucy. The vampire is only seen through the casting of his shadow. As the vampire's shadow approaches her bed, a vase of flowers wilts. The victim first moans and then screams as the bite is delivered off screen. When Van Helsing interrupts the scene, the shadow flees, dripping blood onto the carpet.

The victims of the vampire's INFECTION are willing participants rather than victims. Just before Lucy's first on-screen attack, she leaves behind her cross necklace and sleepwalks into the windy night. Her arms are outstretched and her eyes are fixed in a trance. Later, as she begins to feel the effects of the infection, Lucy is aroused by the prospect of heightened senses. She says, sighing with excitement, "I'm changing. I can feel it." Shortly afterward, Lucy is pale and wheezing on the sofa. As she pries off her choker, the film zooms to an extreme close up of two puncture wounds on her neck. In the second attack by Dracula, Lucy is aroused and waiting for him in bed. Her hands clutch the covers, and then stroke her body in anticipation. The scene ends with her moaning softly. Immediately after, she is seen wheezing and sick.

The syntax of THE INFECTION shows the victim aroused at the prospect of another visit by the vampire, but deathly pale and sick afterward. The same holds true for Mina. She willingly accepts vampirism, yet when Dracula is forced to flee, she appears weak and wheezing.

THE CROSS figures prominently in *Bram Stoker's Dracula*, appearing in the first frame on the top of Constantinople's dome. It falls to the ground and shatters, signaling the rise of Islam. Dracula, the warrior prince, holds a crucifix in prayer and kisses it for his victory. After Elisabeta's death, Dracula thrusts his sword into the altar's cross, which issues blood. He uses a chalice to drink the blood in a perverted version of the Eucharist. In the final scene when Dracula lay dying, the wound on the cross repairs itself. A shaft of light washes over the vampire, showing him in his mortal form. Thus the symbol of the cross, and Christianity, visually bookends the movie.

The traditional syntax for THE CROSS first occurs in Dracula's castle. The vampire sees a reflection of the cross in a straight razor. An extreme close-up of Dracula's eye shows another reflection of the cross in his black pupil. The vampire growls and backs away from Jonathan, calling the cross a "trinket." Jonathan's encounter with the brides shows the ineffectiveness of the symbol. One of the vampire brides opens Jonathan's shirt and growls when she sees the cross. She raises a hand, and the metal melts away. Finally, Van Helsing presents a cross to Lucy as she seduces Arthur in the crypt. Lucy is advancing from the background, and Van Helsing thrusts the cross into the shot. The scene is similar in structure to Van Helsing's repulsion of Lucy in the 1974 *Dracula*. Lucy responds with a look of shock.

In this scene from Bram Stoker's Dracula *(1992, Columbia), Van Helsing (Anthony Hopkins) forces Lucy (Sadie Frost) back into her sarcophagus with a cross.*

She keeps her eyes fixed on the crucifix, hissing as she backs away. Van Helsing forces the cross directly into the vampire's face, driving her back. In a scene reminiscent of *The Exorcist*, Lucy sits up and spews blood from her mouth over the stoic professor.

Van Helsing is THE EXPERT in *Bram Stoker's Dracula*, but he takes a more active role than Van Sloan did in the original. Anthony Hopkins plays the role more closely to Peter Cushing's interpretation of a physical vampire hunter. He is a professor, and his first appearance is at an operating theater with a vampire bat. The debate between science and the supernatural makes it way into the film. Instead of within the library, as with earlier films, *Bram Stoker's Dracula* locates the discussion in the courtyard. Van Helsing proves his point about the existence of the supernatural by seeming to vanish in front of Quincey, Jack, and Arthur, reappearing farther away.

Van Helsing establishes that Dracula is an obsession of his. As he reads from the book *Vampyre*, he calls the creature "the foe I have pursued all my life." This establishes Van Helsing and Dracula as opposing forces, destined to clash. Van Helsing is responsible for the destruction of the vampire brides, and he helps Arthur destroy Lucy, but the final destruction of Dracula is left to Mina. Throughout the film, Van Helsing seems just a little bit off. He dances with Mina in mid-conversation, and laughs at odd moments. He proves himself just as unbalanced as his ultimate foe, Dracula. As an added level of authority, Hopkins's voice narrates the prologue, and the actor also plays the role of the priest who condemns Elisabeta's soul to hell because she was a suicide.

Many consider *Bram Stoker's Dracula* to be the definitive adaptation of the Stoker novel. However the movie deviates from the book in some fundamental ways. The inclusion of the prologue and the emphasis on the love story between Dracula and Mina are all elements added by James Hart. In the original novel, Dracula hardly makes an appearance once he arrives in England. Rather, the book focuses on Van Helsing and the others as they track the vampire through London. The BBC version of the book, starring Louis Jordan, comes closer to the actual tone of Stoker's original work.

Bram Stoker's Dracula finally allows Dracula to be a sympathetic hero. Although cast as the central figure of the 1979 *Dracula*, Frank Langella was still portrayed as a villain. Gary Oldman's *Dracula* is given motivations for his actions—motivations real enough to make the audience empathize with his plight. The film also begins and ends with Dracula's love story. Yet he is still pursued by the other human characters: Van Helsing, and Jonathan. It would take the next film to finally excise the human point of view, and view the world entirely from a vampire's vantage point.

You Can Become a Vampire (The Masquerade)

Role-playing games allow the players to take on the role of a character from fantasy or science fiction. These games alter the event of storytelling by allowing the characters of the story, controlled by the players in the game, to react to events and change the outcome of the story. *Dungeons & Dragons* (D&D) was one of the first role-playing games invented, and set its players in a fantasy world based loosely off of J. R. R. Tolkein's novels, *The Hobbit* and *The Lord of the Rings*.

In 1982, D&D introduced *Ravencroft*, a storyline involving a vampire called Count Strahd von Zarovich. This adventure, written by Tracy and Laura Hickman, grew into a variant of the game, where the vampire theme could be fully explored. Shortly after D&D's introduction of vampires, the company Pacesetter created a horror role-playing game called *Chill*. Here players were members of an organization called the Societas Argenti Viae Eternitata (SAVE or the Eternal Society of the Silver Way), a secret organization dedicated to destroying evil.

By 1991, the popularity of Rice's *Vampire Chronicles* was contagious. Another role-playing game would take this popularity, and infect the gaming world with vampire fever. Mark Rein-Hagen created the game *Vampire: The Masquerade* for White Wolf Studio. The game created its own mythology and hidden society of vampires. This society lived alongside humanity, though hidden by the law of the Masquerade. The Masquerade was an attempt to protect vampires by making humanity believe the creatures were all dead, or had never existed. The vampires are divided into various clans ruled by princes. The newest generation of vampires was brash, and struggled against the authority of the older, elder vampires. These younger vampires drew unwanted attention to their kind and threatened to destroy the Masquerade.

The players of this game, unlike *Ravenloft* or *Chill,* almost always took the role of the vampire. The success of the game created a revolutionary live-action variant where players could act out the roles. The cumbersome dice were replaced with hand gestures, allowing the players to remain in character during the entire game.

Films such as *Blade* and *Underworld* capitalized on the game, borrowing heavily from its mythology. *Blade,* although originally inspired by a Marvel comic book, owes most of its inspiration to *Vampire: The Masquerade.* The movie features twelve clans of vampires that are threatened by a younger upstart vampire. *Underworld* shows parallel societies of vampires and werewolves, and was sued by White Wolf and author Nancy A. Collins. Collins claimed that the entire plot of the movie came from her book, *The Love of Monsters,* which is set in the *World of Darkness* (a supplement to *Vampire: The Masquerade*).

Interview with the Vampire: The Vampire Chronicles

The movie *Interview with the Vampire: The Vampire Chronicles* was eighteen years in the making. Inspired by Anne Rice's immensely popular book of the same name, the themes of the novel had already been seen on film, *Near Dark,* and in a popular role-playing game, *Vampire: The Masquerade.* The prevailing tone of the book and the movie is one of loneliness. The director, Neil Jordan, in the "Special Introduction" to the DVD, announces that the movie is about "the saddest vampires you'll ever see."

Anne Rice claims one of her influences to be *Dracula's Daughter.* This would be apt, considering that Countess Marya Zaleska is the first sympathetic vampire. The earlier movie depicted the vampire as a tragic and sensual figure. Marya seeks only to live a normal life, yet she cannot combat the dark urges inside her. In *Interview with the Vampire,* Louis also struggles against these same afflictions, saying in the film: "I knew peace only when I killed." The idea of a tragic vampire is not new, but what Anne Rice does with her novel, and later the screenplay for the film, is allow the audience into the life of the vampire. In the "Special Introduction" she says, "I wanted you to fall in love with the vampire and see things through his eyes."

THE INFECTION in *Interview with the Vampire* is succinctly presented. When Louis agrees to become a vampire, Lestat bites him on the neck, draining Louis of blood to the point of death. The vampire then bites his own wrist and, in an extreme close-up, lets his blood drip into Louis's open mouth. The sound of a heartbeat enters the scene, beating slowly to mimic the victim's heart. Within moments, Louis grasps Lestat's arm with both hands and drinks from the vampire. Lestat expresses discomfort, and looks as if he will jerk his arm away any moment. The beating heart accelerates until Louis breaks contact with the vampire, allowing Lestat to retrieve his arm.

At this point the victim gradually begins to die. Louis is wracked with cramps and thrashes about on the ground of the cemetery. The heartbeat slows and once it finally stops, Louis transforms. The blood that covers his mouth vanishes. His irises grow lighter, and his deathly pale skin develops well-defined blue veins. Two sets of slightly visible fangs appear in the mouth. Later, Louis shows elongated fingernails. This same transformation occurs with Claudia, with one added detail. When Claudia's heartbeat stops, her hair also becomes more curled and develops a beautiful luster.

One added element of the victim's infection involves the choice to who becomes a vampire. The victim willingly undergoes the infection. The whole process is elaborate enough that there are no accidental vampires (as in *Blacula*). Also, each victim has undergone some form of loss and experiences deep melancholy. Louis had just lost his wife and child. Claudia makes her film appearance by crying over her mother, who succumbed to the plague. Madeleine, the surrogate mother for Claudia, had also recently lost a daughter. Thus the syntax of THE INFECTION bears some similarity to *Son of Dracula*. In that film, Kay willingly accepted vampirism because of her affinity for death. Dr. Laszlo reminds Dr. Brewster that "the girl was morbid." The three characters turned vampires in *Interview* seem to share a love for death.

Louis and Lestat demonstrate opposite responses to the realities of life as a vampire. When attending a social event, Louis chooses to drain the blood of a pair of poodles rather than attack his chosen victim. He holds up his hands in the feeble attempt to clam the hysterical countess, who sees her dogs dead. Lestat's reaction is swift and direct. As the countess cries for help, he twists her neck, killing her. A similar situation plays out when Louis balks at killing a woman in their room at the waterfront. Lestat has confronted Louis, forcing him to realize that he is a vampire and must kill. Louis again refuses to kill, and tries to escape the girl's clinging grasp. He prefers to avoid the issue of killing rather than deal with it head on.

Lestat also shows signs of avoidance. When Louis questions him about the vampire who made him, Lestat becomes suddenly furious. He shouts back at Louis, demanding why he should know anything about being a vampire. Then, just as suddenly, he changes the topic, offering to go on another "hunt" at a New Orleans social gathering. Lestat also dodges a question when Claudia asks why he buys her a doll on the same night each year. Claudia confronts him, saying "You dress me like a doll. You make my hair like a doll. Why?" Lestat quickly changes the subject, suggesting she throw some of her old dolls away.

Interestingly, although Louis remains passive throughout much of the film, Lestat tempers his vicious attacks with an understated gentleness. After Louis is transformed into a vampire, they attack a girl at an outdoor tavern. When the victim is dead, Lestat tenderly lowers her body onto the table. Later, Lestat tempts Louis with two girls at a room by the waterfront. He swiftly bites the victim's wrist. Then, as the blood drains out into a crystal goblet, Lestat recites a poem. When the goblet is full, he gently drapes the arm back on the arm of the couch.

The syntax of THE VAMPIRE is immensely more complex in *Interview with the Vampire* than previous films. The two key characters show many of the flaws and problems as a real person. Lestat is both physical and gentle, while Louis begins reluctant to kill, yet by film's end he easily threatens the reporter, Mallory. The character of the vampire has reached a point where it breaks the mold of any genre syntax.

THE BITE expands the semantic element of the neck, and the vampires in this film bite their victims nearly everywhere, and in various ways. When attacking the woman at the tavern, Lestat begins by biting her neck. Louis then kisses her, biting her mouth. Lestat continues drinking from the wrist, but instead of using his fangs, he pierces her skin with a barbed thimble. Later, Lestat bites another female victim on the breast. Claudia bites her dressmaker on the finger first before draining the victim through the neck. At the Theater of Vampires, Armand bites his victim on the neck, and then passes her back to a gang of other vampires. These creatures feed on the victim in unison.

All the on screen shots of a vampire biting involve female victims.

This even holds for Claudia. Although Lestat feeds from the fop before helping Louis deal with the countess, the bite is not seen on screen. He is seen using his thumb barb to gently scratch the fop's face. Later, the man is dead, with Lestat feeding. Some of this may have been done intentionally, to downplay the homoerotic tone of the book.

Although *Interview with the Vampire* doesn't have an official expert, the syntax of the debate is still present. Louis spends the film seeking answers to his purpose, taking up this debate with Lestat and Armand. Neither provides him with a concrete answer, and much of their discussions revolve around the nature of evil. The syntax of THE CROSS is also absent in the film. When the reporter, Mallory, asks about crucifixes, Louis says he's quite fond of looking at them.

THE DESTRUCTION of the vampire eliminates the stake through the heart (Louis says it is "nonsense"), and revolves around sunlight and fire. Claudia and Madeleine are destroyed when exposed to daylight. The instant the light reaches them, their skin begins to smoke and burn. The girls scream as the camera zooms onto the sun. The next time they are seen, the vampires have been reduced to fine ash. One touch from Louis disintegrates the bodies into powder. The other vampires from the theater are either burned or cut in two. When Louis douses the area in kerosene and sets it aflame, vampires spring from their coffins and attempt to fly away from the fire. Louis cuts those that survive the flames with a scythe, beheading one woman, and gutting another vampire. When faced with Santiago, he slices the vampire into two pieces.

One other possible syntax for destruction is hinted at in the film. When Lestat drinks the blood of a deceased person, he weakens and collapses on the floor. Claudia seizes the opportunity to slit the vampire's throat. All of the vampire's blood pours out onto the rug, and Lestat seems to be choking. His body withers, and the skin shrinks to the bone. Later, he revives himself by draining the blood of snakes, toads, and an alligator in the swamp.

Interview with the Vampire ties together syntactic elements of THE VAMPIRE and THE INFECTION. The vampire must cope with the loneliness that vampirism entails. Even Lestat shows cracks in his otherwise bold visage when he chooses Louis as a companion. These truly are sad vampires, weary of the isolation that comes from immortality. The next television series introduces another vampire who, like Louis, struggles with his own desire for blood.

Opposite: *Lestat (Tom Cruise) is about to bite a victim (Indra Ové) in this scene from* Interview with the Vampire *(1994, Warner Bros.).*

Buffy the Vampire Slayer

The syntax of the expert makes a very definitive shift in the television series *Buffy the Vampire Slayer.* Originally released as a movie in 1992, the film was a failure critically and financially. Creator Joss Whedon retooled the concept, which finally appeared on the small screen in 1997. The concept behind the film, and then the series, was to take the role of the victim, the blond girl running for her life, and reverse it. Now she would fight back and defeat the monster. This was not revolutionary. The syntax for the teenage victim-turned-heroine was laid out in *Halloween* with Jamie Lee Curtis. The series *Buffy the Vampire Slayer* ran for several seasons, and the characters continued to evolve. For the purposes of this book, I am only examining three episodes from the first season.

THE EXPERT has, since Peter Cushing, actively pursued the vampire, using his knowledge to hunt and destroy the creature. In *Buffy the Vampire Slayer* the role of expert is split apart. Rupert Giles, the librarian, appears to match the syntax of the original Van Helsing as played by Van Sloan. He is an older man with an accent, British instead of Hungarian, who is continually holding or reading books through metal-rimmed glasses. The first book to appear on screen is a copy of *Vampyre,* bound in leather, and looking remarkably similar to the book appearing in *Bram Stoker's Dracula.* Giles, however, is not the expert audiences have come to expect. Rather than seeking confrontation with the vampires, he prefers to stay back. He calls himself a "watcher," and his self-proclaimed function is to train the "slayer." Buffy is the other half of the expert, the slayer. She has little knowledge of the lore or history of the vampires. Her function is simple: to fight and destroy the creatures. She fulfills the syntax of Cushing's Van Helsing when he leapt over tables to pursue Dracula. Likewise, she is an extension of Charley, a teenager who rushes into combat without full preparations. Yet unlike *Fright Night* where the syntax showed a novice and experienced expert, the roles are very separate for Buffy and Giles.

Buffy is physically strong and agile. She's able to break open doors and leap over fences. She always carries the tools of her trade, a stake and cross, even to school. She is also a teenager, and subject to the syntax of the teen narrative in high school. She has problems fitting in, worries about her clothes and hair.

Buffy is put in a delicate position when she falls for the vampire Angel. The romantic syntax of their relationship is similar to Julia Hoffman's love for Barnabas in *Dark Shadows.* Giles lays out the state of vampirism as a cut and dry phenomenon: vampires are evil. There is little leeway in his philosophy. In one scene from the episode "Angel," he spells out the scenario clearly for Buffy:

> A vampire isn't a person at all. It may have the movements, the memories, even the personality of the person it took over, but it's still a demon at the core. There is no half way.

Xander further exacerbates the problem by pointing out her duty as a slayer. She was born to hunt and destroy vampires, and therefore must destroy Angel.

THE VAMPIRE syntax loses much of the duality it maintained in previous films. All the vampires, except Angel, are shown to be bloodthirsty creatures that revel in the killing of humans. All the vampires possess great strength, and prefer to subdue their victims physically, with kicking and punching. The duality of social and predatory vampire is merely a shell in this series. The vampire can appear like a normal human, transforming to a predatory form a split second before the kill, yet in both forms, the vampire is remorseless. Some vampires use their mortal appearance to lure the victim into a false sense of security. Darla feigns being scared, and then turns on her victim with viscous speed. Her face becomes distorted, the forehead jutting forward, and the eyes seeming to recede into hollow sockets. The skin turns a deathly pale, and fangs appear. Some vampires, like The Master, or Luke, maintain this form all the time.

Only Angel is sympathetic. He explains the vampire's condition in much the same way as Giles: demonic. "When you become a vampire, the demon takes your body, but it doesn't take your soul. That's gone. No conscience. No remorse. It's an easy way to live." What makes Angel different is his curse. He had his soul given back to him, and therefore cares about the victims he killed. He tries to redeem himself, abstaining from human blood, and attempting to live like a mortal, sleeping in a bed rather than a coffin. Creator Joss Whedon wanted to exemplify the loneliness of the vampire. In the opening to the episode of "Angel," Whedon calls the vampire a creature that's "in the world but not part of it." In this aspect, Angel is syntactically similar to Louis from *Interview with the Vampire*.

The syntax of THE VAMPIRE shows a marked difference between the vampire as hero, and the other vampires. The hero is afforded sympathy. He struggles to overcome his condition. The other vampires are merciless killers, who think of nothing but attaining their goal.

Angel's struggle with vampirism highlights a gray area between good and evil, and Buffy represents a link with his humanity. Although she is not a reincarnation of a lost love, he falls for her just the same. He shadows the slayer, helping her when needed. Darla presses Angel to accept

This publicity still represents the romantic storyline developed between Buffy (Sara Michelle Gellar) and Angel (David Boreanaz) in the television series Buffy the Vampire Slayer *(1997–2003).*

what he is. "Don't whimper and mule like a mangy human," she says. "Kill. Feed. Live." She knows that he still yearns for blood, and tempts him by dangling it before him.

THE BITE for Angel is a syntax of agony rather than pleasure. When he kisses Buffy, he pushes her away panting. He turns to face Buffy again, this time revealing his predatory side—the raised forehead and pale skin. Buffy screams and Angel flees through an open window. Later, when Darla bites Joyce, Buffy's mother, and presents her to Angel, he is hard pressed to refuse. Angel glances at the neck longingly. He looks away, attempting to resist, but he finally succumbs, transforming into his predatory form with a growl.

The rest of the vampires follow a more standard syntax for THE BITE. Darla pretends to be on a date with a potential victim. When she is confident no one is around, she transforms, her face becoming pale and misshapen. She grabs the victim's shoulders and bites his neck. They collapse off camera. Later, the boy falls from a locker, drained of blood and ghostly white. A close-up reveals two puncture wounds, without a single trace of blood. At the Bronze, Luke attacks multiple victims, one at a time on stage. With each, he forces their head to the side, exposing the victim's neck. He then bites each in turn, growling like an animal.

In *Buffy the Vampire Slayer* there is no prolonged INFECTION. The vampire bites only to kill, and their victims stay dead. Only with those where there is an exchange of blood, does the victim rise as a vampire. This exchange is never shown or hinted at in the series. Only the experts, Buffy and Giles, explain the fact. The new vampire rises quickly, often protruding from a freshly dug grave. The transformed victim enjoys vampirism. Jesse calls his old, mortal self a "loser," He considers being a vampire a benefit, and relishes his newfound strength and confidence. This plays upon the syntax of the teenage desire to be cool and different. Jesse tries to talk to Cordelia while still mortal, and is continually rebuffed. As a vampire, he convinces her to dance. She is drawn to his new forcefulness and self-assurance.

Many supernatural aspects of the vampire fail to make an appearance in the series. There are no transformations, flight, or mesmerism (although this last aspect was picked up in future episodes). THE LOOK is not used. THE CROSS, although used syntactically a few times, is mostly costuming for Buffy, as she wears one around her neck. When Luke reaches in to bite the slayer, his hand touches her cross necklace. The sound of sizzling appears, along with smoke. The vampire sits up and looks at his wounded hand. In the "Angel" episode, Buffy leans close to kiss Angel. As they part, the camera pans down for a close-up of the vampire's exposed chest. A cross-shaped burn mark appears on his skin. The expected syntax of shock for the vampire is repressed. The implication is that Angel felt the pain of the burn, but suppressed it while kissing.

Another instance replaces the cross with holy water. Willow tosses a bottle of the liquid at Darla. The vampire grabs her face and screams.

Smoke billows from her skin accompanied by the sound of searing flesh. The only difference in this syntax comes when Darla is next seen. There are no scars or burn marks on her skin. Finally, Xander, Buffy's friend, forcefully presents the cross to a vampire. The creature is held at bay, though does not cover his face or flee. He barks and growls, attempting to get past the instrument.

THE DESTRUCTION of the vampires is achieved almost exclusively through the expert, Buffy. The number of vampires destroyed, along with the speed of the attack, renders the act almost casual. In each case, Buffy uses a stake, thrust through the vampire's heart. The creature gives one singular look of shock, falls to the ground, and explodes into a puff of black dust. Even major characters are disposed of in this way. Only a few instances differ from this syntax. In one scene, Buffy throws a cymbal, decapitating a vampire's head. In another, Angel, rather than the expert, stabs Darla through the back with a stake.

The physical quickness of Buffy's attacks, coupled with her separation from the knowledge syntax of the expert, links her with the hero of an action film. The syntax of the action hero, who combats foes and dispatches them with ease, has been added to the vampire narrative. This paved the way for the vampire, himself, to take on the role of action hero.

Blade

The movie *Blade* is technically based on the comic book character Blade, who first appeared in Marvel comic's *Tomb of Dracula* in July 1973. Although the central character is a vampire slayer (a term used nearly fifteen years before Buffy), little more than his name is carried into the film. Also his enemy, Deacon Frost, is drastically different. Only Blade's origin—being born just as a vampire bit his mother—made it into the film. In the comic *Tomb of Dracula* this rendered Blade immune to vampire infection, while the film makes Blade a half-vampire. *Blade* borrows heavily from the role-playing game *Vampire: The Masquerade* to create the cinematic world of this vampire slayer.

The vampires of the film *Blade* are divided into two groups: the pure blood vampires and the turned vampires. Pure bloods are born as vampires and remain elite, ruling over the other vampires. They are dressed in suits and seen discussing policy and finances around a boardroom table. The syntax of these vampires harkens back to the aristocratic air possessed by malignant and erotic cycle vampires. The turned vampires start out as normal humans, but have been infected by a vampire bite, and the pure blood vampires look down on this. The head of the pure bloods, Dragonetti, says several disparaging remarks about the lack of lineage for Deacon Frost, a turned vampire. This sets up a similar syntactic arrangement as seen in earlier films like *Blacula* or *The Lost Boys*. In those films, the lesser vampires must serve the head or master vampire. The change in syntax in *Blade* has to do with a generation gap.

In the role-playing game, *Vampire: The Masquerade*, the youngest generation of vampires (those represented by Deacon Frost), no longer remember the reasons why the vampire laws were put in place. Thus they oppose the older vampires and their rule. This parallels the historical divergence of the younger generation from the establishment in the 1960s. The role-playing game, and the movie *Blade* simply reflect the tension already felt from the hippie movement.

Physically, these vampires look very human. They have two fangs, but their skin is only slightly pale, and they grow long fingernails only when needed. The younger, turned, vampires dress in fashionable, club clothing. Perhaps the biggest difference these vampires demonstrate over previous examples is their fighting style. The vampires of *Blade* are apt to engage in hand-to-hand combat, using lightning fast martial arts maneuvers. Although predated by *Buffy the Vampire Slayer*, much of this fighting style is due to Wesley Snipes's vision. In the DVD featurette "La Magra," Michael De Luca, president of production for New Line Cinema, says Snipes "wanted to do kind of a take on the Hong Kong action films." Thus the vampires of *Blade* fly into combat, launching into a flurry of kicks, and punches. In addition to the fighting style, these vampires also carry guns. In the opening scene at the rave, the vampires retaliate to Blade's attack by sending in a squad, all armed with automatic pistols.

In terms of the genre pastiche, *Blade* combines the vampire film with the action film. The heavy beat of techno music accompanies several of the fight scenes between Blade and the other vampires. The vampires are dispatched in quick measure, and the body count rises to 88 deaths.

Blade also shows borrowed syntax from the gangster or Mafioso films. The structure of the pure blood vampires, divided into twelve houses, echoes the various competing families in the mafia. The destruction of Dragonetti is syntactically similar to a mob "hit." The pure blood vampire is taken to a remote location along the beach. Frost emasculates the older vampire by pulling out his fangs with a pair of pliers. Dragonetti is then knocked to the ground, mimicking the position of a mob style execution.

The syntax of THE VAMPIRE puts the creature somewhere between action hero and Mafioso gangster. These vampires carry guns, can break into martial arts moves, and quickly rack up an enormous body count. The vampires struggle for control among their own kind, executing a head vampire to further their own agenda.

THE BITE syntax involves the vampire clasping on to the victim for a prolonged period of time. There are only four principal scenes where the vampire bites a victim in the film. Most of the vampire's attacks have changed to hand-to-hand combat or the use of guns. Two of these bites occur in the first twenty minutes of the film. Quinn, the right-hand-man to Frost, revives from being set on fire and bites the medical examiner, Curtis Webb, and hematologist Karen Jenson in quick succession. Both attacks are sudden, with the vampire latching onto the victim's neck. The camera moves from a medium-shot to a close-up as the victim quivers, blood dribbling from the mouth. With Curtis, the vampire finally releases the victim, throwing the body to the ground. Karen's attack is interrupted by the arrival of Blade. Her body is later found slumped on the ground, displaying a bloody wound on the neck. The sound of a slow heart beat is played over the scene.

Displeased with Krieger, Frost attacks his servant familiar in much the same way. He latches on to the neck. The victim quivers and leaks blood from the mouth. When Frost pauses, blood gushes out of the neck wound. Frost later licks the wound, before pushing the body into a pool of water. His teeth and face are covered in blood, and he uses a towel to clean himself.

Even when the victim volunteers, as Karen does, the attack is still swift. Blade begins the scene weak, with Karen propping up his body. As Blade gains strength from the blood, their positions switch. Blade assumes the dominant position, rendering his victim helpless. Their bodies jerk rhythmically before the vampire finally releases his victim. His teeth are covered in blood, one drop oozing from his lips.

The syntax of THE BITE involves a sudden attack by the vampire, and a prolonged bite to the neck. The victim is rendered helpless, blood leaking from the mouth, until finally released or dumped to the ground.

The infection of these victims is somewhat more ambiguous. Curtis and Karen are infected, though nothing more is seen of Krieger. Future scenes with this character were possibly cut. The syntax of THE INFECTION seems to be that anyone who receives a prolonged bite will turn into a vampire. In the case of Curtis, a mutation transforms him into a bloodthirsty zombie that will feed on anything, even other vampires.

Karen actively fights her infection, first with the help of Abraham Whistler, and later with her own research into the scientific nature of vampirism. Whistler injects a solution of garlic into her neck, and smoke immediately wafts from her wound. This gives her a fifty-fifty chance of fighting off the infection. When she later shows signs of continued infection, sensitivity to sunlight and drowsiness, Karen uses equipment brought from her hospital to examine Blade's blood. She describes vampirism as a "sexually transmitted disease," and soon discovers a cure by using gene therapy.

The character of Blade shows a unique syntax for the sympathetic vampire. In *Buffy the Vampire Slayer,* the vampire Angel is intensely remorseful for his past bloodletting, and seeks to live as a human. Blade was born a half-vampire. He has the creature's strength and regenerative abilities, and is not affected by silver, sunlight, or garlic. However, Blade suffers the same longing for blood as every vampire. He combats this craving chemically, injecting a serum. Whistler prepares this drug, which looks like watered down blood. Blade is strapped into a chair. When the serum is injected into his neck, Blade tenses, struggling against his restraints. Like any drug, Blade's body is building up a resistance, and larger and larger doses are needed to quell his thirst.

The syntax of THE INFECTION involves the victim turning into a vampire after a single bite that drains nearly all the blood. The infection can be combated through an injection to the neck. A blood-like serum or garlic is used to either stall or eliminate the infection.

Blade sees a proliferation of experts, following in the tradition of *Fright Night, The Lost Boys,* or *Buffy the Vampire Slayer.* Whistler meets the established syntax of the expert most closely. He is an older man with white hair and a beard. He researches the vampire prophecy on the computer, and explains the vampire condition to Karen. Whistler also fashions the specialized weapons used by Blade, and even dispatches several vampires himself.

As with *Buffy,* the physical and knowledge roles of the expert are split between Dr. Karen Jenson and Blade. Karen, along with Whistler, fulfills the knowledge syntax of THE EXPERT. She is a doctor, and debates the nature of the vampire infection with Whistler. She surmises that vampire blood can't sustain hemoglobin, and can be treated with gene therapy.

Blade is the vampire slayer, specially equipped to destroy vampires with a single deft movement. His weaponry seems designed to explore every conceivable vampire destruction method. Blade uses a shotgun with silver shot, and automatic pistols with silver hollow point bullets filled with garlic. He also engages in physical combat, using a variety of silver edged weapons (silver stakes, a silver boomerang, and a silver sword). The sword experiences an interesting error in details. Silver is the primary method for vampire destruction, and the screenplay describes the sword as being silver. In the film, however, Frost explains that the sword is acid etched titanium.

Blade (Wesley Snipes) is heavily armed and capable of taking on several vampires at once in the New Line Cinema 1998 release Blade.

The viewer must assume that either this is an error, or the sword also contains silver. Finally, Blade, like Buffy, uses his accomplished knowledge of martial arts to combat vampires.

THE EXPERT involves a separation of the knowledge and physical syntactic elements. *Blade* also introduces the vampire as an expert. Blade is the primary source of vampire destruction, disposing of nearly all of the creatures during the film.

Karen destroys Mercury in a twist on THE CROSS syntax. Already this syntax has evolved to include holy water (as in *The Lost Boys*). Here, instead of holy water, Karen uses "vampire mace," which is a mixture of silver nitrate and garlic. The effect is similar to holy water from previous films. When Mercury is sprayed in the face, she chokes, screams, and finally her head explodes.

There are perhaps as many ways to destroy a vampire in *Blade* as there are weapons to battle them. The array of silver armaments, wielded by Blade, makes quick work of the creatures. The vampire expert either shoots or skewers the other vampires through the chest or the head. If he misses, as with Quinn, the vampire survives. If he hits, as Blade often does, the vampire's flesh rapidly burns turning the body to ash. The effect mimics a cigarette burning. Only the blackened bones are left, and these too disintegrate into dust. A similar scenario plays out when Blade slashes at a vampire with a silver sword or garrote. Only when he beheads the vampire or slices through the torso does the vampire perish. Twice Blade slices off Quinn's arm, only to have it regenerate days later.

Sunlight is also used for destruction, but with a semantic twist. Dragonetti is killed in a familiar way. He is exposed to sunlight at the beach, whereupon he immediately begins to smoke, his skin sizzling and turning black. When the full light of day strikes his body, the flesh tears, revealing deep fissures. The vampire screams and then bursts into flame, finally exploding. The other vampires watch this event, safe under a layer of sunscreen. Frost even appears later in the park wearing sunscreen. The experts do not have to rely on daytime to use this form of destruction. Whistler has built a portable ultraviolet light. Karen shines this on the vampire Pearl, who reacts similarly to Dragonetti. She smokes, sizzles, and her skin blackens. Finally Blade attempts to destroy Quinn by lighting him on fire. Unfortunately, the police put the fire out before Quinn can perish.

A new syntax of DESTRUCTION is introduced in *Blade,* one that links closely to THE INFECTION. Both Karen and Blade undergo an injection to the neck in an effort to stall or cure the vampire infection. In her efforts to find a cure, Karen discovers that an anticoagulant, EDTA, has disastrous effects on vampire blood. Blade loads this drug into portable syringes that he then hurls at vampires. Upon impact, the syringe injects the anticoagulant. The vampire bloats grotesquely until the creature literally bursts like a balloon. This is the method with which Blade finally subdues Frost.

Although past films have attempted to update the vampire and bring him into the modern world, *Blade* finally yanks the vampire over. These vampires pack guns, and work as an organized group to defend themselves. The movie acknowledges that we have moved beyond wooden stakes and holy water. The vampire hunter comes equipped with hollow point bullets, and "vampire mace." *Blade* opened the door for other gun wielding vampire films, forever mixing the genre with that of action.

Underworld

The movie *Underworld* rides the edge of two genres so closely it is hard to categorize. Director and writer Len Wiseman addresses the issue in the DVD featurette "The Making of Underworld." He acknowledges that the film has elements from both the action and horror genres, but states clearly "it's more of an action movie" that includes "vampires and werewolves." Even Producer Richard Wright talks about there being a "world of vampires" with a "long and varied history." He sees *Underworld* as a way to take this history apart and piece it back together to suit their needs, calling the film "deconstructivist vampirism."

Underworld is a true genre pastiche. To start, the film borrows heavily from the world created by the role-playing game *Vampire: The Masquerade*. So much so that only four days before the film was to be released, author Nancy A. Collins and White Wolf, Inc. filed suit against Lakeshore Entertainment for copyright infringement. Collins claimed that the entire plot of the film was based on her short story "The Love of Monsters," set in the world of *The Masquerade*. Certainly the film does resemble the game.

The vampires are structured in to two covens ruled by one of three vampire elders. As the vampires age, they gain strength and power. The younger generation, represented by Kraven, seeks to overthrow this power. Additionally, White Wolf Inc. has a werewolf game called *Werewolf: The Apocalypse*, and the two species do not get along. From there it is a short leap to the all-out war in the film.

The film was initially pitched as *Romeo and Juliet* for vampires and werewolves. This structure can still be seen in the basic plot of the film. The two warring families are replaced by warring species. The vampire Selene and the lycan Michael Corvin have developed a mutual attraction that sets them at odds with their own kind. Also, some of the characteristics of Tybalt and Mercucio carry over into Kraven and Lucian. Finally, both the play and the film begin with an unintended altercation that reignites the war.

Underworld also perpetuates the cross over with Mafioso films. *Underworld* itself can be read as either supernatural creatures or the mafia. Several scenes borrow syntactic elements, such as the "hit" performed on the vampire Amelia, and the meeting of Lucian and Kraven in the back seat of a limousine. Both species are continually armed with automatic weapons, the vampires of the film seem more comfortable with shooting than biting, which draws upon the last influence: action films.

The film *The Matrix* is mentioned several times in "The Making of Underworld." Many of the shots and action scenes are heavily influenced by this film, which in itself helped revolutionize the action genre. The opening scene takes place in a darkly lit subway station, mimicking the fight Neo and Agent Smith have in a similar setting. Also, the outfits of the death dealers, with long leather coats and button straps across the front, mimic the coat Neo wears throughout *The Matrix*.

In Underworld *(2003, Lakeshore Entertainment), Selene (Kate Beckinsale) is a death dealer and skilled at shooting and killing lycans.*

Another difficulty in analyzing the film lies with the inclusion of the lycan. I virtually ignored the character of Andreas in *Return of the Vampire* because he was simply the vampire's werewolf servant. His importance lay in his relation to his master, rather than the supernatural qualities associated with lycanthropy. But in *Underworld* we have a different story.

The vampires and lycan are explicitly linked to a single ancestor. Each carries a virus that is deadly to humans, killing most within an hour. But, if an infected human survives and is turned, he or she cannot be turned into the other species. When riding in the car, Selene tells Michael that to bite him would mean death. The species, though two sides of the same virus, are destined to remain apart. The overriding plot in the film is to create a hybrid species that is part vampire and part lycan. Lucian, the lycan leader, displays many vampire characteristics. He remains in human form throughout the entire film, only transforming in flashbacks. When he bites Michael, he does so with the syntax of a vampire bite. Finally, Lucian emphasizes the vampire and lycan connection by calling Kraven cousin. Therefore lycans will be considered a form of vampirism for the purposes of this book.

THE VAMPIRE in *Underworld* (both true vampires and lycans) appears physically similar to humans. Picking up on the syntax established in *Interview with the Vampire* and *Blade,* these vampires can be easily mistaken for

Selene (Kate Beckinsale) walks through a group of other vampires, who lounge about in luxury in Underworld *(2003, Lakeshore Entertainment).*

humans. They have only a slight pale complexion, and although the vampires (not the lycan) retain permanent fangs, they are small, and not used for combat. Both species will develop intense blue eyes when attacking, angry, or hurt. The biggest difference between vampire and lycan comes in their dress and social environs.

The vampires of the film inhabit a richly adorned estate, complete with security guards, a fence, and guard dogs. They dress mostly in black with some accents of red, but all of their clothes are polished and upscale. The vampires represent the ruling class. On the other hand the lycans are disheveled, wearing street clothes. The lair of the lycan is the underground sewer tunnels. In addition, Selene drives a sleek sports car, whereas the lycans operate a functional truck for their assaults.

The lycans are able to transform physically in the film. Raze is the first one to change in his subway battle with Nathaniel. Discarding his shirt, he quickly grows, with much cracking of bones, into a monstrous werewolf. The skin on the lycans darkens and shows off extensive musculature. Rather than being covered with hair, director Wiseman opted for a minimalist approach. Hair only accents the head, chin, and forearms.

Overlooking the obvious transformations of the lycans, the overall syntax of THE VAMPIRE tones down the supernatural aspects of the vampires and lycans. They act and fight more like humans, using guns and fists. In the final conflict between Viktor and Michael, the vampire is forced into hand-to-hand combat. Both species are exceptionally strong, and Viktor punches and hurls Michael across the ruined room. Even when he has the advantage, Viktor tries to choke the hybrid rather than use his fangs.

Because the supernatural aspects are downplayed, many of the syntactic elements associated with the vampire narrative are dropped. No vampire or lycan displays any aspect of THE LOOK. THE EXPERT, also virtually disappears under the syntactic split that occurred in *Buffy the Vampire Slayer* and *Blade*. When the knowledge syntax separated from the physical aspect of slaying the vampire, it opened the door for anyone to destroy the creatures. When the vampire movie is combined with the action film, everyone becomes an expert. All the vampires and lycans are physically armed and trained to destroy the opposite species. The vampires even have a special division for this, called the death dealers.

THE CROSS also takes a highly diminished role in the film. When the semantic evolution of this syntax is considered, however, you can still see it in evidence in the film. When holy water replaced the cross in *Lost Boys*, it paved the way for a total replacement of the old syntax. In more modern films, such as *Blade*, new liquids are used in lieu of holy water. *Blade* used a "vampire mace," and bullets filled with garlic. *Underworld* picks up these semantic elements, combining them into the specialized bullets used in the film.

The lycans develop a hollow bullet with an irradiated fluid that glows blue. The fluid contains ultraviolet light, and acts in much the same way as holy water (or the touch of a cross) did in previous films. When Rigel is shot in the opening scene, blue light emanates from his mouth and the growing wounds on his body. His skin burns blue, then blackens, shrivels, and starts to smolder.

The vampires will not be left out, having two specialized bullets to deal with lycans. At first they use silver bullets, which cause the lycan's skin to smoke upon contact. The wounded creature digs them out with his fingers before the silver causes death. An allergy to silver is the reasoning behind this reaction. Later, to combat the ultraviolet bullets, the vampires develop their own hollow bullets filled with silver nitrate. When Lucian is shot with one, the silver quickly courses through his veins, turning them a dark purple. The effect is similar to being poisoned.

Much of the reason for the supernatural aspects being dropped has to do with story writer Kevin Grevioux. He stated that he "wanted to use science as a basis rather than mysticism." He is also responsible for the virus that both the vampire and lycan carry.

Either species can deliver the virus through a bite. The first on-screen bite comes when Lucian bites Michael Corvin to gain a blood sample. The syntax of the scene complies remarkably with THE BITE for vampires. Lucian remains in human form, and bares his fangs, two upper and two lower to mimic canine teeth. In a close-up, Lucian sinks his teeth into Michael's neck, causing the man to scream. In an extreme close-up, Lucian's eyes turn completely blue with no pupils, and blood leaks from the wound in the victim's shoulder. After he separates from Michael, Lucian has blood coating his mouth and teeth.

In a syntax directly taken from *Interview with the Vampire*, Selene bites her own wrist to deliver blood to the hibernating Viktor. She lets the blood drip into the coffin, and via a conduit, into the sleeping vampire's mouth. This quickly revives the elder vampire. Later, as he undergoes rejuvenation, Viktor is hooked up with several feeding tubes to deliver blood to his entire body.

There are several scenes of lycans ripping out the necks of vampires on the train, but the only other true BITE comes when Selene bites Michael to save him from death. In a scene reminiscent of Blacula biting Tina, she lifts the limp body of Michael, leaning in toward the neck. In an extreme close-up, her teeth puncture the skin.

The syntax of THE BITE centers around the creature's need to propagate rather than for food. Both Lucian and Selene bite Michael, seeking to infect him. The bite is intensely personal, occurring in an extreme close-up.

Both Viktor and Michael receive memories from the person who infected them. Michael begins to have hallucinogenic dreams of Lucian's past. Selene passes her memories along to Viktor when she gives him her blood. These memories are shown in a series of jump-cut images, unorganized and overpowering. Viktor continues to suffer from these disjoint memories. THE INFECTION syntax goes beyond simply creating another vampire or lycan. Memories pass between the vampire or lycan and the recipient of the virus. This creates a personal link between the creator and recipient.

THE DESTRUCTION of vampire and lycan is accomplished primarily through gunfire. Many creatures are gunned down with specialized bullets. Some other traditional and non-traditional methods are also included in the film. Selene demonstrates the need for blood when she passes out from blood loss. Only the quick actions of Michael save her from drowning. Sunlight destroys Viktor's daughter, Sonja, in a flashback. The vampire screams as her skin blackens and smolders. Later, when Viktor returns to view the body, her flesh has turned completely black, looking the consistency of charred wood. Finally, there is Viktor's sword. Selene picks this up and slices Viktor's head in two. Shortly afterward, a section of Viktor's skull slides away, and the vampire perishes.

What makes *Underworld* truly unique is the character of Selene. She is the first vampire to be a heroine, and yet also proud of her condition. Past vampire heroes, *Bram Stoker's Dracula,* Angel from *Buffy the Vampire Slayer* or *Blade,* are all ashamed of their condition, and loathe to perpetuate it with those they love. Yet here we have Selene, the star of the film, unrepentant about her condition. Granted, these vampires are never seen attacking humans for food. It's mentioned that they subsist on livestock and synthetic blood. The vampire film has reached the point where vampires are no longer evil creatures. Gone are the two-dimensional boogeymen. They can now achieve sophisticated roles and complex relationships with other characters.

4

THE FUTURE OF THE VAMPIRE

Again, let us consider the three vampires that visited our door. The first is the malignant vampire, a man with a widow's peak, decked out in a cape and tuxedo. From the films of this period, we would expect him (or her) to be dignified and aristocratic. This vampire enthralls the victim in a trance first, and then moves in for a discrete bite. The second vampire is more physically menacing, having fangs dripping with blood, and a malevolent stare. If the victim happens to be his lost love, he will treat her tenderly and with passion, but if the victim is an obstacle in his path, he or she will be tossed roughly aside. Finally, our third visitor is a young man or woman, not much different from the teenagers who roam our high schools. Only this teen's face will transform into a misshapen demonic visage when preparing to attack. This vampire will bare fangs, and our cross may not protect us.

All of these vampires represent the various semantic and syntactic elements that appeared in film from 1931 to the present day. The character of Dracula has changed remarkably over 70 some odd years, but why has he changed? The character, after all, is a product of Bram Stoker's book, and the text has not been altered. There is also the stage play, by Hamilton Deane and John L. Balderston, to consider, yet that has changed little since its first release. Why then, since many of these films claim to be authentic recreations of Stoker's Dracula, does the Count seem so different in each film? The answer lies with the intertexuality of the horror genre.

New versions of Dracula always look to the films before them for inspiration. No matter how much Dan Curtis wanted to make his Dracula based purely from the text, he could not avoid scenes that evoked the Hammer film from fifteen years earlier. Likewise, James V. Hart desired to make his screenplay for *Bram Stoker's Dracula* as close to the text as possible, yet he added a love story and transformed Stoker's villain into a misunderstood hero. The genre, and the audiences have changed over time.

The Dracula of Bela Lugosi's day is no longer frightening, not only because audiences' tastes have changed, but also the output of horror films in general. How could Lugosi compete with Michael Myers, or Freddy Kruger? He can not, and should not be compared to these films. Likewise, Gary Oldman's portrayal is historically separate from Christopher Lee's or Bela Lugosi's performance. To deem one version a "classic" would relegate these other performances as something substandard, which is simply not the case. The genre evolved, and so too must our views and definitions of genre.

Genres do change, but how and why do they make such drastic leaps? Rick Altman spoke of genre undergoing "unexpected mutations" (22). Some of the reasons for these mutations are now explained, at least in terms of the vampire narrative. Hammer was forced to make distinctive films due to the copyright restrictions placed on them by Universal. Additionally, they exploited the new development of Technicolor and the relaxation of certain film codes to introduce a bloody and fanged vampire. This allowed them to present a Dracula far different from previous versions. When the vampire was portrayed on the small screen, within the confines of a soap opera, much of that genre's syntax rubbed off. The vampire Barnabas became sentimental and guilt ridden over his lost love. This portrayal resonated with audiences, catapulting the vampire from villain to hero status.

As more vampires were added to films, increasingly elaborate methods for their destruction emerged. In the various Hammer films, Dracula perishes from a gigantic cross formed from a windmill (*The Brides of Dracula*, 1960), being impaled on an enormous cross (*Dracula Has Risen from the Grave*, 1968), being struck by lightning (*The Scars of Dracula*, 1970), or being cut by hawthorn thorns (*The Satanic Rites of Dracula*, 1973). After Hammer had exhausted all the semantic and syntactic possibilities, the series of Dracula films ended. Phil Hardy, editor of *The Overlook Film Encyclopedia: Horror*, comments that "although there were some isolated attempts to rework the legend's original formulation, future Dracula movies tended to be either camp parodies or mere injections of vampirism into gore or sex movies" (282). The formula for Dracula, and other vampires based on his legend, had become exhausted. Hardy continues, stating, "The series died from atrophy, to be replaced by disaster movies, cannibalism and body-in-pieces fantasies." The shift from "secure" horror to "paranoid" horror was one that seemed to spell doom for the vampire narrative.

Finally, in 1985, *Fright Night* succeeded in meshing the vampire with the teen horror pictures of the day, finally reviving the narrative. After that point, various syntactic elements, from Western to martial arts, were tried out with vampire characters creating a genre pastiche. Most importantly the vampire was freed from the role of villain, and could now take the place of the film's hero.

Each of these changes within the genre was not planned. They comprise the "unexpected mutations" that Altman discussed. Just as mutations in genetics can create a new species based on environmental factors, so too does genre evolve to meet the demands of its audience. Certain elements, such as THE LOOK or THE CROSS fall to the wayside, and new syntactic elements arise.

As current vampire films include more active and physical vampires, the genre drifts toward the syntax of action movies. Scenes of physical hand-to-hand combat in *Buffy the Vampire Slayer* are replicated in *Blade* and *Underworld.* The vampire and expert share more in common with superheroes than supernatural creatures. The syntax of these fight scenes has been added to the vampire genre. Whether this addition will endure or vanish cannot be determined yet. The roles of the lead characters in these films hardly need to be vampires at all, which begs the question: Do these films still qualify within the sub-genre of the vampire narrative? The answer to this question requires us to look at genre two different ways, from the *very detailed* to the *very broad.*

Syntax is the basic element of genre evolution. When a new syntax, such as the romantic connection between the vampire and the victim, is introduced, it must make an impression on the audience. If it succeeds, the audience will spend money or time to see it. This sends a message to the producers, who want to maximize profits. The producers make other films utilizing the same or similar syntax. Thus the syntactic element has replicated. Borrowing the structure of genetic replication from Dawkins, we can say that one syntactic element may be regarded as a unit that survives through a large number of successive individual films. Thus as more films pick up the syntax of a vampire seeking his lost love, we can say that the syntax had replicated successfully.

As a series of films are broken down into syntactic elements, trends become apparent. Certain syntactic or semantic elements repeat or are varied subtly to add interest. In Hammer's *Horror of Dracula* the expert destroys the main vampire by tearing down the curtains, exposing him to sunlight. The syntax of this scene is repeated through various other films, sometimes with subtle alterations. Dan Curtis's *Dracula* has the expert pull down the curtains, but the vampire does not disintegrate into dust. Rather a stake through the chest finally does him in. In Langella's *Dracula* the expert pulls boards off the walls in the mine. When a shaft of sunlight strikes the vampire (in the form of a bat) it bursts into flames. Finally, in *Fright Night,* breaking blacked-out windows replaces pulling down the curtains. This syntactic element endured faithfully for thirty years. Other syntactic elements fail to repeat in films, and vanish from the genre. In *Lost Boys*, Michael becomes infected by drinking from a bottle of vampire blood, and not a bite to the neck. This does not repeat in subsequent films, and the syntactic element disappears. The delicate point here is where to draw the line separating one syntactic element from another?

Syntax is tied directly to the semantic elements that support it. The action of Van Helsing presenting a cross to a vampire requires there to be, at the very least, a cross, a vampire, and an expert. Yet these three elements coexist on screen in various other moments without initiating the syntax of The Cross. The syntax is linked to the physical action and placement of the characters and elements. The expert holds the cross. The vampire turns in disgust. These actions define the syntax. If it is repeated often, it can be considered stable enough to define and demarcate it from other actions within a series of films.

A *detail-oriented* approach to current films like *Blade* and *Underworld* would be to analyze the use and inclusion of traditional syntactic elements built up over the corpus of films. A critic might simply look for quantity, seeing how many syntactic elements carry over from other films. Yet this implies that there is a "classic" or "correct" combination of elements, and to deviate from that would make the film impure. Another avenue would be to see if there has been an alteration of the syntax or semantic elements, perhaps enough so they are not immediately recognizable. But how far can these syntactic elements stretch?

The film Underworld *(2003, Lake Shore Entertainment) is a combination of the horror and action genres. The vampire Selene (Kate Beckinsale) is equipped with pistols, a hallmark of action films.*

A *broad approach* to vampire narratives will allow narratives to follow one of two patterns: *restricted genre* or *free genre*. In *restricted genre*, a critic can allow the syntactic elements to be altered, but not drastically. The victim of a BITE may change from being asleep, to being aroused, or to being frightened. The basic scene has not been fundamentally altered. Narratives with *restricted genres* would encompass most of the malignant and erotic cycles. Changes were made, yet the essential narrative remained intact. This might fulfill the critics' desire to have a "classic" genre without the implication that this is in any way correct or pure. Simply put, a *restricted genre* is one in which little change happens. Because of this fact, *restricted genre* films or television shows are prone to syntactic and semantic exhaustion. They simply run out of new ways to tell the same narrative. The demise of the Hammer horror series is an excellent example.

In *free genre*, a critic can allow the basic building blocks of the genre to change. The vampire does not need to be aristocratic or a mature adult. Teenagers might become vampires, and they might struggle against their condition. *Free genre* allows the basic narrative structure to alter by borrowing syntactic elements from other genres. This alone revitalizes the genre, allowing syntactic elements to repeat with little change. Compare the various and elaborate scenes of destruction from the films of the erotic cycle to those of the sympathetic cycle. Most of the modern vampires are destroyed with a simple stake. Nearly all the vampires from *The Lost Boys* succumb to this implement, and even Dracula from *Bram Stoker's Dracula* is destroyed with a Bowie knife to the heart. Buffy turns destroying vampires into an everyday occurrence, never varying her routine of staking them in the chest. These films no longer need an elaborate scene of destruction. The addition of other syntactic elements helps to keep the narrative fresh.

The critic analyzing *Blade* might then have two solutions for categorization. The film could be either a vampire film with syntactic elements from action films, or an action film that adds syntactic elements from vampire films. Neither one of these definitions should take precedence over the other. Both are equal in their ability to explain the genre elements in the film. This genre blurring may make it more difficult to categorize films, but only if the critic looks at them holistically. By breaking them down into their constituent syntactic elements, the critic can explain how the genres have combined to create the film.

The next step in this analysis would be to establish the syntactic elements for other genres like the Western or science fiction. A film like *Star Wars* can be appreciated as having syntactic elements from several genres, rather than trying to ignore inconsistencies with earlier films in science fiction. Another question arises concerning the shift from *restricted genre,* where only semantic elements change, to *free genre,* where the entire syntactic basis for the genre changes. Does this shift apply only to vampire narratives, or is it an historical development tied to the rise of the "high concept" film and New Hollywood? In other words, do all genres fundamentally adapt, changing the syntactic elements that make up their core?

Clearly genres do change over time. By examining the basic unit of genre evolution, the syntax, the critic can better understand how unexpected mutations change the direction of genre. Breaking films down into syntactic moments can also untangle genre pastiches that seem to belong to several genres at once. Of course many new questions arise, such as how to divide genres into syntactic elements, but the goal is to help the critic see how and why genre films change over time. Perhaps in future genre criticism, the term "classic" will be put to rest, and genres can be seen as the evolving and complex entities that they are.

APPENDIX A:
SYNOPSES OF FILMS

Theatrical release dates were obtained through the Internet Movie Database.

Dracula

Country: U.S.A.; *Theatrical Release:* February 12, 1931; *Production Company:* Universal; *Director:* Tod Browning; *Writer(s):* Garrett Fort/Dudley Murphy based on the Balderston/Deane stage play; *Cast:* Bela Lugosi (Count Dracula), Helen Chandler (Mina Seward), David Manners (John Harker), Dwight Frye (Renfield), Edward Van Sloan (Professor Van Helsing), Herbert Bunston (Dr. Seward), Frances Dade (Lucy Weston); *Vampire(s):* Count Dracula

Plot summary: The film opens with Renfield, a property agent from London, arriving in Transylvania. When the locals hear he plans to continue his journey after sunset, they warn him of vampires and beg him to wait until morning. He explains that he is expected by his employer, and despite their pleas, carries on, politely accepting a rosary from one of the old women.

At Borgo Pass he is met by a mysterious coachman and is taken on a perilous journey deep into the mountains to Dracula's castle. Renfield enters the ancient fortress and is greeted by Count Dracula. Dracula welcomes him, and is anxious to see the deed to his new home Carfax Abbey. Renfield assures him that everything is exactly as he asked and they set sail for England in just a few days. Dracula reacts violently when Renfield cuts his finger, but the rosary he wears repels him. Dracula leaves Renfield alone to drink drugged wine. Renfield soon collapses and Dracula's three brides slowly approach him, only to be swept away by Dracula who reenters the scene. Dracula descends upon the prone Renfield to bite him (though the actual bite is only implied and not shown).

Dracula sails from Varna to England. When the ship arrives the crew is either dead or missing, and the captain has lashed himself to the wheel. Only the insane Renfield is found below. He is committed to a lunatic sanitarium overseen by Dr. Seward, just next door to Carfax Abbey.

That night Count Dracula arranges an accidental meeting with Dr. Seward at the ballet. He is introduced to Seward's daughter Mina, her fiancée John

Harker, and her friend Lucy Weston. Later that night Dracula enters Lucy's room by flying through the window in the form of a bat. He bites her (again this is only implied and not shown).

Professor Van Helsing, a colleague of Dr. Seward, examines Lucy's body and suspects a vampire. Meanwhile Mina describes a terrible nightmare she's had to John. When Seward and Van Helsing overhear, the professor questions her further and discovers two puncture wounds on her neck. They are interrupted by a visit from Count Dracula, who expresses his concern at hearing that Mina isn't feeling well. Once the Count arrives, Mina appears full of energy and eager to entertain him. Van Helsing notices that Dracula casts no reflection in a mirrored cigarette box. The professor orders Mina to bed. But it is only when Dracula agrees she should retire, does Mina leave the room. Van Helsing confronts the vampire with the mirror. Dracula quickly shatters the mirror and then politely says goodbye. Van Helsing explains to a bewildered John and Dr. Seward that Dracula is a vampire and Mina his new victim.

After questioning Renfield, Van Helsing is sure of a connection. The professor also suspects that the rash of attacks on local children is connected to Lucy. He confirms his suspicions when Mina admits she has seen Lucy since her burial. Van Helsing promises Mina he will free Lucy's soul.

Left alone, Van Helsing is confronted by Dracula. The count attempts to use mind control on Van Helsing, but the professor is too strong, and drives Dracula away with a crucifix. Dracula flees, telling Van Helsing it is too late; he has already mingled his blood with Mina's. Van Helsing and Dr. Seward rush to Mina's room and find her about to bite John. Van Helsing stops her with the crucifix, and convinces John to help him put Lucy to rest.

While Van Helsing and John are destroying Lucy at her grave (none of which is shown on screen), Dracula returns to the sanitarium. Using mind control, Dracula has Mina's maid remove the protective wolfsbane flowers and lets him inside. Dracula abducts Mina and makes his way to Carfax Abbey while Renfield covertly follows. Van Helsing and John see Renfield heading toward the abbey, and follow. Van Helsing tells John that if they can destroy Dracula by sunrise, Mina can still be saved. They desperately search for a way in while Renfield meets Dracula on the stairs inside the abbey. Dracula believes Renfield has betrayed him by leading Van Helsing there. He breaks Renfield's neck and tosses him down the stairs.

John and Van Helsing finally find their way inside as the sun begins to rise. They go to the coffins, fearing the worst. Upon opening Dracula's coffin, they see Dracula in repose. Van Helsing opens the second coffin, but finds it empty. He tells John that Mina is not there. As Van Helsing drives a stake through Dracula's heart (again implied by the sound of a groan), John finds Mina. With Dracula destroyed, she seems to be free of his trance. She tells Van Helsing that the sunrise caused Dracula to flee before he could bite her for the last time. Van Helsing sends the couple on their way, staying behind to wait for the police.

Dracula's Daughter

Country: U.S.A.; *Theatrical Release:* May 11, 1936; *Production Company:* Universal; *Director:* Lambert Hillyer; *Writer(s):* Garrett Fort inspired by the novella "Dracula's Guest" by Bram Stoker; *Cast:* Otto Kruger (Geoffrey Garth), Gloria Holden (Countess Marya Zaleska), Edward Van Sloan (Professor Van Helsing), Irving Pichel (Sandor), Gilbert Emery (Sir Basil Humphrey), Marguerite Churchill (Janet), Nan Grey (Lili); *Vampire(s):* Countess Marya Zaleska

Plot summary: Beginning where Dracula ended, two constables find Professor Van Helsing at Carfax Abbey with the bodies of Dracula and Renfield. Van Helsing admits to killing Dracula. The constables arrest him.

At Scotland Yard, Sir Basil Humphrey questions Van Helsing. The professor tells Sir Basil his fantastic story, and Sir Basil advises Van Helsing that a jury will never believe it. Van Helsing says the vampire's greatest power is that it is unbelievable. Sir Basil respects Van Helsing's reputation and wants to help him, but advises that he is in serious legal trouble. He asks whom the professor will have defend him in court. Van Helsing surprises Sir Basil by choosing Dr. Garth, a respected psychiatrist. Sir Basil is concerned and tells him he needs a good lawyer, but Van Helsing believes his colleague and former student is the only one who might believe him. Sir Basil sends an inspector to Whitby where the bodies of Renfield and Dracula are being kept at the jail.

While waiting for the inspector, the local constable is visited by a mysterious woman in black, Countess Marya Zaleska. She asks to see the body of Count Dracula in order to be sure he is really dead. When the constable refuses, she uses her ring to hypnotize him. When the inspector finally arrives from Scotland Yard, he finds the constable still in a trance, and the body of Count Dracula missing.

Deep in the woods Marya says a prayer of exorcism, shielding her face as she holds a makeshift cross over the body of Dracula. She then makes certain Dracula will never rise again by burning his corpse. She rejoices that she is now free to take her place among the living, but her male servant, Sandor, reminds her that nothing is certain. They hurry back to her studio in London before dawn.

By the next sunset Marya tells Sandor he is wrong. Now that Dracula is destroyed she can have a normal life, but the servant continues to remind her of the darkness around her. She asks him what he sees when he looks into her eyes. He replies by saying, "Death."

Marya walks the streets until finally approaching a man. She again uses her ring to put him into a trance. Just before dawn she rushes into her studio to meet Sandor. She tells him to hurry as it is almost daylight and hands him her cloak. She says sadly, "there is blood on it again," as she closes herself into her coffin. The man Marya hypnotized on the street lies dead on a table in the hospital. The doctors wish they could discover the cause of his blood loss and the wounds on his neck.

Meanwhile, in the country, Dr. Garth is about to go on a foxhunt when his secretary and girlfriend Janet arrives to tell him of Van Helsing's arrest. Returning to Scotland Yard, Garth tells Van Helsing that he should get a lawyer and that any jury will think he is insane. Van Helsing tries to convince Garth to believe his story. He argues that today's science is the past's superstition, and that even Garth's own field of psychiatry was considered black magic just a century ago. Garth reluctantly agrees to help Van Helsing, but has no idea how.

At a society party, Dr. Garth meets the Countess Marya Zaleska, who says she is a newly arrived artist from Hungary. While the partygoers discuss Van Helsing's case, Dr. Garth proposes that perhaps even vampires are just suffering from an obsessive disease of the mind. The countess is greatly intrigued by Garth's idea. She asks to meet him again next evening and he agrees, much to Janet's dismay.

The next night at the countess's apartment, Dr. Garth comments that it is the first woman's apartment he has seen without any mirrors. The countess tells Garth she needs his help. She is under the control of someone from beyond the grave, and he forces her to give in to awful impulses. Garth tells her no one can influence her unless she lets them, and that she should face these impulses like an alcoholic facing a bottle of alcohol. He assures her that by resisting, she will have scored the first victory. He is called away by an emergency and tells her to come to his office the next night. After he leaves, Marya is full of hope despite Sandor's doubts.

The countess tells Sandor she is going to the studio and will need a model. He approaches a young girl named Lili on a lonely bridge, and convinces her to come to the art studio. The countess puts Lili at ease by making small talk and giving her something to eat and drink. Marya stares at Lili, struggling to resist the impulse to attack. She tells Lili she needs her to bare her neck and shoulders, and when Lili complies, it is too much for Marya to resist. She uses her ring to hypnotize Lili, coming closer and closer until Lili screams.

Lili is brought to the hospital near death. The doctors ask Garth to come and examine the girl, who seems to be suffering from amnesia as well as blood loss. Garth says her condition was caused by hypnosis. Janet reads in Lili's file that she had been found on the street, rambling about a woman. When Garth notices the two puncture wounds on her neck, he begins to wonder if Van Helsing might have been right.

Garth goes to Scotland Yard and discusses the case of Lili with Sir Basil and Van Helsing. Reviewing the facts, Van Helsing confirms the marks are those of a vampire bite. Garth plans to question Lili as soon as she wakes up. Van Helsing says that the vampire will have a box of earth nearby where it will sleep during the day. Vampires also cast no reflection in mirrors. Hearing about the mirrors, Garth remembers his visit to Marya's apartment, but keeps the information to himself.

Back at the hospital, the countess comes to Garth's office. She is desperate and tells him she is leaving London. She admits that she put herself to the test as he had suggested and failed. Marya is sure she can only resist if Dr. Garth is there with her and begs him to come with her. Garth, suspecting her more than ever, tries to get her to tell him everything. She refuses, but he confronts her with a hypnosis machine that contains a mirror. They are interrupted by a call that Lili is awake. Garth leaves Marya in his office, telling her that she should not plan on leaving London anytime soon. The countess decides she must force Garth to come with her. Janet appears, looking for Garth, and the countess kidnaps Janet with the help of Sandor.

Garth questions Lili, and learns that her attacker was a woman artist with a large jeweled ring. Lili then dies, and Garth is certain that Marya is the vampire. He rushes back to his office, but finds it empty. Following the clues Lili had given him, Garth finds Marya's art studio and calls Sir Basil. Still skeptical, Sir Basil agrees to come and bring Van Helsing.

Garth enters the studio and confronts the countess. She tells him he is right about her; she is Dracula's daughter and has Janet captive. While Garth confirms on the phone that Janet is missing, Marya escapes. Sir Basil and Van Helsing arrive, and Garth tells them that the countess has kidnapped Janet. Sir Basil lays a dragnet over the city. Back in his office, Sir Basil and Van Helsing wait for news. They learn that Marya has escaped by plane, and Garth has gone after them.

In Transylvania Marya rises from her coffin. Sandor asks why she has left Janet unharmed. The countess knows that she can never be cured, but she still wants Garth as her immortal lover. She knows he will do whatever it takes to save Janet. Sandor is outraged; he reminds her that she had promised him immortality, and tells her that if Garth comes, he will kill him.

Janet lies in a trance while Marya fights the temptation to bite her. Garth arrives outside the castle, and narrowly avoids an arrow shot from Sandor with a bow and arrow. The countess is about to attack Janet when she is stopped by the sound of Garth firing his gun at Sandor.

Garth finds Janet, and Marya explains that Janet is under a powerful trance only she can lift. If he tries to wake her, Janet will die just like Lili. The countess tells Garth that if he wants to save Janet's life, he must become one of the undead and stay with her forever.

Garth agrees and Marya holds up her ring, but before she can hypnotize him, Sandor shoots her through the heart with an arrow. As the countess dies and Janet's trance is lifted, Sir Basil and Van Helsing enter with the police and shoot Sandor dead.

Son of Dracula

Country: U.S.A.; *Theatrical Release:* November 5, 1943; *Production Company:* Universal; *Director:* Robert Siodmak; *Writer(s):* Curt Siodmak (story), Eric Taylor (screenplay); *Cast:* Lon Chaney, Jr. (Count Alucard, aka Count Dracula), Robert Paige (Frank Stanley), Louise Allbritton (Katherine "Kay" Caldwell), Evelyn Ankers (Claire Caldwell), Frank Craven (Prof. Harry Brewster), J. Edward Bromberg (Prof. Laszlo), Samuel S. Hinds (Judge Simmons), Adeline De Walt (Madame "Queen" Zimba), Pat Moriarity (Sheriff Dawes), Etta McDaniel (Sarah, Brewster's Maid), George Irving (Col. Caldwell); *Vampire(s):* Count Alucard, Kay Caldwell

Plot summary: Dr. Brewster and Frank Stanley go to the train station to meet a guest of the Caldwell family named Count Alucard. He has not arrived with the train, but a porter shows them the count's luggage. Dr. Brewster notices that Alucard's name is Dracula written backward. They assume that the count must be coming by car instead.

At the Caldwell family plantation, Dark Oaks, a worker arrives with Alucard's luggage. He informs Kay Caldwell that the count was not on the train. Kay's sister, Claire Caldwell, tells her not to worry. The count would have called if they had a phone at the estate. Kay says that there are other forms of communication and she is sure the count will come.

Kay journeys to a shack in the woods, the home of Queen Zimba, a gypsy that she brought back from Hungary. The gypsy warns Kay that Alucard is not the count's true name. She sees a great house in ruins and Kay marrying a corpse. Before Queen Zimba can elaborate, a bat sweeps down and claws her face, killing her. Kay runs out.

Later that night there is a reception party being held for the count. Alucard lurks outside in the shadows. Inside, Kay and Claire say goodnight to their father, Colonel Caldwell as he is wheeled up to his room by the servant. Alucard transforms into a bat and enters the house. When the servant leaves, he enters the colonel's room.

Downstairs on the veranda, Frank talks to Kay. He says that ever since she met Count Alucard in Budapest she has changed. Kay tells Frank that they have been friends since childhood, and that there is no one in her heart but him. She makes him promise that no matter what happens, he should never doubt her love for him.

The servant calls for Kay as smoke billows out of the colonel's bedroom window. Claire, Kay, Frank, and Dr. Brewster rush upstairs. The servants put out the fire started by the colonel's cigar. The colonel is dead, apparently from fright. Frank then points out the two marks on the man's throat.

Later that night, after all the guests have left, a servant hears a knock at the door. He answers it to find Count Alucard. The count orders the servant to announce his arrival.

Dr. Brewster calls the university to speak to Professor Laszlo, an expert on Eastern European history. First Laszlo tells him that Alucard is not a Hungarian name, and that Dracula is no longer living, having died in the Middle Ages. He informs Brewster that according to legend, the last Dracula became a vampire, but was destroyed many years ago. Dr. Laszlo warns Dr. Brewster to be careful around Count Alucard.

At the reading of Colonel Cladwell's will, Kay produces a new will her father just had made. In it, Kay receives nothing but the plantation. Kay tells Claire that she wanted this because she could not bear to have Dark Oaks sold. After Judge Simmons leaves, Dr. Brewster comments on the fact that all the servants have fled and refuse to return.

Dr. Brewster is suspicious of Alucard, and asks Claire to show him the count's luggage. In the guesthouse they find that two of the trunks are missing, leaving only one large steamer trunk. Dr. Brewster breaks it open and finds it empty. They then see Frank storm off after speaking with Kay. Claire tells Dr. Brewster she was right; Kay called off the engagement. Dr. Brewster says he needs to protect Kay from herself and wants to have her declared legally insane.

That night, Kay takes the car and drives to the swamp. There she watches as Alucard's coffin rises out of the water. A mist leaves the coffin, becoming the count. He glides over the water to join her on land. They get into the car and are spotted by Frank. Alucard and Kay drive to the justice of the peace and demand to be married that night.

Alucard carries Kay across the threshold of Dark Oaks. Kay says everything has worked as they had planned; the house is theirs. Alucard prepares to bite Kay, who willingly gives in, but they are interrupted. Frank bursts in insisting that Alucard leave town at once. Kay tells Franks that she and the count were married, but Frank can't believe it.

Alucard grabs Frank by the throat and throws him across the room. Frank draws a pistol and shoots Alucard. The bullets pass through the count, hitting Kay who is hiding behind him. She falls to the ground. Frank runs out and is pursued by Alucard in the form of a bat. Frank collapses in a cemetery and Alucard prepares to attack. The moon creates the shadow of a cross along Frank's body, and Alucard is repulsed.

Dr. Brewster is reading *Dracula* by Bram Stoker when Frank stumbles into his house. Frank is hysterical and tells the doctor that he killed Kay by shooting through Count Alucard. Frank collapses and Dr. Brewster covers him with a blanket.

At Dark Oaks Alucard shovels dirt into a new coffin. Dr. Brewster arrives to find the front door open, and Alucard sees him enter. Dr. Brewster searches the ground floor and finds it empty. He then moves into the basement where he sees a crate full of earth. Alucard surprises him and informs the doctor that Kay and he were married. He is now the master of the house.

Alucard brings Dr. Brewster up to Kay's bedroom, where Kay sits up in bed. She tells Dr. Brewster that she married Alucard privately. They will be involved in scientific research that will consume all their daylight hours. She asks Dr. Brewster to explain all this to Claire and Frank. Alucard sees Dr. Brewster out and reiterates that the doctor is no longer welcome at Dark Oaks without his express permission.

Dr. Brewster arrives back home to find Frank gone. Judge Simmons arrives and tells him he cannot order Kay insane; she's done nothing to warrant it. The judge gets a call from the sheriff. Frank has surrendered himself, claiming to have murdered Kay.

At the courthouse Dr. Brewster says that Frank did come last night with the same story, but he just visited Kay who was very much alive. The sheriff decides to go to Dark Oaks to see for himself, and he brings Frank along. When they can't find Alucard or Kay, the sheriff has him walk through the events of that night. Frank leads them outside and then cannot remember anything else. The sheriff finds a new coffin in the mausoleum. When he opens the lid, he finds Kay lying dead inside.

Professor Laszlo has arrived at Dr. Brewster's house, and the professor says he is sure that Alucard is a vampire, probably a descendant of Dracula. Laszlo explains the legends of vampires. Dr. Brewster asks if they are immortal, and Laszlo replies only if they return to their coffin before sunrise. As they plan to find the count's coffin, Alucard slips under the door in the form of mist and confronts the men. He grabs Dr. Brewster by the throat, but is stopped when Laszlo presents a cross. Alucard retreats and disappears into mist again.

Dr. Brewster's housekeeper shows in a woman carrying her unconscious child, Tommy. She tells the doctor she found him on the side of the road, and he mumbled something about a foreign man and a fog. The doctor examines the boy and finds two puncture marks on his neck. Dr. Brewster uses iodine to paint crosses over the bites. Laszlo says that the boy is not at risk of becoming a vampire. Dr. Brewster asks about Kay. Laszlo says that because Kay was morbid and into black magic, she may have become a vampire by choice. They decide to have Claire order Kay's body cremated to destroy her.

Kay leaves her coffin in the morgue and enters Frank's cell in the form of a bat. She bites him while he sleeps and then assumes human form to wake him. Kay asks Frank if he loves her enough to spend the rest of his life with her. She tells him she never loved Alucard; it was all part of her plan. He made her immortal, and now she will do the same for Frank. She tells Frank there is something he must do while still human. He needs to find Alucard's coffin and destroy it before he can return at dawn.

The guard outside the cell tells Dr. Brewster and Laszlo that Frank is obviously crazy. He has been talking to himself, first in his voice, then in a woman's voice. Claire visits Frank and tells him she will have Kay's body cremated. Frank becomes hysterical, telling Claire that Kay isn't dead. When Claire leaves, Kay returns. She overheard what her sister said. She tells Frank where to find Alucard's coffin and helps him escape from the cell.

Dr. Brewster and Laszlo return to find Frank out of his cell and armed with a gun. Frank escapes and the guard says he heard Frank say he was going to destroy Alucard in the swamp. The sheriff goes with Dr. Brewster and Laszlo to the morgue only to find Kay's coffin gone. The three head for the swamp after Frank.

Frank makes his way to the drainage tunnel where Alucard has hidden his coffin. He sets fire to the coffin, but Alucard confronts him before he can escape. The count panics and tries to force Frank to put out the fire. The sun rises and Alucard falls to the ground. His skin fades away revealing bone. Frank runs off to meet Kay. She is lying in her coffin. He places his ring on her finger and sets fire to the bed. The others enter as the room goes up in flame.

Return of the Vampire

Country: U.S.A.; *Theatrical Release:* January 1, 1944; *Production Company:* Columbia; *Director:* Lew Landers; *Writer(s):* Griffin Jay, Randall Faye (additional dialogue); *Cast:* Bela Lugosi (Armand Tesla), Frieda Inescort (Lady Jane Ainsley), Nina Foch (Nicki Saunders), Miles Mander (Sir Frederick Fleet), Roland Varno (John Ainsley), Matt Willis (Andreas Obry), Gilbert Emery (Dr. Walter Saunders); *Vampire(s):* Armand Tesla

Plot summary: A frightened girl backs away from Armand Tesla in a foggy alley. He raises his cape as the girl screams. Later, Andreas, a werewolf, prowls through the fog filled Priory Cemetery and enters a crypt. He speaks to a closed coffin, telling his master that it is time for him to go out into the beautiful night.

A hand wearing a tragedy mask ring raises the lid. Armand Tesla questions him about the events of the day. The werewolf tells his master that the girl still lives. Tesla leaves the crypt and disappears into the fog.

Dr. Lady Jane Ainsley and Doctor Saunders examine a slide of the girl's blood. Lady Jane explains that the girl was found suffering from extreme blood loss. They are interrupted by John, Jane's son, and Nicky, Saunders's granddaughter. The adults send the children to bed.

The girl victim recounts that someone was hunting her with burning eyes. Suddenly there is a rush of wind and a wolf howls outside. She shouts and then dies. Later that night, Doctor Saunders reads a book by Armand Tesla called *The Supernatural and Its Manifestations*. The book speaks of the dead returning from their graves.

In the children's room, Nicky is sleeping. The windows blow open and a fog rolls into the room. The shadow of Armand Tesla's cape falls over the girl. Nicky is terrified and screams as the man draws closer.

The next morning, Doctor Saunders takes Lady Jane to see the victim's body. He points to two small wounds on her throat and says that a vampire made them. The doctor quotes from the work of a Romanian scientist who lived 200 years ago named Armand Tesla. The housekeeper interrupts, telling them that something is wrong with Nicky. They rush to the children's room and the doctor discovers the same punctures on Nicky's neck. He orders a transfusion of blood to save her.

Lady Jane and Doctor Saunders search the Priory Cemetery for the vampire's coffin. They see wolf prints and follow them to a crypt. Doctor Saunders opens the coffin and finds a man inside. He says the vampire will cast no reflection and tests the body with a hand mirror.

As Doctor Saunders drives a metal spike through the vampire's chest, Andreas staggers into the crypt, collapsing onto the floor. Doctor Saunders explains that the poor creature must be enslaved by the vampire. Andreas changes back to human form and Lady Jane decides she must help him.

Twenty-three years later, the chief commissioner for Scotland Yard, Sir Fredrick, is going over Doctor Saunders's writings, which were found when the doctor died in a plane crash. Lady Jane explains that the vampire was Armand Tesla. After years of research, he finally became a vampire himself. Sir Fredrick asks about the servant Andreas, and Lady Jane tells him that once Tesla was dead, he had no more control over the man. Andreas is now a valuable assistant to her.

Lady Jane returns home and is greeted by the now adult John and Nicky, who are engaged to each other. Suddenly air raid sirens sound above. The Germans drop bombs across the countryside. One detonates in the cemetery, revealing Tesla's coffin.

The next morning two local volunteers survey the damage at the cemetery. As they begin to clear the rubble, they discover Tesla's body. Believing the spike to be a piece of shrapnel, the men remove it and the body groans.

Lady Jane enters the lab where Andreas is working. She tells him she has word that another scientist, Dr. Hugo Bruckner, has escaped a German concentration camp. She tells Andreas to meet him as he has with the others they've helped.

On his way to meet the scientist, Andreas hears the call of Armand Tesla. He tries to resist, but finally succumbs and transforms back into a werewolf. Tesla tells Andreas that he is back for revenge. His curse caused Doctor Saunders's plane to crash, and now he will make Lady Jane suffer through those she loves. He orders Andreas to find him a new hiding place for his coffin.

Andreas travels through the bombed out shell of a chapel carrying a bundle under one arm. He has killed the German scientist and taken his effects. Tesla will now pose as Dr. Hugo Bruckner.

Lady Jane takes Sir Fredrick to the cemetery to show him the body of Tesla, but the grave has been destroyed from the bombing. Later, they meet at an engagement party for Nicky and John. Sir Fredrick hands Lady Jane the writings by Doctor Saunders. She doesn't want Nicky to ever know about the manuscript, and locks it in a drawer.

Tesla arrives at the party as Hugo Bruckner. Nicky meets Tesla and seems to recognize him. She is instantly taken with the man, and continues to look at him throughout the party. Lady Jane takes Tesla on a tour of her facilities, where he bumps into Andreas working as a lab assistant. Later that night, Lady Jane and Sir Fredrick examine her desk drawer. The lock has been broken and the manuscript removed. Sir Fredrick finds some hairs, which he puts in his pocket. Upstairs, Nicky prepares to go to bed and finds the manuscript on her chair.

As Nicky sleeps, having finished reading the manuscript, Tesla calls to her with is mind. She awakes and journeys to him in a trance. In the laboratory, now flooded with mist, she meets Tesla. He tells Nicky that she is his forever, but first there are things he needs her to do. The next morning, John and Lady Jane discover Nicky passed out on the floor of her bedroom with two wounds on her neck. Lady Jane prepares to give the girl a transfusion.

Lady Jane interviews the two volunteers who cleaned up the cemetery after the last bombing. They remember seeing the body of a very old man with a spike through his heart. They admit to taking the spike out and hearing the body groan. When they show her the area they buried him again, they find the body missing. She tries to convince Sir Fredrick that Tesla is still alive, but he is reluctant to believe in vampires. Still, he has his detectives check out Andreas.

The detectives confront Andreas in an alley as he carries another bundle to Tesla. Andreas transforms into a werewolf and subdues the men, but loses the bundle. The detectives bring the bundle back to Sir Fredrick and describe the ordeal. The chief inspector is not amused, but the detectives produce hair torn from Andreas during the fight. Just then, Sir Fredrick receives a report from the hair he took out of Lady Jane's broken drawer. The report indicates that the hair belonged to a wolf.

Andreas comes to the window of Nicky's room. He enters and grabs the maid, hauling her into another room. Then Tesla calls to Nicky again. He orders her to go to John's room. She visits John and stares longingly at his neck. She kisses him as Tesla watches from the curtains.

Later, Lady Jane finds John passed out in his room with two wounds on his neck. Tesla, masquerading as Dr. Bruckner, examines John. Sir Fredrick asks him if he thinks a vampire could do this. Tesla gives a vague answer that could be interpreted either way.

Sir Fredrick and Lady Jane interrogate Andreas about the missing manuscript and his lurking around the professional club. Sir Fredrick pulls out Andreas's hand, which is covered in hair. Once he is found out, Andreas rushes out a window and escapes. Lady Jane still believes it is not his fault. Andreas is simply under the control of Tesla.

Sir Fredrick takes Lady Jane to the professional club to see Dr. Bruckner. The clerk shows them to the room, but they cannot find the doctor, and he hasn't left for the day. Sir Fredrick reveals that the real Dr. Bruckner is 62, bald and heavily built with a limp, a completely different description from Tesla. Lady Jane notices that the mirror is turned to the wall. She realizes that Dr. Bruckner is Armand Tesla, a vampire, and comes up with a plan to trap him using Nicky as bait.

Lady Jane is playing the organ downstairs. She has removed the cross from Nicky's bedroom and also asked the maid to leave. Tesla appears and confronts her. They discuss Andreas's soul. Tesla sees Andreas as forever his servant, while Lady Jane knows she has placed good in his heart. She reveals that Tesla actually attacked John, making it seem that Nicky did it. She surprises Tesla by unveiling a cross hidden behind the sheet music. Tesla hides his face and disappears in an explosion of smoke.

Sir Fredrick arrives just as Nicky walks down the stairs in a trance. Sir Fredrick and Lady Jane follow her to Priory Cemetery. Andreas and Tesla wait by the crypt to meet her. The air raid sirens begin just as Nicky faints. Andreas goes to pick her up, but is shot by Sir Fredrick. Bombs strike the cemetery, forcing Lady Jane and Sir Fredrick to seek cover. Tesla commands the injured Andreas to take Nicky. They make their escape as rubble falls onto the cemetery.

Andreas carries Nicky to the destroyed chapel. Tesla tells Andreas he does not need him any more and tells him to go die in the corner. Andreas finds a crucifix in the rubble. As he holds it, he returns to human form. He uses the cross to prevent Tesla from biting Nicky. As he drives Tesla up the stairs, another bomb hits the chapel.

In the rubble, Andreas regains consciousness first. He drags the body of Tesla into the sunlight. When the vampire awakes, he hides his face from the sun and tries to escape although he seems to have lost all his strength. Andreas finds a metal spike and hammers it through Tesla's heart, then succumbs to his gunshot wound. Tesla's face melts away in the sunlight.

Sir Fredrick brings Lady Jane to the destroyed chapel where she is reunited with Nicky. She tells Lady Jane that it was Andreas who killed Tesla. Even with the melted body of Tesla, Sir Fredrick still does not believe in vampires.

El Vampiro [The Vampire]

Country: Mexico; *Theatrical Release:* October 4, 1957 (U.S. release 1958); *Production Company:* Cinematográfica ABSA (Mexico); *Director:* Fernando Mendes; *Writer(s):* Ramón Obon; *Cast:* Germán Robles (Count Karol de Lavud and Duval), Abel Salazar (Dr. Enrique/Henry), Ariadna Welter (Marta Gonzalez/Martha), Carmen Montego (Eloisa/

Eloise), José Luis Jimenez (Emilio/Ambrose), Mercedes Soler (Maria/Marilyn), Alicia Montoya (María Teresa/Mary), José Chavez (Anselmo), Julio Daneri (Duval's servant), Margarito Luna (Duval's servant); *Vampire(s):* Count Lavud (aka Duval), Eloise

Plot summary: Señor Duval looks up from the courtyard as a beautiful woman, Eloise, prepares for bed. He transforms into a bat, and flies into the woman's window. Eloise screams as the vampire attacks, biting her neck. He leaves her unconscious with a bloody wound on her throat.

A train arrives and workmen unload a large box of dirt brought from Hungary and addressed to Señor Duval. A young girl, Martha, also gets off the train. Her uncle Ambrose is not there to meet her and she has no way to get to her home, the Sycamores. Another man, Henry, is stranded as well. Henry tells her he couldn't even get someone to take money for a ride. Martha says she must get home. Her aunt is very ill. A cart arrives to pick up the box for Señor Duval. Henry convinces the driver to give Martha a ride to the Sycamores.

A funeral procession makes its way out of the estate. Just behind them Eloise appears out of mist and slowly follows. Before placing the coffin in the vault, Uncle Ambrose asks to see his sister one last time. The coffin is opened to reveal Mary, holding a huge crucifix. The maid Marilyn takes the rosary from the body and the coffin is placed in the vault. The mourners leave, but Marilyn calls the servant, Anselmo, back to read the note she has found attached to the rosary.

The cart comes to a crossroads, and the driver tells Martha and Henry he will not take them any further. As Martha and Henry walk down the path toward the Sycamores, Eloise appears out of the mist. Martha explains that her uncle sent for her because Mary is now very sick. She says another aunt, named Eloise, also lives at the Sycamores. She goes on and on what a beautiful estate it is. Behind them Eloise continues to magically appear, following them until they reach the gates.

Martha is shocked to see the house in complete disrepair. Anselmo tells Martha that after most of the mines shut down, many of the locals left the area. Uncle Ambrose hugs Martha, and she introduces Henry. Eloise turns into a bat and flies toward the house. She next appears walking down the stairs to meet Martha.

Ambrose convinces Henry to stay the night. When they are alone, Henry reveals that he is actually the doctor Ambrose had secretly sent for to investigate if Mary was really crazy or if someone was out to get her.

Señor Duval leaves his coffin and is greeted by the cart driver. With the help of the servants, they open the box, revealing a coffin full of dirt. Duval reveals he plans to resurrect his brother, who the locals destroyed a hundred years ago.

A coach stops in a remote area and Duval exits. He sees two locals walking along the path and turns into a bat. The bat attacks the locals, and while the girl escapes, Duval transforms back into human form and bites the young boy in the neck.

In Martha's room, Eloise explains that Mary has left everything to Martha, so a third of the estate is in her hands now. Eloise says she knows someone who would like to buy the property, and she thinks they should sell. Eloise admits that Ambrose refuses to sell, so the deciding vote is Martha's.

Hearing the arrival of a coach, Eloise hurries to the window. Martha cannot believe her eyes when Eloise doesn't cast a reflection in the mirror. Eloise and Duval communicate telepathically. Eloise warns him that a stranger arrived with Martha and Duval tells Eloise to keep an eye on him.

Ambrose introduces Henry to their neighbor, Señor Duval. Suddenly one of the old books falls from the bookshelf. Henry picks it up and says it is a hand written account of the destruction of a vampire, Count Lavud, a hundred years ago.

Marilyn shows Henry to his room and he asks her about Mary's condition before she died. Marilyn insists that Mary was not crazy. She says her own grandfather was one of the victims a hundred years ago. A vampire began attacking the workers one by one until the mine was forced to close. Finally the remaining men destroyed the creature, but now attacks have begun again. When Marilyn leaves, Henry begins reading the handwritten book. He hears a woman singing a lullaby. He looks around, but finds no one.

In Martha's room, the bookcase opens and Mary enters through a secret passageway. She hurries to Martha's bed and places a crucifix on her pillow, and then runs back, the bookcase closing behind her.

Henry falls asleep and Eloise appears in his room. She goes through his bags and pockets and discovers his stethoscope. Eloise turns into a bat and flies to Duval. She tells him that Henry is really the doctor that Ambrose sent for. Eloise asks what they will do about Martha, and Duval tells her that after he bites the girl twice she will become a vampire like them.

He turns into a bat to flies to Martha's room. Seeing the cross on her pillow, he shields himself with his cape. Martha tosses and turns in bed, knocking the cross off the bed. Duval approaches her bedside and bites her neck. He then turns back into a bat and flies to his lair, closing himself in his coffin as the rooster crows.

In the morning Henry finds Martha sitting in the courtyard. She tells him she had awful dreams about a tall man in a cape that tried to kiss her. Martha is trying to muster the nerve to go inside her old nursery. Her aunt had a special lullaby for her and Martha begins to sing it. Henry says he heard her sing it last night, but Martha says it wasn't her. Martha goes inside the nursery after Henry checks it. As she walks to the center of the room, she sees Mary. Hysterical, Martha runs out of the room, and tells Henry she saw Mary's ghost. Henry checks the room and finds it empty.

That evening Eloise enters Martha's room and tells her to look her best because Señor Duval is coming. She goes to fetch a chest from the dresser, and Martha is terrified when Eloise casts no reflection in the mirror. When Duval's coach arrives, Eloise tells him that Martha knows she has no reflection. Duval tells her to use the ring.

Martha comes down and whispers to Henry that something terrible has happened. Before she can say more, Eloise introduces Duval. Martha is shocked to see the man from her dream. Henry explains that the locals believed that if the vampire were not buried in his native land, then one of his vampire kin would return to seek revenge. While he is talking, Eloise drops a powder from her ring into Martha's glass. When Martha drinks it, she suddenly collapses. Henry checks her pulse, and says that Martha is dead.

As they pray over Martha's body, Anselmo says he saw her finger move. Checking her again, Henry says she is alive, but she's been drugged. He gives her an injection that will help her wake. Ambrose begins to panic that Mary may have been buried alive.

Opening the coffin, they find it empty. Marilyn appears and tells Anselmo there is no need to keep the secret now. The note in the rosary was from Mary. Anselmo and Marilyn had let her out of the crypt and have helped her hide in the old mine tunnels beneath the estate.

They take Henry and Ambrose to see Mary. She says Eloise and Duval drugged her and buried her alive because she would not sell The Sycamores. She knew that they were vampires. Now she has overheard his plans to resurrect his brother Count Lavud. Henry then realizes that Duval is Lavud backwards.

Upstairs, Martha awakes to find Duval at the foot of her bed. She screams, but Duval overpowers her, and carries her off into the tunnels. Hearing her scream, Henry heads down the tunnels while Ambrose goes to his study to get his pistol. Eloise follows Ambrose and bites his neck. Marilyn and Anselmo find Ambrose on the floor just moments later.

In the mining tunnels, Eloise appears behind Henry and is about to attack him when Mary grabs her and the two struggle. Now in his own house, Duval lays Martha on a table. As he leans over to bite her the second time, Henry enters. Duval grabs a sword from the wall and they begin to fight. Henry defends himself with a torch.

Mary succeeds in strangling Eloise, and rushes down the tunnel. Henry and Duval continue to fight, and the torch sets fire to the room. Duval gets the best of Henry, but before he can give the final blow, the rooster crows causing Duval to miss. Duval flees and Henry sees the fire closing in on Martha. Duval's servants enter and begin fighting with Henry.

Duval enters his coffin, but Mary is right behind. Mary pries open the lid and drives a long stake into Duval's heart. Martha comes out of her trance and finds herself surrounded by fire. Henry carries Martha to safety. Mary drives the stake deeper into Duval, and Eloise's corpse ages to dust.

The next day at the train station, Henry tries to say goodbye to Martha. The train appears to leave, but it's revealed that Henry stayed behind. He kisses Martha as the train pulls away.

Horror of Dracula

Country: U.K.; *Theatrical Release:* May 8, 1958 U.S.A. (June 16, U.K.); *Production Company:* Hammer Films; *Director:* Terence Fisher; *Writer(s):* Jimmy Sangster (From Bram Stoker's Novel); *Cast:* Peter Cushing (Dr. Van Helsing), Christopher Lee (Count Dracula), Michael Gough (Arthur Holmwood), Melissa Stribling (Mina Holmwood), Carol Marsh (Lucy Holmwood), Olga Dickie (Gerta), John Van Eyssen (Jonathan), Valerie Gaunt (Vampire

Woman), Janine Faye (Tania), Barbara Archer (Inga), Charles Lloyd Pack (Dr. Seward); *Vampire(s):* Count Dracula, Dracula's Bride (Vampire Woman), Lucy Holmwood

Plot summary: The diary of Jonathan Harker is opened and provides Jonathan's account of arriving at Castle Dracula in Klausenburg. He finds the castle entrance open and the castle itself apparently empty. A note from Count Dracula tells him to help himself to supper.

After starting a fire and finishing his meal, Jonathan turns around to find a young woman in white standing in the room. He introduces himself as the new librarian. The melancholy woman says that *he* is keeping her prisoner. Coming closer to him, she places her hands on his shoulders. Her face then changes and grows quiet as she stares at his throat. Suddenly she then runs away, and Jonathan turns to see Count Dracula standing at the top of the stairs.

The count apologizes for not being there when Jonathan arrived, and offers to show him to his room. In his room, Jonathan tells the count he is anxious to begin working on the library. Dracula tells Jonathan he must be away all day, and gives Jonathan the keys to the library. He comments on a photo and Jonathan tells him it is his fiancée Lucy. Dracula bids Jonathan goodnight and leaves, locking the door.

Jonathan goes to his diary and records that Dracula believes his story of being a librarian. Now all he can do is wait for daylight when he can bring the count's reign of terror to an end.

Later, Jonathan discovers the door is unlocked, and he heads downstairs where he meets the woman again. Jonathan puts his arms around the distraught woman and tells her that he will help. She looks up at his neck and bears her fangs. The woman bites him and he pushes her away. Dracula appears with blood dripping from his mouth. He leaps over the table and grabs the woman. The woman screams and Jonathan watches the count carry her away before he faints.

In the morning Jonathan wakes in his room and finds the door locked again. He examines the puncture wounds on his throat in his mirror. Jonathan opens his diary, and records that he has become a victim of Dracula. Jonathan says it will soon be dark, and he plans to find Dracula's resting place and end his existence.

Jonathan climbs out the window and places his diary at a roadside shrine. He then returns to the castle and makes his way to the cellar. There he finds Dracula lying in a lidless stone sarcophagus. In a second coffin he finds the woman. He opens his bundle and takes out stake and hammer. Placing the stake over the woman's heart Jonathan pounds it into her chest as she screams. Dracula's eyes open.

Outside the sun sets. Jonathan looks at the corpse, now transformed into the body of a very old woman. Jonathan turns to Dracula's coffin and finds it empty. Terrified Jonathan sees Dracula standing at the door, blocking his escape.

Later at the local inn, Van Helsing arrives and asks if another man named Harker had stopped there recently. The innkeeper says no, but the barmaid, Inga, remembers the man. The innkeeper cuts her off. When Inga brings Van Helsing's plate, she hands him Harker's diary and whispers that it was found outside Dracula's castle.

On the road to the castle, a cart carrying a coffin races past Van Helsing. Once inside, Van Helsing finds the castle deserted. Jonathan's things are still in his room, but the frame that held Lucy's photo is now empty.

Van Helsing continues his search until he comes to the cellar. He finds Jonathan lying in one of the coffins, transformed into a vampire. Van Helsing solemnly picks up the stake and hammer Jonathan had dropped on the floor, preparing to destroy his good friend.

Later, at the Holmwood home in Karlstadt, Van Helsing sits with Lucy's brother Arthur and his wife Mina. Arthur is suspicious of Van Helsing's story of Jonathan's death. He refuses to let Van Helsing see Lucy, saying she has been ill.

Upstairs in her room, Lucy lies in bed and assures both Mina and Arthur that when Jonathan comes home she will be better. They both say nothing of Van Helsing's visit and tell Lucy goodnight. Once alone, Lucy locks her door, and opens the French doors. She removes the cross around her neck, and pulls down her collar, revealing puncture wounds on her neck.

In his study, Van Helsing listens to his recorded notes on the phonograph while looking over Harker's diary. The recording says that vampires are allergic to sunlight and it could prove fatal to them. Crosses also repel them because they represent ultimate goodness. Van Helsing adds to his recording that the vampire's victim detests being dominated by vampirism, but is unable to resist, similar to an addiction to drugs.

Back in Lucy's room, Dracula stands on her balcony. He approaches her bed and bares his fangs as he looks at her. Lucy breathes heavily with eager anticipation.

Van Helsing welcomes Mina into his study. She tells him she would like to have Jonathan's things. Van Helsing asks how Lucy has taken the news and Mina tells him she is still too ill to be told. Van Helsing asks what the diagnosis is and Mina tells him anemia. Suspicious, Van Helsing asks if he may see her, and Mina tells him she was hoping for a second opinion.

After examining Lucy, Van Helsing asks Mina about the marks on the girl's throat. Mina says Lucy thought she had been stung by something. Van Helsing tells Mina to keep the windows closed and place garlic flowers all around the room. Later that evening Lucy is in a panic. Gerta enters, and Lucy begs her to open the window and get rid of the flowers. Gerta finally agrees. When she leaves, Dracula appears.

The next morning, Lucy is dead. Van Helsing arrives and goes straight to Lucy's body. Gerta admits that she opened the window and removed the plants because Lucy said she couldn't breath. Van Helsing gives Arthur Jonathan's diary, hoping that he will believe him if he reads Jonathan's own words.

A few nights later, a policeman comes to the Holmwood house with Tania, the housekeeper's little girl. She tells them that Lucy attacked her.

The next night, Arthur goes to Lucy's mausoleum. He then sees Tania walking hand in hand with Lucy. Lucy is about to bite Tania when Arthur screams her name. Lucy turns to Arthur and asks him to let her give him a kiss. Before she can bite him, Van Helsing appears holding a cross between them.

Van Helsing forces Lucy back until it touches her forehead and burns her. Lucy runs into the mausoleum.

Van Helsing explains that Lucy is Dracula's revenge for the woman Jonathan destroyed. Van Helsing tells Arthur he can give Lucy peace, but he asks Arthur to let Lucy go on a bit longer, so she can lead them to Dracula. Arthur refuses.

At daybreak, Arthur watches while Van Helsing drives a stake through Lucy's heart. When it is done, Van Helsing shows Arthur that the burn from the cross has vanished. She is now at peace.

In his study, Van Helsing tells Arthur he saw a cart carry the Count's coffin from the castle, and is sure that the cart would have gone through the customs house in Ingstadt. They plan to go there to find where the coffin was delivered.

While Arthur is away with Van Helsing, a boy comes to the house and tells Mina that Arthur wants to meet her immediately. Meanwhile at the customs house, Arthur bribes the official, who gives them the same address the boy gave Mina. Mina arrives at the address to find a funeral parlor. Inside she comes face to face with Dracula. Later, Arthur and Van Helsing visit the funeral parlor, and the proprietor is shocked that the coffin is now gone.

Back at the house Mina sits quietly while Arthur and Van Helsing plan to search other possible places for Dracula's coffin. Arthur insists Mina wear a cross. Mina tries to refuse, but he puts one into her hand. She screams and faints, revealing a burn mark in her palm.

Arthur regrets not letting Lucy lead them to Dracula and is terrified for his wife. That night, Arthur and Van Helsing watch Mina's window from outside. Mina goes into the hall, where Dracula stands at the bottom of the stairs. He follows Mina into her room, and begins to kiss her, making his way down to her neck.

At sunrise, Arthur and Van Helsing come back inside. Arthur finds Mina passed out on the bed, her throat covered in blood. Van Helsing performs a transfusion to help Mina.

That night Gerta tells Van Helsing that Mina is sleeping peacefully. Van Helsing asks Gerta to bring him another bottle of wine, but she says she does not want to disobey Mina by going to the wine cellar. She explains that a few nights ago Mina ordered her to stay out of the basement.

Van Helsing rushes into the cellar and finds Dracula's coffin. He flings off the lid, only to find it empty. Upstairs he finds Mina is gone. Van Helsing tells Arthur there is only one place left for him to go and that's the castle.

Realizing he is running out of time, Dracula stops outside the castle and tosses Mina into an open grave. Mina wakes as he starts throwing dirt over her. Dracula sees Arthur and Van Helsing arrive and the sun beginning to rise. Dracula abandons Mina and rushes into the castle with Van Helsing right behind.

Dracula and Van Helsing begin to fight. Dracula gets the better of Van Helsing, and he stops for a moment to relish his victory. Van Helsing seizes the moment and leaps at the window, pulling down the drapes. The room is flooded with sunlight. Dracula tries to flee, but Van Helsing grabs two candlesticks and holds them together to form a cross. Van Helsing watches as Dracula disintegrates. Outside the burn disappears from Mina's hand. Dracula has turned to dust, leaving only his ring behind.

Dark Shadows

Country: U.S.A.; *Theatrical Release:* April 17, 1967 (episode 211); *Production Company:* Dan Curtis Productions, Inc.; *Director:* Dan Curtis, Henry Kaplan, John Sedwick, and Lela Swift; *Writer(s):* Sam Hall, Ron Sproat; *Cast:* Jonathan Frid (Barnabas Collins), Grayson Hall (Dr. Julia Hoffman/Natalie du Prés), John Karlen (Willie Loomis), David Henesy (David Collins/Daniel Collins) Kathryn Leigh Scott (Maggie Evans/Josette du Prés), Alexandra Moltke (Victoria Winters), Nancy Barrett (Carolyn Stoddard/Millicent Collins), Joan Bennett (Elizabeth Collins/Naomi Collins), David Ford (Sam Evans/André du Prés), Joel Crothers (Joe Haskell/Nathan Forbes), Anthony George/Mitchell Ryan (Burke Devlin/Jeremiah Collins), Sharon Smyth (Sarah Collins), Robert Gerringer (Dr. Woodard), Lara Parker (Angelique), Louis Edmonds (Roger Collins/Joshua Collins); *Vampire(s):* Barnabas Collins

Plot summary: Because of the nature of television syndication, the synopsis is necessarily brief.

Episodes 205–276

Willie Loomis is fascinated with the portrait of Barnabas Collins and the legend about a secret family treasure. While searching for the treasure in the Collins crypt, he discovers a chained coffin, the perfect place to hide jewels. Unfortunately when he opens the lid, a hand emerges, grasping Willie firmly about the neck. The vampire Barnabas Collins has returned.

Barnabas assumes the identity of a cousin from England and arrives at Collinwood. A weakened Willie is found with puncture wounds on his wrists at the Blue Whale, a local bar. Dr. Woodard, the family doctor, diagnoses Willie with blood loss. Barnabas gains permission to move into the Old House, with Willie as his servant.

A young waitress, Maggie Evans, bears a remarkable resemblance to Josette, Barnabas's long lost love. After several visits by Barnabas to her bedroom, Maggie becomes weaker and is hospitalized. Everyone thinks she has died, until her body disappears. Barnabas is in fact holding her captive. Maggie eventually escapes through the aid of Sarah, the ghost of Barnabas's nine-year-old sister. Maggie suffers from memory loss and has reverted to childhood. Sam and Joe find her and secretly send Maggie to the Windcliff Sanitarium, where Julia Hoffman becomes her doctor.

Episodes 277–329

Barnabas has now switched his intentions to Victoria Collins (Vicki) and hosts a costume ball to get her to wear Josette's dress. The partygoers hold a séance and Vicki falls into a trance, where Josette speaks through her.

Meanwhile, Dr. Julia Hoffman has been probing into Maggie's mind. She finds, under hypnosis, that Maggie is deathly afraid of the name Barnabas. Julia decides to go to Collinwood to find the answers, posing as a visiting historian. While at the Old House she notices that Barnabas casts no reflection. She returns to find Barnabas in his coffin and offers to help him find a cure. Over the course of working with Barnabas, the doctor becomes highly enamored with him.

Dr. Woodard and Burke, Vicki's boyfriend, start to become curious about Barnabas. At the same time, Sarah helps Maggie escape from Windcliff Sanitarium. The young girl stumbles into the Blue Whale and collapses. Julia is forced to hypnotize Maggie to cover her memory of Barnabas.

The ghostly Sarah starts to show up often. She shows David Collins, a young boy, the secret room in the crypt and leaves her shoe in Maggie's room. All attempts by Barnabas to talk to his ghostly sister prove fruitless. He becomes afraid that Sarah will expose him. As David hides from Barnabas and Willie, he becomes locked in a secret room. Barnabas knows Sarah talks to David, and he is afraid that the boy knows the truth. Sarah helps David escape from the room, and Burke arrives before Barnabas can do anything to David. The boy starts to have nightmares about Barnabas.

With Maggie's memory returning, she is once again a threat. The police shoot an intruder outside her bedroom, only to discover it is Willie. Barnabas decides to frame him for Maggie's original kidnapping. Dr. Woodard diagnoses Willie as mentally unsound.

Episodes 330–365

Barnabas has now switched to scare tactics with David. The boy boldly sneaks into the Old House and finds Barnabas's open coffin, but Julia manages to stop Barnabas from killing him. David's story has caused a search to be conducted of the Old House by Burke and Dr. Woodard, turning up nothing. Sarah has been talking to Dr. Woodard, who confronts Barnabas. Later, Dr. Woodard steals Julia's notebook, which contains the specifics of Barnabas's vampirism. Barnabas forces Julia to help him kill Dr. Woddard. The death is made to look like a heart attack.

Vicki becomes distraught when she learns that Burke's plane has crashed without survivors. Barnabas takes this opportunity to get closer to her. Julia becomes jealous and uses hypnosis to convince Vicki that Barnabas is very unattractive. Growing impatient, Barnabas forces Julia to speed up the cure for his vampirism. As a result, he ages to his true age of 200 years. Carolyn comes to the Old House to check out David's story. The aged Barnabas catches her and bites her on the neck. He returns to normal and Carolyn becomes his slave.

Blacula

Country: U.S.A; *Theatrical Release:* August 25, 1972; *Production Company:* American International; *Director:* William Crain; *Writer(s):* Joan Torres, Raymon Koenig; *Cast:* William Marshall (Mamuwalde/Blacula), Vonetta McGee (Tina/Luva), Denise Nicholas (Michelle), Gordon Pinsent (Lt. Peters), Thalmus Rasulala (Dr. Gordon Thomas), Emily Yancy (Nancy), Charles Macaulay (Dracula); *Vampire(s):* Dracula, Blacula

Plot summary: In 1780, an African Prince Mamuwalde and his wife Luva tour Europe to meet with members of the ruling class, hoping to persuade them to stop the slave trade. In Transylvania, they meet Count Dracula, who scoffs at the idea and thinks slavery has its merits. When he offers to purchase Luva, Mamuwalde takes offense. Mamuwalde accuses Dracula of acting like an animal to which Dracula replies, "Really ... let us not forget sir it is you that comes from the jungle." When they try to leave, several servants enter and overpower Mamuwalde, knocking him unconscious. A group of vampire women take hold of Luva, and Dracula goes to the unconscious Mamuwalde and bites his neck.

Luva watches in horror as Mamuwalde lies in a coffin. Dracula stands over him with bloody fangs and curses him with his name saying, "You will be Blacula." He locks Mamuwalde in the coffin to be tormented by his lust for blood. He then seals Luva in the tomb to listen to her husband's screams until the flesh rots from her bones.

In 1972, an interracial gay couple, named Bobby and Billy, purchase all the contents of Castle Dracula, and plan to sell the contents through their antique business. In a Los Angeles warehouse, they anxiously start pricing everything, and notice the coffin. Bobby goes to work on the coffin lid, breaking the lock. Billy cuts his arm working on another crate, and the two tend to the wound, unaware that the coffin lid opens behind them. Mamuwalde steps outside, and attacks the two men. He remembers the words of Count Dracula: "I curse you with my name, you shall be Blacula."

Dr. Gordon Thomas visits Bobby's body at the funeral parlor with his girlfriend Michelle and her sister Tina. Mamuwalde watches from the shadows and is struck by Tina's incredible resemblance to Luva. Dr. Thomas sends the girls to visit Bobby's mother and stays behind to examine the body. The funeral director begins to object, but Dr. Thomas informs him he works for the Police Science Division. Dr. Thomas is shocked that the body is drained of blood. The funeral director says that he had not embalmed the body at the request of the family, and shows Dr. Thomas the puncture wounds on Bobby's neck.

On the way from Bobby's wake, Tina and Michelle part ways. Tina notices someone following her. Mamuwalde emerges from the shadows and grabs Tina's arm calling her Luva. Tina screams and pulls away, dropping her purse. Tina runs away, and Mamuwalde loses track of her when a cab hits him. Angry at losing Tina, Mamuwalde bites the cab driver, Juanita Jones.

The next day at the police station Dr. Thomas goes to the morgue to examine the body of Juanita Jones, and finds it drained of blood, with the exact same puncture wounds on her throat that were on Bobby. He shakes his head and begins to laugh, telling himself "that's ridiculous."

Dr. Thomas complains to Lt. Jack Peters that the police reports on Billy and Bobby's deaths are missing. Peters calls in Officer Barnes and tells him to find the reports and deliver them to Dr. Thomas immediately. Dr. Thomas tells them he'll be at the club tonight for Michelle's birthday.

Back in his office, Dr. Thomas calls the funeral parlor and tells the director he is sending men to collect Bobby's body. Michelle, who is also his assistant, tells Dr. Thomas that Tina was hassled the night before and is still shaken up because the guy got her purse.

At the club that night Mamuwalde arrives and returns Tina's purse. Joining the others, Mamuwalde introduces himself and apologizes for scaring Tina.

He explains that he was surprised by her remarkable resemblance to his former wife, who he had recently lost.

Dr. Thomas is called away to the phone. The funeral director tells him Bobby's body is now gone. When he returns to the table and informs the others of the news, Mamuwalde says, "Perhaps he wasn't dead."

Nancy, the club photographer, comes to the table and Mamuwalde tries to avoid the camera by leaving, but Tina follows. He asks her if he could see Tina again. She agrees to see him just as Nancy snaps their picture. Mamuwalde leaves and Nancy tells the table she is going to develop the pictures. In the darkroom, Nancy is shocked that Mamuwalde doesn't appear in the picture. She turns around and is attacked by Mamuwalde. Officer Barnes pulls up outside the club to deliver the report to Dr. Thomas, and sees Nancy stumble out of her house and collapse. He goes to help the woman, but she has already turned into a vampire and bites him.

In Dr. Thomas's office, Michelle returns from the library with a stack of books on the occult. Lt. Peters calls and tells Dr. Thomas he can't get the order to exhume the body. Dr. Thomas tells Michelle that they are going to the graveyard to dig up Billy anyway.

Mamuwalde arrives at Tina's apartment. He says that her strange feelings for him are because she is the reincarnation of his wife Luva. He tells her he is a vampire and asks her to be with him. He tells her he will never force her to accept him, and moves to leave. Tina stops him, and asks Mamuwalde to stay with her. They kiss.

In the graveyard, Dr. Thomas digs up Billy's grave while Michelle holds the flashlight. He opens the coffin and Billy leaps out with his fangs bared. They fight and Dr. Thomas stakes Billy in the heart, cutting his head off with the shovel. Dr. Thomas calms Michelle down and she asks about Bobby. Dr. Thomas tells her Bobby is a vampire too.

Dr. Thomas remembers that the cab driver, Juanita, is still in the morgue. Dr. Thomas stops at a pay phone and calls the morgue. He tells Sam, the attendant, to take Juanita's body out of the freezer and lock her in the exam room. Sam hangs up and brings out Juanita's body, but the phone rings again, and he leaves the room without locking the door. While Sam is on the phone, Juanita wakes and attacks him.

Lt. Peters and Dr. Thomas arrive at the morgue to find the office in shambles. They discover Sam is gone and then are attacked by Juanita. Dr. Thomas uses a cross to force her back into the sunlight, which destroys her. Dr. Thomas explains that the vampires are reproducing geometrically.

Dr. Thomas and Michelle meet Tina and Mamuwalde at the club. Dr. Thomas tells Mamuwalde that even though many in the department won't believe a vampire is responsible for the recent murders, the police are organizing a search for the creature's resting place. Mamuwalde tells Dr. Thomas that the fact that no one believes is the vampire's best defense. Mamuwalde and Tina leave together.

A friend named Skillet stops by their table and asks if they have seen Nancy, the photographer. Dr. Thomas goes across the street to Nancy's house. He finds it open and ransacked. In the darkroom, he sees the photo that Mamuwalde should be in but is not. Realizing Mamuwalde is a vampire, Dr. Thomas rushes out.

Lt. Peters gets word that a police car has spotted Bobby and is following him. Lt. Peters and Dr. Thomas meet the police car at the warehouse. They enter, but soon find themselves surrounded by vampires including Bobby, Sam, Nancy and Officer Barnes. The vampires quickly kill the other policemen. Lt. Peters and Dr. Thomas are cornered. They use oil lamps to set fire to the vampires, and Dr. Thomas stakes Sam.

As they escape, they come face to face with Mamuwalde. He tells them that he has moved his coffin, thanks to Dr. Thomas's suggestion. Dr. Thomas asks Mamuwalde if he plans for Tina to become a vampire as well, and Mamuwalde angrily answers that her life means more to him than his own. Mamuwalde then turns into a bat and escapes.

Back at Tina's apartment, the police clear the streets outside. Mamuwalde watches from a rooftop. In her room, Tina senses Mamuwalde calling her to him. He turns into a bat and takes off. When Dr. Thomas returns, he discovers that Tina has left the apartment. Lt. Peters instructs the police not to stop her, just follow. Tina walks in a trance to a chemical plant.

Tina meets Mamuwalde inside and they kiss. They hear the sirens outside and they rush down the tunnels of the plant while the police search for them. A cop spots them and opens fire. Tina is shot and Mamuwalde retaliates, killing the man. As Tina lies dying, Mamuwalde tells her he cannot lose her again. He asks her to forgive him, but it is the only way. He bites her.

Dr. Thomas, Lt. Peters, and Michelle enter the plant and hear Mamuwalde's voice as he yells that none will escape his vengeance. While Mamuwalde goes about killing the police, Dr. Thomas, Lt. Peters, and Michelle find a coffin. Dr. Thomas opens the lid and Lt. Peters plunges the stake into what he thinks is Mamuwalde's heart. It is in fact Tina lying in the coffin. Mamuwalde appears, and tells them to get away from Tina.

Mamuwalde goes to the coffin and looks at Tina, now dead. He asks what is left for him now that his only reason for living has been taken away. He kisses Tina's hand and walks past the others, climbing the stairs toward the sunrise. Mamuwalde reaches the roof and collapses in the sunlight. Dr. Thomas and Lt. Peters follow and watch in amazement as Mamuwalde melts away, leaving only a skeleton behind.

Dracula

Country: U.S.A.; *Theatrical Release:* February 8, 1974; *Production Company:* Universal; *Director:* Dan Curtis; *Writer(s):* Richard Matheson (based on Stoker's novel); *Cast:* Jack Palance (Count Dracula), Simon Ward (Arthur Holmwood), Nigel Davenport (Dr. Van Helsing), Pamela Brown (Mrs. Westenra), Fiona Lewis (Lucy Westenra), Penelope Horner (Mina Murray), Murray Brown (Jonathan Harker); *Vampire(s):* Count Dracula, Vampire Brides

Plot summary: Jonathan Harker arrives at the inn and is given a letter from his client, Count Dracula. The letter informs him that Dracula's carriage will meet him at the Borgo pass the following evening. The next morning, Jonathan travels by coach to the Borgo pass and is unnerved by the strange looks the other passengers give him. Dracula's carriage and a mysterious driver meet Jonathan, and speed him through the woods, followed by a pack of wolves.

At the castle, Count Dracula greets Jonathan and then abruptly leaves in the middle of the conversation. Dracula offers him dinner, but interrupts him to ask for pictures of the properties in London. As he looks over the properties, Dracula notices a photo of Jonathan, Arthur, Mina, and Lucy. The count fixates on Lucy's image.

Dracula asks about the Carfax Estate, the property nearest to Lucy. Jonathan admits it is an old house, but Dracula says he is of an old family and prefers an old house. Dracula speaks of his family's history until he hears the clock chime, indicating sunrise. He tells Jonathan to write home, saying he will stay with the count for a month. Jonathan is shocked, but Dracula merely leaves the room and locks the door.

Jonathan wakes the next evening. While he shaves, Dracula enters. Jonathan is startled and cuts his neck. Dracula sees the blood and stares until Jonathan starts to become nervous. Dracula turns his back and tells him to write the letters home. Jonathan tries to leave, but Dracula locks the door again.

Later, a frustrated Jonathan notices a door hidden behind a tapestry. He leaves and wanders into the library. He looks through the papers on the desk and is surprised to find a newspaper clipping with Lucy's photo circled. He notices a coffin at the other end of the room beneath a portrait labeled: Vlad Tepes, 1471. The man in the painting is the exact image of Count Dracula. The woman standing beside him looks startlingly like Lucy.

Jonathan turns around and sees three women in the room with him. They growl and rush toward him. As the women attack, Dracula enters the room and screams at the women. He pulls them off of the man, and forces Jonathan back to his room.

Dracula orders Jonathan to write the letters home. As Jonathan complies, Dracula sees the photo again and remembers a woman in his past who resembles Lucy. They fondly kiss in the sunlight. Jonathan finishes and hands over the letters. Dracula says that now he will go to England and grabs Jonathan by the throat, hurling him across the room.

Jonathan wakes the next morning and sees through the window that gypsies are transporting several oblong crates. He grabs hold of the ivy growing along the wall and climbs up to the roof. Entering the castle, he travels down into the cavernous tunnels of the crypt. There he discovers more of the oblong boxes, filled with earth. He then finds a box with Dracula inside. He tries to kill Dracula with a shovel, but is stopped by gypsies and knocked out. When he awakes, it is night and the boxes are gone. Jonathan is surrounded by the three women, who close in and attack him.

Five weeks later, in the village of Whitby, England, the wreckage of a ship lies on the beach. Dracula stands alone next to the wrecked vessel. The captain is lashed to the wheel.

Lucy's mother, Mrs. Westenra, meets Mina at the train station. Mina explains that she's had no news of Jonathan from the continent, and Mrs. Westenra says that Lucy has taken to walking in her sleep. They are bringing in a new doctor named Van Helsing to check on her. On the ride back to the Westenra estate, she relates the news of the recent shipwreck. The crew was killed and the only cargo, some large boxes of earth, survived.

Dr. Van Helsing examines a very pale looking Lucy in bed. He leaves with Arthur, her fiancée, and asks about the wounds on her neck. Arthur says they've been there for three weeks and thinks they might be have been caused by a snake. Van Helsing suspects more but will not say until he is certain.

That night, Arthur and Van Helsing stand guard over Lucy. She's wearing a necklace of garlic flowers and sleeps restlessly. Later, Van Helsing wakes Arthur, asking him to take the shift until dawn. Outside the window, Dracula wills Arthur to sleep and Lucy to wake.

Lucy leaves the house and meets Dracula on the lawn. She removes the garlic flowers and the bandage from her neck. Dracula kisses her passionately, and then bites her. At dawn, Van Helsing wakes and notices that Lucy is gone. He and Arthur find her outside with fresh wounds on her neck.

Van Helsing uses the maid to transfuse blood into Lucy. He explains to Arthur that his fiancée is a victim of a vampire. Arthur doubts that such a creature can be real, but Van Helsing insists. He tells Arthur they must continue as before, and this time they must be sure to stay awake.

In the days that follow, Lucy grows strong and spends time with Mina and Arthur. Believing her to be cured, Van Helsing says goodbye and tells Arthur to continue watching her at night. When Van Helsing returns, they will begin their search for the vampire.

That night at the London Zoo, a groundsman confronts Dracula who has pried apart the bars of a cage. A wolf escapes and attacks the man. Back at the Westenra estate, Mrs. Westenra begs Arthur to tell her what is going on. As Lucy sleeps, they hear the sound of a wolf howling. Arthur takes out a pistol and places it on the table. Suddenly the wolf from the zoo breaks through the window, leaping onto Arthur. Mrs. Westenra collapses and the gun is knocked to the floor. Arthur manages to reach the gun, shoots the wolf, and then passes out. Dracula appears in Lucy's room. She wakes and tears off the garlic flowers.

Later the butler and maid arrive and find Arthur regaining consciousness. He and the butler hurry outside. They find the sprawled body of Lucy, lying slumped by a tree, dead.

Lucy is buried in the Westenra mausoleum. After the funeral, Arthur stares at Lucy's portrait. He turns and is shocked to see Lucy standing outside the window. He rushes to her and kisses her. She tells him they will always be together, and when they embrace, she tries to bite Arthur. She is interrupted by Van Helsing, who holds up a cross. She runs out and Van Helsing keeps Arthur from following. At sunrise, Van Helsing takes Arthur to the mausoleum where they find Lucy back in her coffin. He drives a stake through her heart.

Van Helsing wants Mina to take Mrs. Westenra into Whitby for while. When Mina demands to know what is happening, he explains that the man who killed Lucy is a vampire and may return. He and Arthur will hunt the vampire down, find his box of earth, and destroy him. That reminds Mina of the ship-wreck with the boxes of earth.

That night, Dracula goes to Lucy's coffin and calls to her. When she does not answer, he reluctantly opens her coffin. He sees that she has been destroyed and becomes enraged. He overturns Lucy's coffin and upends everything in the mausoleum.

Van Helsing and Arthur take Mina and Mrs. Westenra into town and check them into a hotel. As they leave, Dracula enters the hotel. When a hotel clerk stops him, Dracula crushes the man's throat. He rushes out of the hotel, past several more clerks and customers.

After following a trail of several delivery companies, Arthur and Van Helsing learn that the boxes of earth were delivered to Count Dracula at the Carfax Estate. They go there immediately and discover the boxes. They pile them together and burn them, but there is still one box missing. When they return to the hotel, they learn that there was a commotion and Mina and Mrs. Westenra have checked out.

Back at the Westenra Estate, Mina and Mrs. Westenra decide to spend the night in the same room. Dracula breaks in through the locked door. Arthur and Van Helsing arrive and rush upstairs where they find Dracula leaning over Mina. Van Helsing holds out a cross, but Dracula tightens his grip on Mina's throat and orders him to put it away. Dracula cuts open his chest and forces Mina to drink the blood. Van Helsing and Arthur watch in horror. Finally Dracula throws Mina aside and calmly walks out. He returns to Carfax only to find all his boxes burned. Dracula is enraged and howls at the night.

Van Helsing hypnotizes Mina and questions her about Dracula's where-abouts. She says she hears the sound of water. Van Helsing regrets destroying the boxes because now Dracula has fled England. Arthur wonders if that wasn't what they wanted. Van Helsing explains that if they do not destroy Dracula, Mina will be under his influence until she dies. They decide to check Varna, and then notice Mina react to the name Dracula. Van Helsing brings her out of the trance and asks Mina if she has ever heard the name Dracula. Mina tells them that Dracula was the name of Jonathan's client in Transylvania.

Van Helsing, Arthur, and Mina give chase by train, hoping to catch up to Dracula's ship in Varna. At the inn in Transylvania, Mina has grown worse. The men leave her there and ride through the night to reach Dracula's castle. In the crypt beneath the castle, they discover the three women in their coffins. Van Helsing stakes each woman through the heart. Jonathan leaps out of the shadows, now transformed into a vampire. They push Jonathan into a pit lined with stalagmites.

Mina wakes in the inn and the innkeeper's wife tries to comfort her. Mina grabs the cross around the innkeeper's neck, burning her hand. She screams and throws the cross away.

Back at the castle Van Helsing and Arthur find Dracula's library. They see the portrait and the woman's resemblance to Lucy. Dracula enters but is held at bay by Arthur, who holds up a cross. The count overturns a table, knocking both men down. Dracula begins choking Arthur when Van Helsing notices that the sun has risen. He pulls down the curtains, flooding the room with sunlight. Dracula stumbles, seemingly drained of strength. Van Helsing uses a spear from a suit of armor and stabs Dracula through the heart, impaling the vampire to the overturned table. Dracula finally dies.

Dracula

Country: U.S.A.; *Theatrical Release:* July 13, 1979 New York (Wide Release July 20); *Production Company:* Universal; *Director:* John Badham; *Writer(s):* W. D. Richter (based on Stoker's novel); *Cast:* Frank Langella (Count Dracula), Laurence Olivier (Prof. Abraham Van Helsing), Donald Pleasence (Dr. Jack Seward), Kate Nelligan (Lucy Seward), Trevor Eve (Jonathan Harker), Jan Francis (Mina Van Helsing), Tony Haygarth (Milo Renfield); *Vampire(s):* Count Dracula

Plot summary: The Demeter is tossed by a storm. The remaining crewmembers desperately try to remove a huge box from the cargo hold, to throw it overboard. A clawed hand bursts through the wooden box and tears out a crewman's throat. The men panic as an animal of some kind erupts out of the box.

In Whitby, Mina goes to the window and sees the Demeter sail dangerously close to the rocks. She runs down to the shore where the ship is breaking apart, and sees a wolf leap from the deck. Inside a nearby cave, she finds Count Dracula lying under a fur pelt.

In the morning the villagers are assessing the wreckage. Renfield comes to collect Dracula's crates. Later, he delivers the boxes to Carfax Abbey as the sun sets. Dracula transforms into a bat and attacks the man on the stairs.

At Dr. Seward's house, everyone is discussing the shipwreck and the dead crew. Count Dracula is announced and he goes immediately to Mina, whom he thanks for saving his life. After dinner Dracula causes Mina to collapse with a wave of his hand. He then offers to help her using hypnosis. Impressed by this stunt, Lucy, Dr. Seward's daughter, insists on dancing with the count.

Lucy waits for Mina to fall asleep, and then meets Jonathan, her fiancé on the patio. He teases her about flirting with the count. Dracula crawls down the wall to Mina's window. She awakes to see Dracula clawing open the window. When he enters, Mina is completely enthralled, leaning back to expose her neck for him.

Lucy sneaks back into the room, and finds Mina gasping for air. Lucy calls for help and Dr. Seward and Jonathan quickly enter. They watch helplessly as Mina suffocates in front of them. Lucy screams at the sight of the puncture wounds on Mina's throat.

The next morning, at breakfast, Dr. Seward dictates a telegram informing Mina's father, Van Helsing, of the girl's death. Lucy asks what could have caused the wounds, and Dr. Seward assumes it might have come from pinning on a shawl.

Jonathan goes to Carfax and uses his key to enter. Dracula signs the deeds to the property, and tells Jonathan to give Dr. Seward and Lucy an invitation to dinner, knowing full well that Jonathan will be out of town. On the way back, a hysterical Renfield springs up from the back seat of Jonathan's car. The man is quickly committed to Dr. Seward's sanitarium.

Jonathan attends Mina's funeral with Lucy, and then leaves for London on business. As Dr. Seward and Lucy walk back from the cemetery, Dr. Seward tells her that he must meet Professor Van Helsing on the evening train. Lucy decides that she will attend Dracula's dinner alone.

Dr. Seward meets Van Helsing at the train and they journey back to the sanitarium by coach. Dr. Seward tells the professor that there were no physical signs except that Mina had been sleepwalking and having nightmares. Van Helsing is concerned at the great loss of blood.

At the sanitarium a woman leaps out the window while an inmate screams. Dr. Seward and Van Helsing rush in and find her young baby dead. The inmate claims that Mina murdered her baby, and had fangs like a wolf.

In the courtyard of Carfax Abbey Dracula comments that the howling wolves sound sad and lonely. Lucy thinks they sound lovely and adores the night. Dracula kisses her and moves toward her neck, but stops himself. He asks her to forgive him for intruding on her life. She pulls him closer saying she came of her own accord.

Lucy finds Van Helsing sitting by Mina's grave, and asks him about the garlic flowers placed there. Van Helsing telling her about the Eastern European legends of the vampire. Lucy can't believe that Mina was attacked by one of those creatures.

Van Helsing gives her a cross, and asks that she wear it in Mina's memory. Dracula arrives on horseback and introduces himself to Van Helsing. Van Helsing and Lucy return to the house, where Van Helsing watches from the window as Dracula's horse first spooks at the garlic flowers, then stomps on the ground to remove them from Mina's grave.

Dr. Seward is bewildered when Van Helsing insists on bringing a white horse to the cemetery as part of a gypsy custom to locate the grave of a vampire. In the cemetery, the horse goes wild when it reaches Mina's grave.

As Lucy prepares for bed, she removes the cross Van Helsing gave her. A fog appears in front of her window, and Dracula enters. He picks her up and carries her to bed, kissing her. He tells Lucy he needs her blood, and then bites her neck. They embrace and consummate their union as rippling red smoke surrounds them. Dracula uses his fingernail to cut open his chest. Lucy willingly drinks from the wound.

Van Helsing and Dr. Seward dig up Mina's grave and find her body missing. A hole in the side of the coffin leads to the mining tunnels that run under the town. Van Helsing takes a long stake and a cross and heads into the tunnels.

He stumbles and drops his cross into a puddle, and sees Mina in the water's reflection. She looks pale with rotting skin. Seward arrives and keeps Mina from attacking Van Helsing, finally subduing the girl by placing his cross against her forehead. She turns to rush away, but is impaled on Van Helsing's stake. He cradles his dead daughter, crying at her loss.

Jonathan arrives back from business and sneaks into Lucy's room. He finds her sprawled on the bed. Van Helsing and Dr. Seward arrive and find only a slight pulse and punctures on her neck. Van Helsing orders a blood transfusion.

Afterward, Dracula greets Van Helsing. Van Helsing comments on how he can't see the count's reflection in the mirror. Dracula responds by throwing a candlestick and shattering the glass. Dracula asks about Lucy's condition. Van Helsing offers to show his treatment, producing several cloves of garlic. Dracula cowers and tells the professor he should return to Holland. When Van Helsing refuses to leave, Dracula tries to hypnotize him. Van Helsing resists and Dracula is forced to approach. The professor pulls a cross from his pocket. Dracula yells sacrilege and jumps through the window, transforming into a wolf.

Lucy watches from the window as Van Helsing prepares to perform surgery on Mina's body. Van Helsing holds a mirror up to show that Mina has no reflection. He explains that in order to save Mina's soul, he must remove her heart. He begins to cut open the girl's chest.

Van Helsing returns to find that Lucy has escaped. They take Jonathan's car and chase after her, finally forcing her carriage to stop. Jonathan tells her Dracula is a vampire. Lucy tries to force her way through the men, and it takes all three to subdue her.

Dr. Seward takes Lucy home while Van Helsing and Jonathan head to Carfax Abbey. In the lower levels they discover Dracula's coffin, but it's empty. Dracula materializes out of thin air beside them. He explains that he can move around in daylight so long as he is inside. Jonathan holds up a cross, but Dracula grabs it and it bursts into flames. He tells them that he is the king of his kind and he will make Lucy his queen.

Jonathan attempts to strike the count with a shovel, but Dracula transforms into a bat. He then attacks Jonathan, clawing the man's face. Van Helsing tears away a board and sunlight floods in, causing the bat to catch fire. Dracula flees into the dark tunnels. Van Helsing places pieces of communion wafer into Dracula's coffin.

Back at the sanitarium, Dr. Seward explains that he had to lock Lucy in one of the padded cells because she was uncontrollable. Jonathan goes in to see her. Lucy begins kissing Jonathan, and tries to bite him. She is stopped by the appearance of Van Helsing bearing a cross. He forces Lucy back until she seems to pass out. Lucy then revives looking more human and takes the cross, holding it to her face.

Renfield sees Dracula crawling up the side of the wall toward his window and screams for help, but his cries are ignored. Dracula pulls out the bars of the window and breaks the man's neck. The other patients start to go wild. Dr. Seward, Van Helsing, and Jonathan rush to Renfield's cell.

Dracula sneaks into Lucy's cell in the form of a mist. When the others return, there is a hole in the side of the wall and Lucy is gone. They see Dracula crawling down the wall with Lucy. They pursue in Jonathan's car.

They meet a cart on the road carrying Dracula's crate to the seaport, and give chase. The driver of the cart can't control the horses, and is thrown off. He lands in front of Jonathan's car, forcing it run into a ditch. The cart continues, but the car is stuck. Dr. Seward stays with the injured driver while Jonathan and

Van Helsing proceed on foot. At the seaport, a ferryman takes them out to Dracula's ship.

In the ship's hold, Jonathan and Van Helsing find Dracula's crate, with both Lucy and Dracula sleeping inside. Lucy wakes and attacks Jonathan while Van Helsing attempts to stake Dracula. The count grabs the stake and stabs Van Helsing through the chest, pinning him to the wall.

Jonathan tries shooting Dracula, but it has no effect. He then throws a massive hook used for hauling cargo, but this misses. As Dracula attacks Jonathan, Van Helsing throws the hook back, stabbing Dracula in the back. As the count struggles to free himself from the hook, Jonathan releases a lever causing Dracula to be hoisted up into the sunlight.

Lucy watches as Dracula screams, his face aging and flaking away. Finally the count seems to perish in the sunlight. Mina smiles as the remains of Dracula's cape flutters away in the wind.

Salem's Lot

Country: U.S.A.; *Theatrical Release:* November 17, 1979; *Production Company:* Warner Bros.; *Director:* Tobe Hooper; *Writer(s):* Stephen King (novel), Paul Monash (screenplay); *Cast:* David Soul (Ben Mears), James Mason (Richard K. Straker), Lance Kerwin (Mark Petrie), Bonnie Bedelia (Susan Norton), Lew Ayres (Jason Berk), Julie Cobb (Bonnie Sawyer), Elisha Cook, Jr. (Gordon "Weasel" Phillips), George Dzundza (Cully Sawyer), Ed Flanders (Dr. Bill Norton), Clarissa Kaye-Mason (Marjorie Glick), Geoffrey Lewis (Mike Ryerson), Barney McFadden (Ned Tebbets), Kenneth McMillan (Constable Parkins Gillespie), Fred Willard (Larry Crockett), Marie Windsor (Eva Miller), Barbara Babcock (June Petrie), Bonnie Bartlett (Ann Norton), Joshua Bryant (Ted Petrie), James Gallery (Father Donald Callahan), Robert Lussier (Deputy Constable Nolly Gardner), Brad Savage (Danny Glick), Ronnie Scribner (Ralphie Glick), Ned Wilson (Henry Glick), Reggie Nalder (Kurt Barlow); *Vampire(s):* Kurt Barlow, Susan Norton, Marjorie Glick, Mike Ryerson, Ned Tebbets, Danny Glick, Ralphie Glick

Plot summary: An older man, Ben Mears and a teenage boy, Mark Petrie, pray in a church in Ximico, Guatemala. They fill a bottle with holy water, and Ben gasps as the bottle starts to glow.

We shift back two years to Salem's Lot, Maine. Ben arrives in town and drives to Larry Crockett's realty office. He asks about renting the Marsten House and is surprised to find it sold. Larry suggests he try a room at Eva Miller's boarding house.

Later, Ben comes across Susan Norton drawing in the park with a copy of his novel next to her. Ben asks her out to dinner. Later, he drives to Susan's house and has dinner with her mother and father, Dr. Bill Norton. As Susan and Ben leave, Ben reveals that it's been two years since his wife died, and he returned to Salem's Lot to write about the Marsten House. They drive to the lake where they kiss.

A man named Straker meets with Larry Crockett in his antique shop and asks him to arrange for two men to pick up a sideboard shipped from Europe. He wants the item taken into the cellar of the Marsten House, and the doors chained and padlocked.

A teenage boy, Mark Petrie, performs a monologue at a school play rehearsal as Jason Berk, the schoolteacher, watches. Ben surprised his former teacher.

Ben meets Susan at school and offers to walk her home. She glances across the street and sees Ned Tebbets. She excuses herself and confronts her former boyfriend. He knows she was up at the lake with Ben and drives off in a huff.

A man named Cully approaches Mike Ryerson, the groundskeeper at the Harmony Hill Cemetery, and asks him to find another guy to handle a delivery for him. Later, Cully says goodbye to his wife, Bonnie, who works as a secretary at Larry Crockett's office. Cully lies and says that the delivery for Mr. Straker will take him at least until midnight. After he leaves, Larry worries that Cully knows about his affair with Bonnie.

Mike says goodbye to his dog in the cemetery as he and Ned take the truck from Cully to pick up the sideboard. At the docks, Mike and Ned load the huge crate onto the truck. Ned feels the side of the crate and is spooked by how cold it is. On the drive back, Ned notices that the crate moves closer and closer to the truck cab. He wants to open the crate, but Mike disagrees.

Ben and Jason Berk meet for dinner. Ben relates a story about when he entered the Marsten House as a boy. He went in on a dare, and imagined he saw Hubie Marsten, the man who built the house, hanging from a noose. He thought the corpse opened its eyes and looked at him. Ben thinks the house is evil and that it attracts evil men to it.

Mark Petrie and the Glick boys, Ralphie and Danny, have been rehearsing the school play in Mark's room. The boys question Mark about his collection of monster figures. Mark replies that he's always liked that sort of stuff. Mrs. Petrie comes in to tell the Glick boys that their mom wants them to come home.

As the Glick boys walk home, Ralphie is nervous about cutting through the woods. Danny dismisses the fear and leaves his brother alone. Ralphie calls to Danny to wait, but a wind suddenly surrounds him. He turns as a tall dark figure appears.

Mike and Ned finally arrive at the Marsten House. The crate is freezing to the touch, and the men hurry to deposit it in the cellar. Ned insists that the cold isn't natural and wants to open it. Mike hears a noise upstairs and they both run out of the cellar. Ned tosses the locks and chain into the cellar before they drive away.

Marjorie Glick and her husband call the Petrie house. They are concerned that the boys haven't come home yet. Marjorie sees Danny stagger into the yard and collapse.

Straker returns to the Marsten House and is concerned to see the cellar doors unlocked. He takes a large bundle wrapped in black plastic from the trunk of his car and carries it into the cellar. There he sees the crate splintered as if it had exploded. Straker lays the bundle on the table and removes the plastic, revealing the unconscious body of Ralphie Glick.

Cully watches from the shadows as Bonnie welcomes Larry inside the house. After retrieving his shotgun from the shed, he bursts into the bedroom catching Larry and Bonnie in a compromising position. Cully takes Larry into the living room and makes him hold the shotgun barrel to his face. He then pulls the triggers and the gun clicks empty. Larry stumbles outside where a massive shadowy figure rises up before him.

Danny lies in his bed at home. Outside the window a fog appears. Ralphie floats into view and begins scratching the windowpane. Danny gets out of bed in a trance and opens the window. Ralphie floats into the room toward Danny.

Down at the lake, Ben and Susan hear two cars pull up. They investigate, only to find Larry Crockett dead in his car. When Constable Parkins Gillespie comes to question them about what they heard, he tells Ben not to leave town.

As Ben and Susan return to the Norton house, they meet Dr. Norton, who is heading to the hospital. Danny has collapsed again. That morning, a search party, including Ben, look for Ralphie Glick. Ben finds a piece of black material and Parkins bags it. Ben comments that Straker always wears a black suit.

Parkins drops in to visit Straker, and asks to see the man's black suits. Later, Parkins calls the FBI and asks them to check out Ben Mears, Richard Straker, and Kurt Barlow, Straker's mysterious partner that no one has seen.

Dr. Bill Norton and Ben meet to discuss the mysterious goings-on in Salem's Lot. Bill doesn't see any link between Larry's death and the Marsten House. Ben insists that there has to be a connection. Dr. Norton also explains that he thinks Danny Glick is suffering from pernicious anemia.

In the hospital, Danny wakes to see fog outside his window, and Ralphie floating outside. When Danny gets out of bed, he pulls his intravenous tube and the bottle crashes to the ground. He opens the window and Ralphie floats inside, grabbing his brother. He opens his mouth to reveal two fangs, and bites Danny in the neck. That morning, the nurse discovers Danny sprawled out in his hospital bed, dead.

Danny Glick has a funeral service at Harmony Hill Cemetery. After everyone leaves, Mike starts to shovel dirt over the coffin. The sun begins to set, and a tremendous wind howls across the cemetery. Mike stares at the coffin and is overcome by a trance. He jumps into the grave and opens the coffin lid. Danny awakes and bites Mike in the neck.

Ben is having dinner with Berk when Mike Ryerson stumbles to their table. Mike is pale and has two visible puncture wounds on his neck. Berk and Ben question him about what happened. He says that after the funeral he fell asleep in the cemetery. Berk insists that Mike spend the night at his house, and they'll see Dr. Norton in the morning.

Mark wakes up in his bed and sees a fog. Danny Glick appears floating outside his window. Mark gets out of bed, and walks toward the window in an apparent trance. Danny scratches at the glass, and Mark takes hold of the latch. But instead of opening the window, he locks it. Mark takes a cross from one of his models and holds it out toward the window. Danny hisses and retreats into the fog. Mark goes to bed holding the cross.

As Berk sets up Mike in the guestroom of his house, he notices the marks on the man's neck. Mike can't recall how they got there. Later that night, Berk tosses and turns in bed. He hears a child's laughter and wakes.

Berk calls Ben and has him bring a cross over. When Ben arrives, Berk takes him to the guestroom where Mike lies in bed. Ben thinks that Mike is only sleeping, but Berk points to the open window, insisting he locked it. There is a single drop of blood on Mike's collar. Ben tries to wake Mike and discovers that the man is dead. Berk asks if there are marks on the neck. Ben checks and sees none. Downstairs, Ben convinces Berk not to mention his suspicions about what happened to Mike. They decide to call the authorities and let them take over. After the coroner takes the body away, Ben and Berk reveal their suspicions of vampirism to Dr. Norton.

When Ben comes back to his room at the boarding house, Ned Tebbets jumps him and beats him up. Ben awakes in the hospital. Dr. Norton informs him that he'll be staying overnight and that Ned is in jail. Ben asks if anyone else has become sick, and Dr. Norton says no. When questioned about Ben and Berk's suspicions of vampires, Dr. Norton says it's out of the question. No one will believe them.

That night Berk sits up in his study amid a pile of books on vampires. He hears a noise upstairs and goes to investigate, carrying the cross Ben brought earlier. A pale Mike Ryerson sits in a rocking chair in the guestroom. Mike's eyes glow and he orders Berk to look at him. Berk seems to fall victim to the trance, but gains strength when he looks at the cross. He holds the object up toward Mike, who hisses and crashes backward through the window. Berk begins to have a heart attack, and stumbles to the phone.

Ned lies in his jail cell but wakes when he hears the cell door click open. He rubs his eyes and looks again. Suddenly the ghastly face of Kurt Barlow appears. The creature is pale blue with pointed ears and multiple sharp fangs. Barlow drapes his cape over Ned.

Ben checks out of the hospital the next day, and runs into Susan. She tells him Ned died last night in his jail cell, and Marjorie Glick died that afternoon. She also says that Berk is in intensive care from a heart attack.

Ben asks Susan to take him to the town priest. Father Callahan tells them that the concept of evil has changed in the last century. When questioned about noticing anything strange, Callahan mentions that some of his most regular parishioners have missed mass.

Later at the Norton house, Ben tells Susan to get some hawthorn branches and put them up around the house. He believes the vampires are breeding in a geometric progression. Dr. Norton informs them that Ned's body has disappeared from the morgue. He and Ben head to the funeral parlor to check on the body of Marjorie Glick.

At the Petrie house, Father Callahan questions Mark about Danny visiting his window last night. Mark's parents insist all this is a result of his morbid interest in monsters. Mark steadfastly insists that what he saw wasn't a dream. Suddenly the lights flicker and the whole house shakes violently. The window shatters and a dark object, like a rock, flies to the ground. The black shape rises to reveal Barlow. He quickly knocks Mr. and Mrs. Petrie's heads together, killing them. Mark rushes Barlow, but the creature easily captures the boy. Father Callahan holds out his cross to protect himself.

Straker arrives, telling Callahan that there's nothing he can do against the master. He offers a deal with the priest: toss away the cross and the boy will be let go. Straker considers it a test of faith. Callahan agrees and Barlow releases Mark. Instead of honoring the bargain, Callahan clings to his cross. Barlow approaches, unaffected by the cross. He grabs the object and tosses it to the floor.

At the funeral parlor, Dr. Norton checks Marjorie's body, saying she is similar to Mike's body. He leaves to call Susan. Ben fashions a makeshift cross out of two tongue depressors and tape. As he says a blessing over the cross, Marjorie sits upright on the table. Ben panics, screaming for Dr. Norton. Marjorie rushes toward him, but Ben uses the cross to keep her at bay, finally touching it to her forehead. She screams as the cross scalds her skin, and fades away.

On the ride back to town, Ben reveals that they must get to Barlow during the day and drive a stake through his heart. Ben assumes that Straker is just a human watchdog, and can be killed with a gun or a knife. When they arrive at the Norton house, Ben tells Susan she has to leave with her mother before sunset.

The next morning Ben drives through the abandoned town to the police station. He finds only deputy Nolly, who says he dreamed Ned came to see him last night. Meanwhile Susan goes to the boarding house where she finds Eva exhausted in a chair. She's been dreaming of her old flame, Weasel, kissing her on the neck.

Susan drives up to the Marsten House and sees Mark carrying two wooden stakes. The boy enters the house through the cellar doors. She follows and wanders through the dark and filthy house. On the second floor, Mark leaps out and nearly attacks her with a stake. They hear a noise, and Mark rushes toward it. When Susan follows, Straker tosses Mark's unconscious body to the ground. He then tells her to come with him.

Later, Straker ties Mark to a chair. When the boy asks what happened to Susan, Straker responds that he took her where she wanted to go. As soon as he leaves the boy, Mark begins working his way out of the ropes.

Ben pulls into Parkins's driveway and finds that the constable is leaving town. He gives Ben his pistol. Ben meets Dr. Norton at the hospital. Bill asks if he's seen Susan. Ben is surprised, saying she should have left by now. They rush out to search for her. Driving up to the Marsten House, they spot Susan's car.

As they're about to enter the house, Ben freezes. He's not sure he can go inside. Just then, Mark rushes out of the doors. He tells them that Susan and Straker are inside. Ben tells Mark to keep running, and the two men enter the house. Dr. Norton heads upstairs while Ben is distracted by Mark's return. The boy is determined to stay, and Ben can't convince him otherwise.

Upstairs, Straker kills Dr. Norton by forcing him onto a wall full of animal horns. Straker then appears at the top of the stairs, and rips off a piece of the banister to use as a club. As Straker slowly descends the stairs, Ben unloads the pistol into him. Only by the fourth shot does Straker show any sign of weakness. After the fifth shot, the man collapses and finally dies.

Mark warns that it's getting dark, and rushes toward the basement. Ben follows to discover that Straker has sawed away the stairs to the basement. Mark has fallen to the ground and twisted his ankle. Ben jumps down and the two search for Barlow's coffin. Mark notices a padlocked door to the root cellar. Ben breaks the lock.

Inside they find Barlow's coffin and the other townspeople sleeping on the ground. Ben and Mark drag the coffin into the basement, and Mark notices that the sun has set. Ben opens the coffin and grabs a stake. Mark looks at Barlow, who opens his eyes. Ben yells not to look at it, and shoves Mark away. As Ben pounds the stake into the creature's heart, Barlow claws and hisses. Behind Mark, the other townspeople, now vampires, begin to crawl toward the exit of the root cellar. Mark slams the door shut and secures it with a screwdriver. Barlow finally dies and withers away into bones.

Ben and Mark pour gasoline around the house and set it on fire. As the Marsten House burns, the other vampires scream.

We flash forward two years to Ximico, and Ben and Mark refilling their bottles with holy water. They see the water glow and Ben knows they can't leave yet. They return to the house they've been staying in, where Mark starts packing. Ben enters the bedroom and sees Susan lying on the bed. She says that they'll always be young and in love. Ben kneels beside her. As he draws closer, she makes ready to bite his neck, but Ben pulls a stake out, and drives it into her chest. Ben returns to Mark and they grab their bags and head out into the night.

Fright Night

Country: U.S.A.; *Theatrical Release:* August 2, 1985; *Production Company:* Columbia Pictures; *Director:* Tom Holland; *Writer(s):* Tom Holland; *Cast:* Chris Sarandon (Jerry Dandridge), William Ragsdale (Charley Brewster), Roddy McDowall (Peter Vincent), Amanda Bearse (Amy), Stephen Geoffreys (Evil Ed Thompson), Jonathan Stark (Billy Cole) Dorothy Fielding (Judy Brewster); *Vampire(s):* Jerry Dandridge, Evil Ed, Amy

Plot summary: Charley Brewster and his girlfriend, Amy, are making out on the floor while his favorite show, *Fright Night*, plays on television. Charley notices that someone has moved into the empty house next door. He watches as two men carry what looks like a coffin into the basement.

The next evening, Charley sees a sexy call-girl go to his neighbor's house. The day after Charley sees a news report on a murdered body, and recognizes the victim as the call-girl. Charley tires to break into the basement next door. The live-in handyman, Billy Cole, catches him and warns Charley to stay away.

Charley stays up with binoculars watching his neighbor's window. He sees another young woman being undressed by a handsome man, Jerry Dandridge. The man opens his mouth wide, showing fangs. Jerry senses that he is being watched and pulls down the shade with long pointed fingers. Charley rushes outside and hides in the bushes. He watches as Billy carries out a body-shaped garbage bag. Something flies down from the roof, and suddenly Jerry is standing next to the handyman. Charley's mother opens the door and starts calling his name. Jerry tosses the apple he was eating toward the exact bush where Charley is hiding. The boy panics and runs back into his house.

Charley has convinced a police detective to check out his neighbor. Billy Cole tells the detective his roommate, Jerry Dandridge, is away, and he explains that he was dumping some trash the night before. Charley tells the detective to look in the basement, where he will find Jerry sleeping in a coffin. The detective thinks Charley is crazy and leaves.

Charley rushes to visit his friend, Evil Ed, asking him for help with vampires. Evil does not believe Charley, but tells him to get some garlic and crosses. Most importantly Charley should be safe as long as no one invites the vampire into his home. Charley hurries back to his house only to find his mother entertaining Jerry in the living room. Jerry makes Charley squirm, saying that now that he's been invited over, he might drop by anytime.

That night, Jerry appears in Mrs. Brewster's room, and jams the door shut. Jerry surprises Charley in his room, grabbing the boy by the throat. He offers Charley a choice: if Charley forgets about him, Jerry will leave the boy alone. Charley tries to use his cross, and Jerry shakes his head, calling Charley a fool. Opening a window with a single finger, Jerry proceeds to push the boy through it.

Charley grabs madly at the windowsill, finally taking a wooden pencil off his desk, and jabbing it through Jerry's hand. Jerry clutches his injured hand. He has transformed into a monster and growls in anger, but when he hears Mrs. Brewster struggle with her locked door, he leaves. Charley releases his mother.

Jerry calls Charley and says that he will come for the boy tomorrow night. As Charley hangs up the phone, he sees Peter Vincent, star and host of *Fright Night*, stake a vampire in one of his films. The following day Charley goes to visit Peter Vincent, but finds that the actor has just been fired. Charley tells him a vampire is living next to him, and he wants Peter to destroy it. Peter thinks Charley is crazy and drives away.

Amy and Evil arrive at Charley's house only to find him holed up in his room, filled with candles, crosses, and recently sharpened stakes. He says he will drive a stake through Jerry's heart. Amy finally convinces Charley to wait.

She and Evil pay a visit to Peter Vincent. They want Peter to perform a vampire test on Jerry Dandridge and pronounce him human. Peter only agrees after Amy offers him $500. They call Jerry and tell him the plan. He agrees as long as they don't use crosses or real holy water because he is a born-again Christian.

The next evening Billy lets Peter, Amy, Evil and Charley inside the house. When Jerry arrives, he is instantly entranced by Amy's appearance. Peter hands Jerry a small vial of ordinary tap water that he claims is holy water. Jerry drinks it, but Charley insists that it wasn't true holy water.

Peter politely ushers the group toward the door. He removes his mirrored cigarette case, and notices that Jerry casts no reflection. Shocked, he drops the case, shattering the mirror. He nervously hurries the kids outside and jumps into his car. When pressed, Peter admits that Jerry didn't have a reflection.

Inside the house, Jerry comments on how much Amy looks like his lost lover. Billy knows that no one will believe Charley now, but Jerry steps on a sliver of mirror from Peter's cigarette case.

As the group walks through town, Evil splits off to take a shortcut. He screams, making Charley believe a vampire bit him. Charley is furious at the joke and leaves. As Evil travels alone through the alley, Jerry corners the teenager in a dead-end. He offers to turn the boy into a vampire, and Evil accepts.

Charley and Amy hear another scream, but think it's only Evil playing another joke. Suddenly the power on the street goes out and they realize they are being followed. They run, but Jerry always appears in front of them. Finally they duck into a nightclub.

Evil knocks on Peter Vincent's door and is invited in. Once inside, Evil shows Peter his bite mark and turns on the actor. He calls Peter a coward and a fake, but Peter presses a cross to the teenager's forehead. The skin burns and Evil cowers, finally escaping through a window.

Jerry enters the nightclub and draws Amy onto the dance floor while Charley is busy on a payphone. Amy falls into a trance and dances seductively with Jerry. When Charley tries to break them up, a bouncer steps in to help. Jerry growls and breaks the bouncer's arm. The club-goers panic and rush for the exit. In the confusion, Charley and Amy are separated. Jerry captures Amy again and tells Charley to bring Peter to his house if he ever wants to see his girlfriend alive again.

Charley goes to Peter's apartment and must touch a cross to gain entrance. He tries to get Peter's help, but the actor can't bring himself to go through with it. He tells Charley that he was paid to perform the vampire test.

Amy wakes up lying on a bearskin rug before a roaring fire. She sees the painting that looks like her and Jerry explains that it was someone he knew a long time ago. He seduces Amy, who is frightened at first, but then willingly lets him bite her.

Charley approaches Jerry's house alone, only to be joined by Peter Vincent. Peter has brought along his box from the movies. He and Charley equip themselves with crosses and stakes, as well as a gun for Billy. They enter through the front door and meet Jerry at the top of the stairs. Peter stands his ground and presents a cross. Jerry merely laughs, telling him that he has to have faith for it to work. He crushes the cross and tosses it away. Charley then steps forward and holds up his cross. Jerry cringes back, but Billy appears and knocks Charley over the banister. Terrified, Peter runs outside and goes to Charley's house to get help.

Peter tries to use the phone, but the lines have been cut. Concerned about Charley's mother, Peter rushes upstairs, but finds Evil in bed instead. Peter runs for the stairs, tripping on a hallway table. Evil transforms into a wolf and follows. Peter uses one of the broken table legs to impale the wolf, sending it over the banister. Evil slowly transforms back into human form, trying to pull the stake from his chest. When he finally dies, Peter removes the stake. With renewed confidence, he returns to Jerry's house.

Jerry drops a knocked-out Charley next to Amy. He leaves him with a stake, saying he will need it before dawn, and locks the door. Charley wakes and sees that Amy has grown fangs. Peter returns, and breaks down the door. He reassures Charley that if they can destroy Jerry before sunrise, Amy will be cured.

Peter and Charley confront Billy in the main hall. The handyman slowly climbs the stairs and Peter shoots him once. Billy rises and seems unaffected by repeated gunshots. Charley stabs the handyman in the chest with a stake. Billy liquefies into green slime, finally turning into dust and bone.

Jerry bursts through the stained-glass window. Peter holds up his cross. At first Jerry laughs, but Peter redoubles his efforts and causes the vampire to cower. The sun begins to rise, and Jerry leaps up, transforming into a bat. Peter rushes downstairs and pushes Charley out of the way as the bat attacks. He holds up a stake for the bat to bite, and hoists the creature up into the sunlight. The bat bursts into flames, finally flying into the basement.

Charley and Peter follow and begin searching for Jerry's coffin. Peter finds a secret room. Inside is a locked coffin, and Peter must use his tools to break it open. Meanwhile Charley comes face-to-face with Amy transformed into a vampire. When he holds up a cross, she turns and starts to cry. Charley lowers the cross, and Amy attacks with an oversized mouth of fangs.

Peter breaks the locks and pounds a stake into the vampire's heart. Before he can finish, Jerry rises up from the coffin and pulls the stake out. When he tosses the stake aside, he inadvertently breaks a blacked-out window, letting in sunlight. The light forces Amy away from Charley. Charley breaks more of the windows, and soon Jerry is surrounded by sunlight. He runs for his coffin, but Peter closes it before he can get there. In the only dark room left, Jerry advances on Peter. Charley rushes forward and removes the last boarded window. Sunlight floods into the basement, striking Jerry in the chest. The vampire explodes into a giant ball of flame, leaving nothing behind.

Charley and Amy watch *Fright Night* come on the television inside Charley's room. Peter welcomes his viewers back to his new show. Charley gets up and turns off the light, but notices something from Jerry's darkened window across the street. Amy looks up at him, worried. Charley smiles and says that it's nothing. He jumps on the bed and kisses her. Evil's voice laughs from the darkened window.

The Lost Boys

Country: U.S.A.; *Theatrical Release:* July 31, 1987; *Production Company:* Warner Bros.; *Director:* Joel Schumacher; *Writer(s):* Jeffrey Boam, Janice Fischer; *Cast:* Jason Patric (Michael Emerson), Corey Haim (Sam Emerson), Dianne Wiest (Lucy Emerson), Barnard Hughes (Grandpa), Edward Herrmann (Max), Kiefer Sutherland (David) Jami Gertz (Star), Corey Feldman (Edgar Frog), Jamison Newlander (Alan Frog); *Vampire(s):* Max, David, Star, Laddie, Vampire Gang

Plot summary: David and his gang saunter along a merry-go-round. They meet a rival gang leader and start a fight, but before things escalate, a security guard stops them. The guard kicks them all off the boardwalk. Later, after the boardwalk has closed up for the night, the security guard walks to his car in the parking lot. David and his gang fly down and attack. The guard tries to get into his car, but he ends up ripping the door off by the hinges.

Lucy, a recently divorced mom, drives into town with her two sons, Michael and Sam. They see a sign welcoming them to Santa Clara, but on the back, spray-painted, is the message: Murder capital of the world. They plan to live with her dad until Lucy can get back on her feet. Michael and Sam find their grandpa a little odd. The rustic house has no television and comes complete with a taxidermy workshop.

That night Lucy and the boys go to the boardwalk. Lucy meets Max, the owner of a video store, who offers her a job. Michael spots a girl in the crowd and begins following her, but she gets on the back David's bike and rides away. Sam meets the Frog brothers who help their parents run a comic book store. The Frog brothers ask Sam if he has noticed anything strange about the town and give him a vampire comic.

The next night Michael returns to the boardwalk and the girl from the night before finds him. He learns that her name is Star and she agrees to go get some dinner with him. They are about to leave on Michael's motorcycle when David pulls up with his gang. She leaves Michael and gets on David's bike. David invites Michael to follow along to the point. Michael races with David and his gang, spinning out just before going off the cliff. The gang takes Michael down into a collapsed hotel that was destroyed by the 1906 San Francisco earthquake. The gang lives there along with Star and a little boy named Laddie.

In the hotel cavern David plays tricks with Michael's mind, making him think he is eating maggots instead of rice. He then offers Michael a drink from an old wine bottle. Star tells Michael not to drink because it's blood. Michael thinks it is only another joke and drinks anyway. He begins to feel drugged and ends up on the railroad bridge with the gang. David and the gang jump off, hanging to a girder under the tracks. They convince Michael to join them. As a train goes over, the bridge begins to shake, and one by one the gang members drop off. David tells Michael to let go and then drops into the mist below. Michael tries to hold on but finally falls.

Michael wakes up the next afternoon on his bed. The light is too strong and he puts on his sunglasses. Sam brings him the phone and Lucy tells Michael her boss has asked her to dinner and she needs him to stay with Sam. Grandpa goes out to visit his girlfriend and Sam offers to make Michael something for dinner, but Michael refuses.

Michael goes to the refrigerator and is overcome by an intense pain in his gut. Possessed by hunger, Michael climbs the stairs toward the bathroom. Inside Sam is taking his bath and the family dog, Nanook, sits near the tub. Michael opens the door as Sam goes under the water. Nanook, sensing the change in Michael, attacks.

Sam rushes into the hall and finds Michael holding his bloody hand. Michael tells him Nanook bit him. Sam sees that Michael casts no reflection in the mirror. He runs upstairs, telling Michael that he is a vampire and locks his door. Sam calls the Frog brothers. They advise him to stake Michael, but Sam says he cannot do it. Michael passes out on his bed, only to wake up floating on the ceiling. Sam calls Lucy at the restaurant, and tells her she needs to come home.

Michael struggles as he floats out his open window. He grabs hold of the phone. Hearing all the commotion, Lucy runs out of the restaurant. Michael floats outside of Sam's window, still holding the phone. He begs Sam to let him inside and finally Sam opens his window. Michael asks Sam not to tell their Mom. He'll fix everything. Sam reluctantly agrees. When Lucy runs in, Sam says he had a nightmare.

Michael sneaks out and goes to the ruined hotel. There he finds Star alone. She tells him she tried to warn him. She stops his questions by kissing him. They make love on the bed, falling asleep as the vampires return, flying into a dark cavern at the back of the cave.

The next day Michael comes home and Lucy tries to talk to him, but he tells her he needs to sleep. Lucy takes Sam to stop by Max's house and apologize for running out on him at dinner. Lucy goes inside the gate to leave a bottle of wine by the door, but she is nearly mauled by Max's dog, Thorn.

Sam goes to the comic store and tells the Frog brothers that Michael is only a half-vampire and that the comic book says that if the head vampire is killed, all the half-vampires return to normal. He tells them about Max and what happened with his dog. They suspect Max may be the head vampire.

That night at the house Michael runs into Max, who is coming to have dinner. Michael invites him in and heads out. Sam surprises Lucy with extra dinner guests, the Frog brothers. The boys test Max to see if he is a vampire. They give him shredded garlic instead of Parmesan, throw holy water on him, and put a mirror in front of his face. Max seems unaffected by the tests. He says he understands that Sam is worried he will take his father's place and he hopes they can be friends.

Michael confronts David and the gang on the boardwalk when he cannot find Star. David tells Michael he has to go with them if he ever wants to see Star again. They ride out near a group of "surf nazis" having a bonfire at the beach. David and his gang suddenly change into fanged vampires and David tells Michael its time for him to join the club. David and his gang sweep down and attack the surfers while Michael watches, both horrified and tempted by the blood. Michael resists, falling backward onto the sand.

Later, Star appears and flies up into the room. She explains that Michael won't be a full vampire until he makes his first kill. Michael was supposed to be her first kill, but she couldn't do it. She wants Michael to help her and Laddie.

The next day, Michael and Sam borrow their grandpa's car and pick up the Frog brothers. They all drive to the ruined hotel. Michael carries Laddie and Star up to the car and then passes out under the rays of the sun. The Frog brothers and Sam follow the tunnel at the back of the cave. They end up in a large cavern where David and his gang hang upside down from the ceiling, sleeping. Edgar Frog climbs up and stakes the nearest vampire, who falls to the floor writhing in pain. David wakes and jumps down. The boys try to escape through the tunnel, and a shaft of sunlight saves them from David.

They only have two hours before sunset. The Frog brothers collect holy water, and prepare squirt guns and stakes. The vampires arrive as the sun sets. One gang member bursts through the fireplace and knocks Michael out. Upstairs the Frog brothers meet another gang member. They knock him into a bathtub filled with holy water, where he dissolves. Downstairs Sam shoots an arrow through the chest of another gang member.

Michael wakes up and is confronted by David, who eggs Michael on, finally causing the half-vampire to transform to his vampire persona. The two fly together and fight in mid-air. David tells him it is too late. His blood is in Michael's veins. Michael refuses and throws David onto a pair of animal horns, killing him.

The others run downstairs, but Michael and Star have not changed. Lucy and Max arrive. Max reveals himself to be the head vampire. His plan was to lure Lucy by first turning her boys into vampires. The Frog brothers are shocked because he passed the tests. He informs them to never invite a vampire into a house; it renders them powerless. He grabs Sam, nearly choking the boy, and extends a hand to Lucy. As he tries to bite her, Grandpa appears in his truck. He crashes through the wall, launching enormous stakes out of the vehicle. One stake strikes Max in the chest. He is knocked back and explodes in a ball of fire.

Grandpa gets out of his truck and heads toward the refrigerator. Michael, Sam, and Lucy follow him. He says that the one thing he cannot stand about Santa Clara is all the vampires. The three stare at him, dumbfounded.

Near Dark

Country: U.S.A.; *Theatrical Release:* October 2, 1987; *Production Company:* F/M Entertainment; *Director:* Kathryn Bigelow; *Writer(s):* Eric Red, Kathryn Bigelow; *Cast:* Adrian Pasdar (Caleb), Jenny Wright (Mae), Lance Henricksen (Jesse), Bill Paxton (Severen), Jenette Goldstein (Diamondback), Tim Thomerson (Loy), Joshua Miller (Homer), Marcie Leeds (Sarah); *Vampire(s):* Caleb, Mae, Jesse, Severen, Diamondback, Homer

Plot summary: Caleb Colton crushes a mosquito feeding off his arm. He is a teen cowboy in a little Oklahoma town. A pretty new girl, named Mae, arrives in town one night. She says she is staying in a trailer park with some friends and could use a ride. Caleb takes Mae for a drive to his house to show off his horse, but the animal spooks and runs away. Caleb comments that he has never seen a girl like her before, and she agrees. She points to the stars, telling him it will take a billion years for their light to reach here, and that she will still be around to see it.

She begins to panic when she thinks the sun might rise, telling Caleb to drive her home. Caleb drives part of the way and stops, telling her if she wants him to take her home, she will have to kiss him. Mae becomes suddenly calm, leaning across the seat to kiss Caleb. After moment she bites his neck, and then jumps out of the truck, running for her home. Caleb gets out and tries to follow her, holding onto his bleeding neck.

His truck refuses to start, so he walks home. The sun begins to rise, and smoke smolders from under his clothes. His dad Loy, the town veterinarian, and his daughter, Sarah, are up tending to one of the animals when they see Caleb collapse on the dirt field. They rush toward him, but a motor-home with windows covered in aluminum foil speeds down the road. It opens its door and someone inside scoops Caleb off the ground. The motor-home drives away before Loy can catch up.

Sick and confused, Caleb is confronted by a group of strangers, one of whom is Mae. The group is going to kill Caleb, but Mae throws herself over him, saying he's been bit, but not bled. Because he is already turned into a vampire, the group leader, Jesse, tells Mae he has a week to show he is one of them. They pull over for the day and sleep.

Loy reports Caleb's kidnapping to the town sheriff, but the sheriff offers very little help. Loy and Sarah begin driving around, trying to find Caleb themselves. That night the group steals a new car and sets fire to the motor-home. They go their separate ways for the evening, and Caleb tells Mae he has to go home. Mae tells him he will be back soon.

Caleb grows more and more ill. He finds his way into the town bus station. A police officer questions the boy, thinking he is taking drugs. Caleb tells him he just wants to go home. The officer gives him the three dollars he needs for a ticket and tells him to be good. Caleb grows worse on the bus and asks the driver to let him off. He stumbles back to the group's car and finds Mae. She bites her wrist and offers it to Caleb to drink.

Loy and Sarah continue to search for Caleb while the group sleeps during the day. The next night Mae tells Caleb that he has to learn to kill. Caleb responds that he cannot, but Mae tells him not to think of it as killing. The other members of the group all use their own methods to secure a victim and a meal. Mae and Caleb pick up a ride with a truck. The driver makes small talk, explaining how to properly brake an eighteen-wheeler. Mae encourages Caleb to attack, but he cannot bring himself to do it and gets out of the truck on the side of the road. Mae kills the truck driver, and then lets Caleb drink from her again. She finally yanks her arm away from Caleb, telling him he could kill her if he drinks too much.

When the group joins up for the day, Jesse is outraged that Caleb still has not made a kill. He says it isn't right for him to let Mae carry him. If he does not make a kill the next night he's dead. Meanwhile, Loy and Sarah learn about the police officer that met Caleb in the bus station. They head in that direction.

The next night the group enters an isolated bar. Severen starts a fight with a patron and makes the man punch Caleb in the gut. Caleb finally hits back, knocking the patron across the bar. He is surprised at his own strength. A waitress brings Jesse a beer, but he tells her to just leave the glass. Then Diamondback, Jesse's girlfriend, uses a butterfly knife to slit the waitress's throat. Jesse fills the glass with her blood and slams it on the table. Severen breaks another patron's neck and then bites him. The bartender grabs a shotgun from under the bar and shoots Caleb. The shot seems to have no effect on the boy. Severen jumps up onto the bar and backs the bartender into a corner. He then slits the man's throat with his spurs. The man Caleb knocked out wakes up, and Homer, the little boy, shoots him from behind.

The group looks to Caleb to kill the last surviving patron. Mae makes the man dance with her as Caleb approaches. Caleb hesitates allowing the man to jump through the window and escape. Caleb chases him while the others set fire to the bar. He catches up with the man, but cannot make the kill. Caleb lets the man go. The others arrive in a new vehicle, a van, and they all speed to a motel with only minutes to spare before sunrise.

Later that day the cops surround the motel room. The man that Caleb failed to kill sits in one of the squad cars. The group members all grab guns and they decide to shoot their way out. The slightest ray of sunlight causes the vampires to blister and smoke. As the cops shoot at the motel room, the holes let in more sunlight. Caleb tells Jesse he is going for the van outside. The rest of the group covers him. He wraps himself with a blanket, but even with the protection, he bursts into flames. Caleb drives the van through the wall of the motel, and the other members pile inside. Jesse is pleased with Caleb for saving them.

The group switches vehicles again and check into another motel. Homer goes out to the parking lot and meets Sarah, who is also staying at the same motel. He is immediately taken with the young girl and brings her to the room to watch television. Diamondback is concerned and asks if the girl is there with family. She says she is there with her dad, and Severen goes to fetch him.

Just as Sarah tries to leave the room, she runs into Caleb. Caleb informs the group that Sarah is his sister. Severen returns with Loy. Caleb wants the group to let them go, but Homer grabs Sarah. He had turned Mae into a vampire for himself, but she chose Caleb. Now he is going to turn Sarah into a vampire to replace her. Caleb threatens Homer, but Jesse intervenes. Loy tries to shoot Jesse, but the man simply spits up the bullet and returns it to Loy. Caleb begs Jesse to let them go. Jesse says they have seen too much and must die. Sarah breaks free from Homer and opens the door. The morning sunlight pours in, temporarily catching the vampires off guard. Caleb, Loy, and Sarah hurry out to Loy's truck.

Loy wants to take his son to a hospital, but Caleb shows his father how the sun burns him. He asks if Loy has ever done a transfusion on a person before. After having all of his blood transfused, Caleb revives and goes into the sun with Sarah.

That night Caleb goes outside to check on a noise and meets Mae. She asks why he left and he kisses her. She is shocked that he is warm again. Caleb tells her that he belongs with his family. Mae runs off. Caleb returns only to find Sarah missing. All the tires of their truck are slashed, so he takes his horse to follow the group.

He rides down the road of the abandoned town until the horse spooks and throws him. Severen appears and throws Caleb across the street. Caleb flags down an oncoming eighteen-wheeler and asks the driver for help. Severen shoots the driver, and Caleb takes over driving the rig. He runs Severen down in the street, but the vampire climbs up the hood and begins ripping apart the engine. Caleb brakes the truck, causing it to jackknife. He jumps out just before the truck explodes.

Caleb turns around and sees Jesse and Mae standing by their car. Homer holds Sarah in the back seat. Diamondback sneaks up behind Jesse, ready to throw a knife into his back. Sarah breaks free of Homer and warns Caleb. He moves out of the way just as Diamondback throws her knife. It hits Jesse in the mouth. Jesse pulls the knife free as Caleb grabs Sarah and runs. Jesse shoots at Caleb, but Mae pushes him, making the shot miss. Jesse, Mae, and Diamondback get into the car to chase after Caleb.

Caleb falls and tells Sarah to keep running. The car speeds alongside the girl and pulls her inside. The sun begins to rise and the gang struggles to black out the windows. Caleb chases on foot. Mae watches as Homer struggles with Sarah, about to bite her. She grabs the girl and jumps out the back window of the speeding car. Mae begins to instantly smolder in the sunlight. Caleb catches up and protects her from the sunlight. Homer leaps from the car, and quickly catches on fire. He falls to the ground and explodes. Jesse and Diamondback turn the car around, but they explode into fire before reaching Caleb.

The next day Mae sits up terrified on the exam table. Caleb opens the door to let in the sunlight. She does not burn and sees that Caleb has given her a transfusion as well.

Bram Stoker's Dracula

Country: U.S.A.; *Theatrical Release:* November 13, 1992; *Production Company:* Columbia; *Director:* Francis Ford Coppola; *Writer(s):* James V. Hart; *Cast:* Gary Oldman (Dracula), Winona Ryder (Wilhemina Murray/Elisabeta), Anthony Hopkins (Prof. Abraham Van Helsing), Keanu Reeves (Jonathan Harker), Richard E. Grant (Dr. Jack Seward), Cary Elwes (Lord Arthur Holmwood), Bill Campbell (Quincey P. Morris), Sadie Frost (Lucy Westenra), Tom Waits (R.M. Renfield); *Vampire(s):* Dracula, Vampire Brides

Plot summary: In 1492, after the fall of Constantinople, the Muslim Turks sweep upward into Europe. In Transylvania prince Vlad Dracula takes up arms to face them in hopes of saving his homeland and protecting the Christian faith.

Dracula leaves his young bride, Elisabeta, to face certain death on the battlefield. Against all odds he wins against the Turks. Dracula drops to his knees and praises God by kissing the crucifix. An overwhelming feeling of dread for Elisabeta seizes him, and he rushes back to the castle, where he finds his bride lying dead on the chapel floor. The Turks had shot an arrow into the castle claiming that Dracula had been killed in battle. She responded to the news by hurling herself from the tower.

The priest tells Dracula that since she had taken her own life, Elisabeta's soul will be forever damned. Dracula shouts at the priest, asking if this is his reward for defending God's church. He renounces God, promising to arise from the dead to avenge Elisabeta's death. Dracula drives his sword into the altar's cross, which starts to bleed. The prince takes the sacramental goblet, catches the blood issuing from the cross, and drinks it.

In 1897 London, a young solicitor named Jonathan Harker is taking over Mr. Renfield's assignment. He will travel to Transylvania and assist Count Dracula in his purchase of property in London. Later, Jonathan meets with his fiancée, Mina, to say goodbye.

Jonathan sets out across Europe recording his journey in his diary. A coach drops Jonathan at the Borgo Pass, and a passenger gives him a crucifix. A mysterious black coach appears and whisks Jonathan through the mountains to Dracula's castle.

An elderly Count Dracula greets the solicitor and serves him supper. Jonathan completes the paperwork and informs Dracula that he is now the owner of Carfax Abbey. Dracula is stunned when he sees a picture of Jonathan's fiancée, Mina. She looks exactly like his lost bride, Elisabeta. Jonathan tells the count that he and Mina will be married when he returns to England. Dracula's shadow seems to strangle Jonathan, though the solicitor doesn't notice. Dracula orders Jonathan to write home and tell his loved ones that he will stay for a month.

Back in England, Mina types in her diary. Lucy Westenra enters and complains that she has not had even one marriage proposal. Later, at the party, Mina watches as Lucy juggles the affections of the three men in her life: Dr. Jack Seward, the Texan Quincey Morris, and Lord Arthur Holmwood. All three are desperately in love with Lucy. As Mina admires Lucy's free spirit, she is suddenly struck by a strange sensation. The shadow of Dracula covers the room, speaking to her in Romanian.

At the sanitarium, Dr. Seward records his notes on the patient Renfield. Once a respectable solicitor, he returned from Transylvania and suffered a complete mental breakdown. He now possesses a bloodlust, and has taken to eating insects.

Back in Dracula's castle, Jonathan is shaving and is surprised when Dracula places a hand on Jonathan's shoulder, causing him to cut his neck. Dracula shields himself from the mirror, which shatters. He asks for the letters he told Jonathan to write. After he counts the letters, Dracula takes the razor from Jonathan and proceeds to shave the young man. The count catches a reflection of Jonathan's crucifix in the razor blade, and backs away. Dracula tells him not to put faith in such trinkets of deceit. Outside wolves howl, and Dracula seems to vanish from the room. When Jonathan goes to the window again, he is shocked to see Dracula crawling down the castle wall.

As Jonathan searches the castle, he begins to be mesmerized by whispers telling him to lie on a bed. Suddenly three women appear from under the covers. They seduce him, revealing fangs and biting Jonathan. Dracula bursts in and shouts at the women for touching Jonathan. They crawl to the count, and Jonathan watches in horror as Dracula hands them a crying infant. The women feast on the baby as Dracula laughs.

In England, Mina reads the letter Dracula forced Jonathan to write. She is worried because it is so short and unlike Jonathan. Lucy joins Mina in the garden and announces that she is engaged to Arthur. Suddenly the two are caught in a thunderstorm. Dracula's eyes appear in the clouds. Lucy and Mina play in the rain while at sea Dracula grows younger in a box of earth in the cargo hold of the Demeter, a ship bound for London.

That night, Lucy sleepwalks through the garden and Mina rushes to follow. She finds her friend lying on a stone bench, copulating with Dracula, who appears in a wolf-like form. Dracula sees Mina and commands her to forget. Mina is momentarily hypnotized, and when she recovers, Dracula seems to have vanished.

Now young again, Dracula walks through the busy streets of London. He follows Mina, commanding her to notice him. They meet, and he introduces himself as Prince Vlad Dracula.

Dr. Seward arrives to examine Lucy. She is being fitted for her wedding gown and tells the doctor that she is changing and having horrible nightmares. After a few moments, she begins to wheeze, and must lie down on the sofa. Arthur and Quincey arrive and look shocked at Lucy's condition. Seward tells Arthur that he cannot find the cause for the illness and has cabled Professor Abraham Van Helsing for help.

At the cinematograph in London Dracula is amazed at the state of modern technology. Mina realizes she is alone with a strange man and tells Dracula she must leave. He pulls her close to him, and they both drift into a corner. Mina struggles but then relaxes. Dracula prepares to bite her, but upon seeing her face, forces himself to stop.

In Dracula's castle, Jonathan lies limp in bed with numerous bite marks along his body. The three women lie with him, still drinking his blood. His diary entry mentions that the women drain his blood to keep him at the castle. He vows that he will attempt one more escape.

In Amsterdam, Professor Van Helsing receives the telegram from Dr. Seward. Later his coach arrives at the Holmwood estate, where Dr. Seward meets him. They hear Lucy moan from upstairs and rush to see her. They enter the room just as Dracula's shadow retreats. Van Helsing sees the wound on Lucy's throat and tells Dr. Seward that he must give her a transfusion at once.

Later, Arthur, Quincey, and Dr. Seward stumble into the garden, each having given blood to Lucy. Van Helsing is there and questions Dr. Seward about the facts of Lucy's case. Dr. Seward cannot accept that some monster attacked the girl, but Van Helsing convinces him that it is possible.

Mina sits in a private dining room with Dracula. They both drink absinthe and she begins to speak of Transylvania as though she had lived there. Dracula tells her of the princess Elisabeta. Mina forms a connection with the long lost woman and begins to cry.

Jonathan manages to escape from the castle, plunging off the roof into the river. He stumbles, half dead, to a convent and is taken in by the nuns. Mina then receives a letter from the convent explaining that Jonathan is recovering from a grave illness. Mina is thrilled to hear the news. She vows to never see Prince Dracula again.

As Lucy says goodbye to Mina from her bed, she goes into a fit, and tears off her necklace of garlic flowers. Quincey tries to calm her, and she nearly bites the man. She faints and Van Helsing shows Dr. Seward the fangs that Lucy has grown.

That evening, Dracula sits alone in the private dining room, and receives a letter from Mina. She tells him she is going to marry her fiancée and they can never meet again. Dracula cries, but his sorrow quickly turns to rage.

Quincey patrols the grounds outside Lucy's room, while Arthur guards from her bedside. Dracula approaches the estate, incapacitating Quincey and Arthur. He then appears at Lucy's window, no longer handsome but transformed into a horrible looking creature. He crashes through the window fully transformed into a wolf. As he sinks his teeth into her throat, Mina and Jonathan exchange vows and kiss as a newly married couple.

After her funeral, Van Helsing leads Dr. Seward, Arthur, and Quincey to Lucy's mausoleum. They open the sarcophagus and find it empty. Arthur becomes hysterical, and pulls a gun on the professor. Van Helsing calmly explains that Lucy is now a vampire, feeding on the blood of the living.

Lucy enters the crypt carrying a baby. When she sees Arthur, she drops the infant and attempts to seduce her former fiancée. Van Helsing intervenes holding a cross, and Lucy growls, backing into her sarcophagus. Arthur drives a spike into his fiancée's chest as Van Helsing cuts off her head.

Mina and Jonathan arrive back in London. Jonathan tells Van Helsing that he knows where the count is hiding. Everyone meets outside Carfax Abbey. Dr. Seward takes Mina to his apartment at the sanitarium where she can be safe. On the way she stops to speak with Renfield, who tells her to leave at once.

The men enter the abbey and begin sanctifying and destroying the boxes of earth. Dracula hangs from the ceiling in the form of a giant green bat. He flies out of the abbey and transforms into mist. First he kills Renfield for betraying him, and then he enters Mina's room.

Mina opens her eyes and Dracula lies over her in bed. She wants to be with him forever, but Dracula resists. He tells her he is the monster the others are hunting. To be with him would mean that she would have to die. She insists, and Dracula finally bites her. Using his fingernail, he cuts open his chest, and Mina drinks his blood.

Van Helsing and the others burst in, and Dracula confronts them in the form of a giant bat. He tells Van Helsing that Mina is now his. The count backs into the shadows and transforms into hundreds of rats to escape. Van Helsing hypnotizes Mina. She tells him Dracula is on a ship, and they realize that the count is heading back to Transylvania. They pursue the count over land in order to beat him to the castle. At the port of Varna, they split up. Arthur, Jonathan, and Quincey travel by horseback, while Van Helsing and Mina travel separately to the castle.

As they near the castle, Mina and Van Helsing camp at the base of the castle. The vampire women arrive and take control of Mina. She seduces Van Helsing and tries to bite him. He drives her back by placing a holy wafer to her forehead. He then creates a circle of fire around himself and Mina. The vampire women attack and kill their horses. At dawn Van Helsing enters the castle, finds the women in their coffins, and chops off their heads.

The gypsies carrying Dracula's coffin race toward the castle, followed by Arthur, Jonathan, and Quincey on horseback as the sun begins to set. The men catch up to the wagon, and Jonathan leaps on board, forcing open the box of earth. During the battle, a gypsy stabs Quincey in the back. When the sun finally sets, Dracula bursts free from the box. Jonathan slashes at the count's throat. Dracula stumbles away, but Quincey rams his Bowie knife into the count's heart.

Mina screams and helps Dracula enter the castle's chapel. He collapses on the very spot where Elisabeta died long ago. Mina kisses him. He asks for her to give him peace, and she drives the knife the rest of the way through his chest. Suddenly a light shines on Dracula and the altar cross that Dracula stabbed repairs itself. She removes the knife and cuts off Dracula's head.

Interview with the Vampire: The Vampire Chronicles

Country: U.S.A.; *Theatrical Release:* November 11, 1994; *Production Company:* Warner Bros.; *Director:* Neil Jordan; *Writer(s):* Anne Rice; *Cast:* Tom Cruise (Lestat de Lioncourt), Brad Pitt (Louis de Pointe du Lac), Kirsten Dunst (Claudia), Stephen Rea (Santiago), Antonio Banderas (Armand), Christian Slater (Daniel Malloy); *Vampire(s):* Lestat, Louis, Claudia, Santiago, Armand

Plot summary: A reporter, Daniel Mallory, sets up his tape recorder in a barren hotel room. Another man, Louis, stands on the balcony, his back to the camera. When Louis says that he is a vampire, Daniel laughs. The man turns, revealing a pale face. He then seems to disappear, and the light flicks on. Daniel sees that Louis has reappeared on the other side of the room. Louis gestures for Daniel to sit, and he begins to retell his life.

The scene shifts to a plantation along the Louisiana coast in 1791. Louis had recently lost his wife and child and is stricken with a grief so powerful, he yearns for death. His plight has caught the eye of a vampire, Lestat. Louis stumbles arm in arm with a prostitute onto a darkened dock. As a pimp comes forward to rob Louis, Lestat arrives and quickly dispatches the man and prostitute. The vampire leans in and bites Louis on the neck. Grasping the young man, the vampire floats several stories up. When Louis admits he still wants to live, Lestat drops him into the water.

Later, Lestat visits Louis in his bedroom, and offers a life without any sickness or death. He says he will give Louis the choice he never had. Louis agrees and meets Lestat in the cemetery. The vampire suddenly bites the man in the neck again, nearly killing him. Lestat then bites his own wrist, letting the blood drip into Louis's mouth. When Louis has drunk enough blood, his body begins to convulse in pain, and he dies. Louis transforms into a vampire. His face becomes pale and he grows fangs.

Louis relates to Daniel that many of the vampire myths are false, but coffins are a necessity. Back in 1791, Louis goes to sleep in a coffin, and wakes with a powerful hunger. The two vampires travel to a local tavern where Lestat bites a barmaid, and passes her over to Louis. The two drink her blood, and Lestat finally kills her.

At the plantation dining room, Louis resists biting his maid, Yvette. Lestat captures a rat, kills it, and squeezes the blood into a wineglass. Louis is astounded that they are able to live off animal blood. Lestat doubts Louis can last a week without drinking human blood.

They travel to New Orleans on one of Lestat's "hunts." Lestat singles out an older woman, the countess, and her young fop lover. Louis cannot bring himself to kill the countess, and instead kills her two poodles. After finishing with the fop, Lestat rushes over and twists the woman's neck, killing her. Lestat calls

Louis a coward, and Louis responds by saying that he is condemned to a living hell.

At the plantation, Louis questions Lestat about the one who made him. Lestat says he learned nothing. When pressed by Louis, Lestat becomes furious. As he calms down, he begs Louis to come to New Orleans for another "hunt," but Louis can't bring himself to kill yet. Lestat leaves.

Later, Louis can no longer resist the urge, and bites Yvette. He is so furious at lapse of willpower that he sets fire to the manor house. Lestat crashes through a window at the last moment, saving Louis. They end up sleeping the night in a crypt.

After renting rooms along the New Orleans waterfront, Lestat entertains two prostitutes, killing one surreptitiously with a bite on the neck. He then moves on to the second girl, biting the woman's breast. The girl sees the blood and panics. Lestat snatches her wrist, bites it, and empties some blood into a goblet while reciting poetry. He offers the blood to Louis, telling him to pretend that it's wine. Louis refuses to drink or kill the girl. Lestat, finally fed up at Louis, ends the girl's life.

Louis wanders the rainy streets, and stumbles across Claudia clinging to her mother's rotting corpse. She asks Louis to help her. He hugs her and ends up biting the girl. Lestat arrives, laughing. Louis is overcome with guilt, and rushes out into the night.

Lestat tracks down Louis by following the trail of rats. He leads him back to their room, where the girl is still alive. Before Louis's eyes, Lestat lets Claudia drink his blood. After dying and arising as a vampire, Claudia greedily drinks from a servant girl. Lestat cautions her not to drink the last drop of blood.

The three become a family, and Claudia proves to be an effective killer. Louis has fallen in love with the girl and considers her a daughter while Lestat sees her as an apt pupil. Time passes, and New Orleans has become part of the United States. The three stroll through the streets, and Claudia looks up at a window where a grown woman bathes herself. She says she wants to grow up and be like that girl.

Later, Lestat gives Claudia a doll. She questions him as to why he gives her a doll the same day each year. She tosses the other dolls off her bed, revealing the corpse of the girl seen in the window. Grabbing scissors, Claudia cuts her hair, wanting desperately to change, but the hair quickly grows back.

Claudia learns that it was Louis who killed her, and Lestat who changed her into a vampire. When she asks Louis why they did this, he points to an old woman on the street, telling her that she will never be like that, and never die. Claudia wants to leave Lestat by any means.

Claudia apologizes to Lestat and offers a pair of twin boys for him to drink. He accepts the gift, but falls ill shortly after biting one boy. Claudia admits to killing them with laudanum. She then takes advantage of a weakened Lestat, and slits his throat. He withers into a corpse on the rug. Louis and Claudia dispose of the body in the swamp.

They prepare to sail to Europe, and Claudia researches myths about vampires. On the day they are to leave, Lestat returns looking ravaged and covered in grime. He explains that he fed off the fauna of the swamp to survive. He rushes Claudia, but Louis hurls a lamp, setting Lestat on fire. The two escape to the ship.

In Europe they find no other vampires. Finally, ready to give up, they arrive in Paris in 1870. While walking one night, Louis is approached by Santiago, another vampire. He also meets Armand, who invites him to the Theater of the Vampires.

They arrive at the theater and watch as the vampires pretend to be humans pretending to be vampires. Santiago plays the character of Death, and culminates the show by bringing a live victim on stage. Before he can bite her, Armand appears and takes over. He bites the girl and then passes her back to the waiting vampires, who descend on the body in unison.

Armand shows Louis and Claudia the crypt under the stage where the vampires live. In Armand's private chamber, Louis discovers that Armand is four hundred years old. As they leave, Santiago reads Louis's mind, and discovers that he killed Lestat. This is the only crime among vampires.

Claudia confronts Louis. She knows he will leave her for Armand. Later, she meets Madeleine in a doll shop. She then pleads for Louis to transform the woman into a vampire, so she can be Claudia's companion. Louis finally succumbs and transforms the woman. Only moments after, the vampires from the theater arrive and carry all three off.

Louis is locked in a coffin and walled alive in a tunnel niche. Claudia and Madeleine are thrown into a cell that has a grate open to the streets of Paris. When the sun rises, Claudia and Madeleine cling to each other. They scream as the sunlight burns their flesh. Armand pulls down the wall and rescues Louis from the coffin. When he goes to see Claudia, he finds her body turned to ash.

The next morning, just before sunrise, Louis hurls kerosene over the coffins under the theater. He sets them on fire, and uses a scythe to cut down those that survive the burning. Santiago rushes him, and Louis cuts him in half with the scythe. Louis staggers outside into the morning light. Armand rescues him from inside his personal coach.

Louis and Armand walk through a hallway filled with paintings. Armand reveals that he knew Louis would kill the other vampires. Louis rejects Armand and his lack of remorse. He refuses to be Armand's companion, preferring his suffering and regret.

Louis finally comes back to America, and in 1988, he discovers Lestat living in a ruined mansion. Lestat is still shriveled, hardly at full strength. He wants Louis to stay, so he can venture out and regain strength. Louis leaves Lestat there.

Daniel can't accept that the story ends there. He is convinced that Louis has chosen him to be the next companion. Louis becomes furious, grabbing Daniel by the neck and raising him up toward the ceiling. When he drops Daniel, the reporter rushes outside and gets into his car.

As he drives away, he quickly checks his neck. Daniel pushes one of the tapes into the deck. Louis's voice begins retelling the story again from the beginning. Suddenly a bony hand pulls Daniel's seat back. Lestat bites the reporter. Instantly color returns to the vampire's face. Lestat takes over driving, and pops the tape out. He says that he will give Daniel the choice he never had.

Buffy the Vampire Slayer

Country: U.S.A.; *Theatrical Release:* "Welcome to the Hellmouth" and "The Harvest" March 10, 1997, "Angel" April 14, 1998; *Production Company:* Mutant Enemy Inc.; *Director:* "Welcome to the Hellmouth" and "The Harvest" Charles Martin, "Angel" Scott Brazil; *Writer(s):* "Welcome to the Hellmouth" and "The Harvest" Joss Whedon, "Angel" David Greenwalt; *Cast:* Sara Michelle Gellar (Buffy Summers), Nicholas Brendon (Xander Harris), Alyson Hannigan (Willow Rosenberg), Charisma Carpenter (Cordelia Chase), Anthony Stewart Head (Rupert Giles), Mark Metcalf (the Master), Brian Thompson (Luke), David Boreanaz (Angel), Ken Lerner (Principal Flutie), Kristine Sutherland (Joyce Summers), Julie Benz (Darla), Mercedes McNab (Harmony), Andrew J. Ferchland (the Anointed One); *Vampire(s):* the Master, Luke, Angel, Darla, the Anointed One

Plot summary: Because of the nature of television syndication, the synopsis is necessarily brief.

"Welcome to the Hellmouth" and "The Harvest"

Buffy Summers, a 16-year-old girl, moves to Sunnydale, California from Los Angeles with her mom. The principal offers her a clean slate, but is then alarmed to learn that she was kicked out of her last school for burning down the gym. She tries to explain that it was full of vampires, but decides to keep that information to herself.

She meets Cordelia Chase, the most popular girl in school, who invites her to go out that night. Buffy also meets three other students, Xander Harris, who instantly develops a crush on her, his best friend Willow Rosenberg, the smartest girl in school, and their friend Jesse.

When Buffy visits the library to pick up a textbook, she meets Rupert Giles, the new school librarian. He slams a massive leather bound tome titled *Vampyr* on the counter and tells her he is her new Watcher. Buffy looks shocked, and quickly leaves the library. When a boy is found dead on campus, Buffy goes to investigate, finding that a vampire killed him.

She returns to Giles to inform him about the body. She also tells him she no longer wants to be a slayer and has left that life back in Los Angeles. He informs her she has no choice in the matter and that her moving in Sunnydale was no coincidence. It is a center for mystical events.

On her way to the Bronze, Sunnydale's only nightclub, Buffy meets a tall dark stranger, Angel. Whether Angel is a friend or a foe is yet to be determined. Buffy first confronts vampires in the cemetery, trying to save Willow and Xander. Luke, a hulking vampire, overpowers her. Only the cross about her neck saves her.

Buffy searches for the vampires through tunnels running under Sunnydale with some unwanted help from Xander. They meet Jesse, who is now a vampire. Again, they use a cross, and barely escape a trap set by the vampires.

After researching in the library, Giles and Willow find out that Sunnydale is literally built on top of a mouth to Hell. An earthquake trapped an ancient vampire, called the Master, underground when he tried to open the entrance to Hell in 1937. The Harvest is a mass feeding where a chosen vessel can drain victims of blood in order for the Master to gain enough strength to break out of his underground tomb. Xander tells them the vampires will go to the Bronze because it is the perfect place for a mass feeding.

Luke is anointed by the Master to be his vessel. When Buffy and friends reach the Bronze, it turns out to be too late. Luke and several other vampires have already entered and are beginning the Harvest. They break into the club, and destroy Luke and the other vampires. The Master remains trapped.

"Angel"

Escaping a trio of vampires, Buffy invites Angel inside her house. They are safe because the vampires must be invited in before they can enter. Angel tells her that he cannot be around her because when he is, all he wants to do is kiss her. They kiss, but as the kiss intensifies, Angel cannot control himself and reveals his vampire persona. Buffy screams and Angel jumps out of the window.

The next day at school, Buffy tells Giles and friends that Angel is a vampire. She hopes that Giles knows if a vampire could ever be good, but he says no. Xander encourages her to do her duty as the slayer and kill Angel. She says that she cannot kill Angel because she loves him. But then she finds her mother in Angel's arms. He looks ready to feed, and she quickly changes her mind.

Buffy, armed with a crossbow, finds Angel at his apartment. They talk and Angel tells her that he was cursed with a soul after feeding off a gypsy girl. For the past hundred years, he hasn't fed off a living human being. Darla comes out of the shadows and attacks, but ultimately ends up skewered by Angel.

Days later Buffy and Angel share a good-bye kiss at the Bronze. As Buffy walks away, a burn mark is revealed on Angel's chest. When she leaned in to kiss him, the cross pressed against his skin.

Blade

Country: U.S.A.; Theatrical Release: August 19, 1998; Production Company: New Line Cinema; Director: Stephen Norrington; Writer(s): David S. Goyer; Cast: Wesley Snipes (Blade/Eric Brooks/"The Daywalker"), Stephen Dorff (Deacon Frost), Kris Kristofferson (Abraham Whistler), N'Bushe Wright (Dr. Karen Jenson), Donal Logue (Quinn), Udo Kier (Dragonetti), Arly Jover (Mercury), Traci Lords (Raquel), Kevin Patrick Walls (Officer Krieger), Tim Guinee (Dr. Curtis Webb), Sanaa Lathan (Vanessa Brooks), Eric Edwards (Pearl); Vampire(s): Blade, Deacon Frost, Quinn, Dragonetti, Mercury, Raquel, Pearl

Plot summary: In 1967, a pregnant woman is wheeled into an emergency room with a bloody wound on her throat. The child is born, but the woman dies on the table.

The film flashes forward to the present. A beautiful woman, Raquel, leads her date into a rave held at a meatpacking plant. The dance floor is packed with people writhing to a techno beat. Soon the overhead sprinklers turn on, spraying the entire crowd with blood. The sign behind the DJ reads "Blood Bath." The dancers, now covered with blood, bare their fangs and turn on Raquel's date. As he scrambles to escape, he runs into Blade, dressed in black leather and body armor. The vampires in the crowd whisper the name "Daywalker."

Blade proceeds to attack the vampires using first a shotgun, and then silver stakes. Each vampire he assaults, burns into ash and disintegrates. The vampire in charge, Quinn, sends vampire guards armed with automatic pistols in retaliation. Blade uses a silver boomerang and then a katana to slice and disintegrate these vampires. Retrieving his shotgun, Blade fires two spikes into Quinn's shoulders, pinning him to the wall. He sets the vampire on fire and escapes before the police arrive.

At the hospital, the charred body of Quinn is prepared for autopsy by Dr. Karen Jenson, a hematologist, and the medical examiner, Dr. Curtis Webb. As Curtis begins his Y-incision, Quinn revives and bites the man in the neck. After draining the man, he turns on Karen. Blade arrives before he can drain too much of Karen's blood. Blade slices off the vampire's arm, but the police arrive before he can finish off the vampire.

Blade grabs the prone body of Karen, and escapes by jumping across to an adjacent building. He takes her back to an industrial warehouse where he meets up with Abraham Whistler, a grizzled older man. Whistler is dubious about Blade bringing back Karen. He injects the woman with garlic to combat the vampire's bite.

In a boardroom, twelve older vampires, dressed in suits, discuss the attack on the rave. Seated at the head of the table is Dragonetti, who calls in Deacon Frost, a younger vampire, to answer about the attack. Frost is openly defiant of the other vampires, and comments that the vampires should be ruling the humans, not making deals with them. Dragonetti reminds Frost that all the members of the board are pure bloods, born vampires, while he was merely turned into a vampire.

Karen wakes up at the warehouse. She sees Blade undergo some kind of treatment. Whistler straps him into a chair and injects him with a serum. Blade stiffens and struggles as the drug takes effect. When they discover her eavesdropping, Whistler explains to Karen that they hunt vampires, who will soon come after her. He gives her "vampire mace," a combination of silver nitrate and garlic.

Dragonetti catches Frost in the vampire archives trying to translate the ancient vampire texts using a computer program. Dragonetti is suspicious about what Frost is after.

Blade drops Karen at her apartment. Inside she is startled by a policeman, Officer Krieger. He questions her about being kidnapped, and then attacks. Blade arrives and saves her. He explains that the man is a vampire familiar, a human servant who hopes someday to become a vampire. Outside Krieger escapes, and Blade and Karen wait until the familiar returns and leads them to a vampire safe house.

Blade makes his way inside and confronts Officer Krieger. He beats the man, getting him to reveal a secret entrance. Blade and Karen travel to the same vampire archives Frost was recently in.

Officer Krieger arrives at Frost's penthouse party, and apologizes for leading Blade to the archives. Frost responds by biting the man's neck. He then kisses Mercury, a female vampire dressed all in white, as Krieger dies in the penthouse fountain.

Blade and Karen meet Pearl, a nearly two ton obese vampire who is watching multiple computer screens. Karen uses an ultraviolet light to burn Pearl until he tells them Frost has translated the vampire texts, and discovered something about a prophecy to awaken La Magra, the blood god. Blade takes the hard drive for further analysis.

Blade enters the vault and finds ancient pieces of parchment suspended in glass. They are ambushed by a group of vampires lead by Quinn. The vampires subdue Blade, and Quinn shows off his recently regenerated arm. A well-timed explosion from Whistler saves Blade, and the three run into the subway tunnels. Blade escapes by grabbing onto a moving subway train. Karen finally realizes that Blade is also a vampire.

Back at the warehouse, Whistler explains Blade's history to Karen. Because his mother was bitten while pregnant, he is a half-vampire. He can walk around in daylight, and has the vampire's strength and regenerative abilities, but he also has a lust for blood. Recently Blade has built up a resistance to the serum that controls his bloodlust.

At the beach, Frost and the other vampires apply sun block. They bring Dragonetti to the shore in a mob-style hit. The pure blood vampire begins to smolder in the dawn light. Frost uses a pair of pliers to pull out the vampire's teeth. When the sun finally does rise, the pure blood vampire explodes. Later, Frost sits in Dragonetti's chair in the boardroom. He tells the other pure blood vampires that he needs twelve volunteers.

Blade hands over the hard drive to Whistler. Karen shows Blade a new weapon, an anticoagulant that causes vampire blood to explode. She has also been working on a cure for vampirism, and draws some of Blade's blood.

In the city park, Frost offers Blade a truce. When Blade rejects it, Frost escapes. Back at the warehouse, Frost and his vampires overpower Karen and Whistler. When Blade returns, he finds Karen gone and Whistler near death and infected. Whistler reveals that Frost needs Blade's blood to resurrect a vampire god. He asks for a gun and shots himself, rather than go on as a vampire.

Blade assaults Frost's penthouse, killing multiple guards and vampires along the way. He injects the anticoagulant into two vampires, causing them to explode. When Blade arrives in Frost's bedroom, the sight of his mother surprises him. She survived the pregnancy and was turned into a vampire. Frost and the other vampires subdue Blade with stun guns.

Frost leads the twelve pure blood vampires, Blade, and Karen into a giant stone atrium, several stories high. Blade is overcome with his bloodlust. When Frost sees the vials of anticoagulant, he thinks these are Blade's serum. He tosses these over the side, where they disappear.

Karen is brought to a pit and dropped inside where she meets Curtis. The vampire infection turned him into a zombie. He attacks Karen, but she escapes by using a bone fragment to climb out.

Blade is strapped to a huge stone block, molded to fit his body. The stone block slowly drains his blood, and it travels down to the atrium below. The twelve pure blood vampires are arranged so that Blade's blood falls on their foreheads.

Frost positions himself at the center, where another droplet of Blade's blood strikes him in the forehead.

Karen releases Blade, and offers her own blood to revive him. He drinks, regaining full strength. His mother arrives, and the two fight. Finally, Blade stabs her with the bone fragment, and she disintegrates.

The spirits of the twelve pure blood vampires fly out of their bodies, circling the atrium. These spirits then pass into Frost. Blade arrives, and quickly dispatches the other guards. Above, Karen uses her vampire mace on Mercury, which causes her head to explode.

Blade and Frost duel with swords. Each time Blade slices Frost, his body heals itself, making him impossible to kill. Seeing the anticoagulant lodged in a stone, Blade knocks it loose, and injects it into Frost. The vampire swells up and explodes.

Outside, Karen and Blade witness the sunrise. Blade rejects her cure. There are still more vampires to destroy. The film moves to Moscow, where a male vampire leads a girl to a dance club. Blade intervenes just before the vampire leans in to bite.

Underworld

Country: U.S.A.; *Theatrical Release:* September 8, 2003 (Toronto Film Festival, Canada), September 19, 2003 (USA and UK); *Production Company:* Lakeshore Entertainment; *Director:* Len Wiseman; *Writer(s):* Screenplay by Danny McBride, Story by Kevin Grevioux, Len Wiseman, and Danny McBride; *Cast:* Kate Beckinsale (Selene), Scott Speedman (Michael Corvin), Michael Sheen (Lucian), Shane Brolly (Kraven), Bill Nighy (Viktor), Erwin Leder (Singe), Sophia Myles (Erika), Robbie Gee (Kahn), Wentworth Miller (Dr. Adam Lockwood), Kevin Grevioux (Raze); *Vampire(s):* Selene, Kraven, Viktor, Erika, Kahn (the following are werewolves) Lucian, Singe, Raze

Plot summary: Selene crouches atop a high building, observing the street below. Her voice-over explains that vampires and lycans (short for lycanthropes or werewolves) have been warring for hundreds of years. Six hundred years ago, the great lycan leader, Lucian, had finally been killed, and now the vampires hunt the creatures to the brink of extinction. Selene explains that she is a death dealer, a vampire who kills lycans. Yet, as the creatures dwindle in number, she is becoming obsolete.

Selene steps off her perch, and falls 100 feet to the street below. She begins to trail two lycans, who are tracking a human named Michael Corvin into the subway. The larger of the two lycans, Raze, senses he is being followed, and initiates a gun battle with Selene and two other death dealers, Rigel and Nathaniel. Rigel is shot, and begins to smoke and burn, his wounds glowing with blue light.

The shootout spills onto the subway train. Raze and Nathaniel switch to hand-to-hand combat, with the lycan transforming into wolf form. Selene pursues the other lycan into the subway shaft, killing him with silver bullets. She takes the gun that killed Rigel, ejects the magazine, and sees that the bullets glow blue.

She hears the sounds of grunting and fighting from somewhere in the tunnels, but is chased away by Raze before she can investigate. Elsewhere in the tunnels, two transformed lycans fight, while a group of onlookers cheers them on. The lycan leader stops the fight, calling the group a pack of wild dogs.

Selene returns to a vast estate, protected by a security fence and guards. She shows the gun she retrieved to Kahn, the vampire weapons expert. He says the bullets are an irradiated fluid, liquid ultraviolet light, which is lethal to vampires. The head of the vampire estate, Kraven, refuses to let Selene investigate the lycans further.

Upstairs, Selene analyzes the photos of the lycans taken by Rigel. She sees a hospital badge around Michael's neck, and tracks down his address. Violating Kraven's orders, she escapes through the window and leaves the estate.

A lycan scientist, Singe, analyzes the blood of a chained man. The lycan leader from earlier appears, and watches as the test proves unsuccessful. Singe crosses James T. Corvin off a scrap of paper pinned to the wall. All the names and notes point to a single word: Corvinus. Raze returns to inform them that he lost Michael Corvin because of the death dealers. The lycan leader decides he will take matters into his own hands.

Michael Corvin returns to his apartment, and is surprised by Selene, who has broken inside. Suddenly lycans storm the building. Michael escapes into the elevator, but on the ground floor, the lycan leader grabs him and bites his shoulder. Selene appears and drags Michael away. The lycan leader spits Michael's blood into a vial.

Selene and Michael escape in her car, but not before the lycan leader stabs her through the shoulder. She loses blood and faints, flipping the car into the river. Michael saves her, but passes out on the riverbank.

The lycan leader returns and delivers the vial of blood to Singe. The leader says that, because he bit the human, Michael will soon become a lycan as well. Singe tests the blood and this time it comes out positive.

Selene brings Michael back to her room at the estate where he awakes from a strange dream of the past. Selene is called to speak with Kraven, who is jealous of Michael, and wants Selene for his own. Erika, a vampire friend of Selene's, discovers that Michael has been bitten by a lycan. Michael panics and jumps out the window.

Later, at the firing range, Kahn shows Selene the new ammunition he's developed. Using the lycan bullets as a template, he's put silver nitrate into the bullets. Selene asks Kahn if he believes that Lucian is really dead. Kraven was supposedly the one who killed the great lycan leader.

Selene breaks into the estate library and reads the account of how Lucian died. She recognizes the amulet in a picture of Lucian as being the same one worn by the lycan leader who attacked Michael. She realizes that Lucian is still alive, and that Kraven lied about killing the lycan.

In a dark alley, Kraven meets up with Lucian in the back seat of a car. Lucian tells the vampire that their arrangement still stands.

Knowing she needs advice, Selene does the unthinkable. She enters the vault where the vampire elders sleep, unlocks Viktor's coffin, and bites her own wrist, using the blood to revive him.

Michael arrives at the front gate, asking to see Selene. She picks him up in her car and takes him to a safe house in the city, where she explains about the war between vampires and lycans. She also tells him that if she were to bite him, he'd die. No one has ever survived an infection from both species, lycan and vampire. Selene reveals why she hates lycans. They butchered her whole family. Viktor saved her and took her in as a daughter. Selene locks Michael up to prevent him from transforming on the full moon, and returns to the estate.

Selene faces a revived Viktor, whose body is still being rejuvenated by blood. Viktor accuses Selene of wakening him too early, a crime among vampires. He also admonishes her for having a fondness for Michael, a lycan and their sworn enemy. Kraven locks Selene in a room to await judgment for her crimes.

Kraven switches the team that will pick up the vampire elder, Amelia, from the train station. Soren and the vampires arrive at the station, but stand by and watch as the lycans descend and massacre the vampire elder and her entourage. Raze arrives and uses a syringe to draw Amelia's blood.

Erika, who has always wanted Kraven to be with her, helps Selene escape. Selene arrives at the safe house, but the lycans have followed her. Selene keeps them at bay while Michael jumps out a window. He is picked up in the alley by two other lycans, dressed as police officers. Michael is kept from transforming into a wolf by an injection of special enzymes.

Singe is wounded, but not killed in the attack on Selene. She brings him back to the estate as proof for Viktor. Singe reveals that the lycans have been trying to combine the vampire and lycan bloodlines. They realized they needed a direct descendant of the first infectee, Alexander Corvinus. Michael's blood allows for a perfect union of the two species. Viktor cannot accept such a concept. Singe also divulges that Lucian is still alive. Viktor kills the lycan and apologizes for doubting Selene. He orders her to kill Michael.

Michael is brought before Lucian, and strapped to a table. Lucian draws some blood from his captive and sends Michael into another vision of the past. He relives Lucian's memories, and sees how Viktor destroyed his own daughter, Sonja, rather than let her be with a lycan like Lucian. Lucian then injects Michael's blood into his own arm.

Kraven arrives, having escaped the estate before Viktor learned of his treachery. He asks Lucian what to do now that Viktor has awoken. They hear gunshots as Selene, Kahn, and the other death dealers arrive. Kraven shoots Lucian in the back with the silver nitrate bullet, which seems to kill the lycan.

Raze finally returns with Amelia's blood and sees Lucian's fallen body. He transforms and quickly attacks the invading death dealers, dispatching Soren.

Selene breaks off from the group, and finds Michael. She wants him to escape before Viktor arrives. As they leave together, they run into Kraven. He shoots Michael with the silver nitrate bullets. As Michael lies dying, Kraven reveals that it was Viktor who murdered Selene's family, not lycans. Viktor saved her because she reminded him of Sonja.

Lucian returns for one last attack. He survived being shot, and stabs Kraven through the leg. Lucian urges Selene to bite Michael and combine the bloodlines. She does, just as Viktor arrives. The vampire elder throws her aside, and tosses Michael through a wall.

Michael begins to transform as both bloodlines create a hybrid of the two species. He and Viktor fight, and for a while Michael holds his own. Selene finally takes Viktor's sword and slices the vampire elder's head in two.

The film ends with Singe's blood dripping into the coffin of Marcus, who is also a descendent of Corvinus. In a voice-over Selene states that soon Marcus will take the throne, and she will be hunted.

APPENDIX B:
SEMANTIC-SYNTACTIC TIMELINE

This timeline will show at a glance how the syntactic and semantic elements change over time. They are divided into seven parts: THE LOOK, THE BITE, THE INFECTION, THE EXPERT, THE CROSS, THE VAMPIRE, and THE DESTRUCTION.

The Look

THE LOOK covers the film moment when the vampire stares down an adversary or victim, the hypnotic stare the vampire uses to control his victims, and also the unspoken communication inherent in the scene.

Movie	Syntax	Semantic Elements
Dracula (1931)	Vampire and victim are alone, away from others. The vampire's gaze enthralls the victim andallows unspoken communication.	• Vampire • Victim • Close-up of vampire's face • Eyes highlighted by light • Victim's eyes fixed in a trance
Dracula's Daughter (1936)	Vampire and victim are alone. The victim is in a deep trance, similar to death.	• Vampire • Victim • Close-up of vampire's face • Gleaming ring • Victim's eyes fixed in a trance
Son of Dracula (1943)	The vampire uses a menacing glare to show his displeasure.	• Vampire • Close up of vampire's face
Return of the Vampire (1944)	The vampire and victim are alone. A mist covers the floor. The vampire's	• Vampire • Victim or servant

Movie	Syntax	Semantic Elements
	gaze enthralls the victim, and allows unspoken communication.	• Close-up of vampire's eyes • Eyes highlighted by light • Mist • Victim's eyes fixed in a trance
El Vampiro (1957) [*The Vampire*— 1958]	Although the opening credits show the vampire staring up at the balcony, the look is one of menace, rather than control. Also the two vampires each stare blankly into space as they share a telepathic conversation via voiceover.	• Vampire • Victim or another vampire • Extreme close-up of eyes • Eyes highlighted by light • Voiceover for telepathy
Horror of Dracula (1958)	The vampire only uses an intense look once in the film, as he prepares to bite a victim. There is the implication that the vampire may be controlling his victim through this look.	• Vampire • Victim • Medium-shot of vampire's face • Eyes highlighted by light
Dark Shadows (1967) Television Series	The vampire has no special abilities conferred via a look. The close-up simply shows the vampire brooding. Once, a victim describes the vampire's eyes as burning.	• Vampire • Close-up of vampire's face
Blacula (1972)	The vampire stares toward his victim, who seems to hear his thoughts accompanied by whistling sound.	• Vampire • Victim • Medium-shot of vampire's face
Dracula (1974)	The vampire stares at the bedroom of his victim, who rises from her bed. She walks toward him, eyes fixed in a trance.	• Vampire • Victim • Zoom onto vampire's eyes in extreme close-up
Dracula (1979)	The vampire stares at a victim, who then must follow his verbal commands. If the vampire wishes to give the commands silently, he swirls his hand, with two fingers curled like a bat's claw.	• Vampire • Victim • Close-up or extreme lose-up of vampire's eyes • Movement of hand • Victim's eyes fixed in a trance
Salem's Lot (1979) Television	The vampire stares at the victim with eyes that seem to glow yellow. The victim appears in a trance. After the	• Vampire • Victim • Medium-shot of

Movie	Syntax	Semantic Elements
Mini-series	bite, the victim only recalls the incident as a dream.	vampire's eyes • Victim's eyes fixed in a trance
Fright Night (1985)	The vampire zigzags through a crowded nightclub, fixing his stare on his victim. She is drawn toward him. Her eyes are fixed in a trance.	• Vampire • Victim • Long-shot of vampire • Victim's eyes in a trance
The Lost Boys (1987)	The vampire has no control over his victims. He merely stares at them hungrily.	• Vampire • Victim • Close-up or extreme closeup of eyes
Near Dark (1987)	Not Applicable	Not Applicable
Bram Stoker's Dracula (1992)	The vampire is able to control various victims from as far away as a ship at sea. A shadow of his form appears to stroke the victim's neck, and a voice-over speaks to her. Later, the superimposed image of his face appears in the clouds. The victims giggle and seem to loose their inhibitions. When faced with his lost love, vampire is able to cause her to remember her past life. Both the vampire and the victim have an extreme close-up of one eye.	• Vampire • Victim • Close-up or extreme close-up of vampire's eyes • Victim's eyes fixed in a trance • Superimposed vampire face or shadow • Voice-over for telepathy
Interview with the Vampire (1994)	The vampire is able to calm and sedate a victim by staring intently at the victim's eyes. The victim becomes calm and pliable to the vampire's will. Another reference to eyes comes with the vampire's altered sight, and seeing through "vampire eyes."	• Vampire • Victim • Two-shot of vampire and victim • Victim's eyes fixed in a trance
Buffy the Vampire Slayer (1997) Television Series	Not Applicable	Not Applicable
Blade (1998)	Not Applicable	Not Applicable
Underworld (2003)	Not Applicable	Not Applicable

The Bite

THE BITE explores how the vampire bites his or her victim, and how the victim reacts to the attack.

Movie	Syntax	Semantic Elements
Dracula (1931)	Vampire attacks the victim only when helpless (drugged, sleeping, or entranced). He moves toward the victim, arms raised, yet the bite is never seen.	• Vampire (male) • Victim (female or male) • Bedroom setting • Cape • Victim sleeping or entranced
Dracula's Daughter (1936)	The vampire attacks the victim only when helpless (entranced). She moves toward the victim, yet the bite is never seen.	• Vampire (female) • Victim (male or female) • Street or bedroom setting • Victim entranced
Son of Dracula (1943)	All bites are implied, however the wounds are shown on camera as two grey splotches on the neck. One failed bite scene is composed like a lover's kiss.	• Marks on neck (dark splotches) • Two-shot of vampire and victim, facing each other
Return of the Vampire (1944)	The vampire attacks the victim, who appears shocked. There is often a scream as the cape is drawn up over the victim.	• Vampire (male) • Victim (female) • Street or bedroom setting • Cape • Scream from victim • Marks on neck (pin-pricks)
El Vampiro (1957) [The Vampire— 1958]	The vampire approaches victims when they are awake. The victim responds with fear, finally screaming. The fangs are visible as the vampire leans down to bite the neck, finally covering the act with the cape. Shortly after the vampire departs.	• Vampire (male or female) • Victim (female or male) • Fangs • Bedroom setting • Cape • Scream from victim • Marks on neck (fresh blood)
Horror of Dracula (1958)	The vampire approaches victims when they are awake. The victim is in a state of expectation, mixed with fear. The vampire bears his fangs, and bites.	• Vampire (male or female) • Victim (female or male) • Fangs • Kiss • Bedroom setting • Cape • Victim appears aroused • Marks on neck with rills of blood

Movie	Syntax	Semantic Elements
Dark Shadows (1967) Television Series	The vampire approaches the bed of a sleeping victim. He stares at the victim, opens mouth to show fangs, and approaches. The scene fades before the actual bite is delivered.	• Vampire (male) • Victim (female) • Fangs • Bedroom setting • Victim asleep
Blacula (1972)	The vampire only attacks when transformed into his predatory form. He growls and pants heavily as he approaches his victims. He forcefully turns the head and delivers a bite to the throat. His fangs are visible even when the mouth is closed. The lesser vampires attack by charging and jumping their victims.	• Vampire (male or female) • Victim (female or male) • Fangs • Kiss • Growling • Arms raised like claws • Victim struggles and screams • Marks on neck with blood
Dracula (1974)	The vampire brides hiss and charge at their victim, who struggles to escape. The main vampire brings his victim to him in a trance. He kisses her, finally baring fangs and delivering a bite to the neck. She responds with aroused moans as though performing sex.	• Vampire (male or female) • Victim (female) • Fangs • Kiss • Bedroom setting • Growling and hissing • Arms raised like claws • Victim struggles or is aroused • Blood on the neck
Dracula (1979)	The vampire brides approach the victim slowly, playing on the victim's sympathies. They bare their fangs and bite the victim on the neck. The main vampire seduces his victims, kissing them as though they are lovers. His fangs are never visible.	• Vampire (male or female) • Victim (female or male) • Fangs • Kiss • Bedroom setting • Victims struggles or is aroused • Bite marks on neck
Salem's Lot (1979) Television Mini-series	The main vampire suddenly appears, stunning the victim. He then drapes the victim with his cape, hiding the actual bite. The lesser vampires float or approach as their victims remain in a trance. They bare their fangs and bite the neck.	• Vampire (male or child) • Victim (child or male) • Fangs • Bedroom setting • Growling and hissing • Victim entranced • Bite marks on neck

Movie	Syntax	Semantic Elements
Fright Night (1985)	When the vampire bites his lover, the scene is set romantically on a rug with a burning fire. The lover accepts the bite willingly. The lesser vampires physically attack their victims with arms raised.	• Vampire (male or female) • Victim (female or male) • Fangs • Kiss • Arms raised like claws • Victim struggles or is aroused • Bite marks on neck
The Lost Boys (1987)	Most of the bite scenes are implied. Victims are attacked from above, as the vampires swoop down to attack from the air. In one rapid cut, a vampire bites a victim on the head, releasing a geyser of blood. Another victim shows his throat ripped open. The bite between the head vampire and his lover shows the traditional scene of vampire biting the neck.	• Vampire (male) • Victim (male) • Fangs • Raised forehead • Wolf eyes • Victim struggles • Torn out throat
Near Dark (1987)	The vampire's fangs are implied, but never seen. One vampire bites a victim, and then afterward, he has bloody wounds on his neck. The other bites do not show the neck after the bite. A new type of bite occurs between two vampires. One vampire bites her wrist, and offers it to another vampire. The sound of a heartbeat accompanies the scene. Finally the first vampire pulls her wrist away.	• Vampire (male, female, or child) • Victim (male or female) • Victim struggles • Cutting device (knife or spur) • Bloody puncture wound on neck or wrist • Sound of beating heart
Bram Stoker's Dracula (1992)	All the bite scenes are erotically charged. The vampire mixes sex with the attack. The victim is aroused as the vampire kisses, bites, and licks the wound. The vampire growls or purrs, assuming an animal quality. In some scenes, the vampire appears hairy, part wolf, or fully transformed as a wolf.	• Vampire (male or female) • Victim (female or male) • Fangs • Kiss • Vampire licks wound • Bedroom setting • Growling or purring • Victim appears aroused • Puncture wounds on neck
Interview with the Vampire	There are numerous bite scenes in the movie. The vampire bites primarily on	• Vampire (male or female)

Movie	Syntax	Semantic Elements
(1994)	the neck, but bites also include a finger, a breast, and multiple wrists. Most of the bites involve the vampire using his or her fangs, but Lestat often pierces his victims using a barbed thimble. The vampire bites his or her own wrist in order to transform a victim into a vampire (see infection).	• Victim (primarily female, with one male, and rats and dogs) • Fangs • Piercing device (thimble with barb) • Victim struggles or is aroused • Bloody wounds on neck, wrist or other body part
Buffy the Vampire Slayer (1997) Television Series	All the vampires transform physically when attacking victims. The transformation is accompanied by a growl and happens in s split second. The vampire either lures the victim, feigning helplessness, or forcing the victim's head to the side, exposing the neck.	• Vampire (male or female) • Victim (female or male) • Fangs • Pale skin • Raised forehead and sunken eyes • Growling
Blade (1998)	The vampire quickly latches onto the victim's throat, and holds the bite for a very long time, during which the victim quivers in a state of helplessness and blood dribbles from the mouth. When released, the victim shows a bloody wound on the neck, and the vampire has blood smeared over his mouth.	• Vampire (male) • Victim (male or female) • Fangs • Growling • Blood dribbles out of victim's mouth • Victim stiffens • Bloody wound on neck • Blood on vampire's mouth
Underworld (2003)	The lycan attacks the victim's throat, sinking the fangs into the skin. The victim initially screams, and then seems overwhelmed by the experience. In one instance, a vampire bites its own wrist to deliver blood to a dormant vampire.	• Vampire (female) • Lycan (male) • Victim (male) • Fangs • Growling • Blood leaks from wound • Victim screams and stiffens • Bloody wound on neck or wrist • Blood on lycan's mouth

The Infection

THE INFECTION deals with how the victim of a vampire attack ultimately responds to vampirism, and how the new vampire deals with the life and conditions of vampirism.

Movie	Syntax	Semantic Elements
Dracula (1931)	The victim is under the control of the vampire. Unspoken communication allows the victim to hear the vampire's thoughts.	• Victim (female) • Bite marks (not seen) • Glazed, trance-like stare
Dracula's Daughter (1936)	The vampire's victims appear in a death-like trance. One victim recalls some details before dying.	• Victim (male or female) • Bite marks (not seen) • Glazed, trance-like stare • Victim remembers some details, then dies
Son of Dracula (1943)	The victim is a willing convert to vampirism. She has a morbid fear of death and attains immortality through the vampire. Another child victim appears faint and helpless.	• Victim (female or child)
Return of the Vampire (1944)	The victim is under total control of the vampire. She hears his voice from far away, and must follow his commands. Another victim recalls some details, but then dies.	• Victim (female) • Bite marks—close-up (pin-pricks) • Glazed, trance-like stare • Victim remembers some details, then dies • Voice-over signals telepathic communication
El Vampiro (1957) [The Vampire—1958]	The victims of both vampires faint, falling onto the bed or floor. The camera zooms in for a close-up of the bite marks.	• Victim (female or male) • Bite marks—close-up (fresh blood) • Victim passes out into unconsciousness
Horror of Dracula (1958)	The effects of vampirism are likened to drug addiction. One victim appears aroused, wanting another bite from the vampire.	• Victim (female or male) • Bite marks—close-up (rills of blood)
Dark Shadows (1967) Television Series	The victim appears weak and tired, collapsing from exhaustion. The victims change their personalities, often becoming more subservient.	• Victim (female) • Victim weak and tired

Movie	Syntax	Semantic Elements
Blacula (1972)	The victims of the vampire quickly become vampires themselves, the infection multiplying geometrically.	• Victim (female or male) • Bite marks—close-up • Pale skin
Dracula (1974)	The victims appear weak and bedridden. One victim wears a bandage around her throat. The vampire states that his victims will become his slaves and helpers. Once a victim dies, he or she rises as a vampire.	• Victim (female or male) • Blood spattered on neck • Glazed look on eyes
Dracula (1979)	One victim suffers from pale skin, has trouble breathing, and dies. The second victim, the lover of the vampire, attempts to protect the vampire, and goes to him willingly.	• Victim (female) • Puncture wounds on neck • Pale skin
Salem's Lot (1979) Television Mini-series	Some victims are next seen as full fledged vampires. They fully adopt the new lifestyle, always hungering for blood. One victim is seen slowly wasting away, until he dies in bed. Susan Norton retains romantic feelings for the hero, Ben. She attempts to seduce him into a bite.	• Victim (child, male, female) • Puncture wounds on neck • Sick and tired feeling • Victim recalls the vampire's bite as a dream
Fright Night (1985)	Both victims become vampires shortly after being bitten, in only a few hours. The victims take to vampirism readily, accepting the new condition with zeal.	• Victim (female or male) • Puncture wounds on neck • Fangs • Wolf-eyes
The Lost Boys (1987)	The separation between victims as food and victims as potential vampires is made explicit. The hero drinks the vampire's blood from a bottle, and within hours starts to transform into a half-vampire. These half-vampires sleep in beds, rather than the cave/coffin of the others. The infected victim struggles with the state of vampirism, fighting off the urges to kill and drink blood. The struggle for acceptance of vampirism is both internal, and external in the form of peer pressure. When the urge to feed hits the vampire, he doubles over, coughing from severe stomach pains. The sound of a beating heart accompanies his urges.	• Victim (male, female, or child) • Fangs • Wolf-eyes • Raised forehead • Long fingernails • Coughing • Pale skin • Sweaty skin • Stomach pains • Sound of beating heart

Movie	Syntax	Semantic Elements
Near Dark (1987)	Biting a victim, without draining all the blood, instantly creates a vampire. The infected victim transforms within a matter of minutes. If the vampire does not drink blood, he experiences severe stomach pains. The vampire staggers, and finally collapses to the ground, his face pale and sweaty. Once he drinks blood, his health instantly returns.	• Victim (male) • Coughing • Pale skin • Sweaty skin • Spitting up food or drink • Stomach pains
Bram Stoker's Dracula (1992)	The vampire is remorseful of his condition. He longs to bite his lost love, but cannot bring himself to do it. He hesitates even when she is willing. The victims become pale, wheezing and gasping for breath. They soon develop fangs of their own.	• Vampire (male) • Victim (female) • Pale skin • Wheezing • Fangs • Throws away food
Interview with the Vampire (1994)	The victims become vampires as a matter of choice. Each has endured a traumatic event, and is willing to undergo the transformation. The vampire drains the victim of blood up to the point of death. The vampire then bites his wrist and drips the blood into the victim's mouth. The victim then seizes onto the vampire's wrist with two hands and drinks. Afterward the victim experiences extreme pain as his or her body dies. Upon the instant of death, the skin becomes pale, the irises lighten, fangs and fingernails grow, any blood on the skin fades away, and the hair transforms into a perfect, beautiful state.	• Vampire (male) • Victim (male or female) • Bloody wound on wrist • Sound of beating heart • Wracking body pains • Pale skin with visible blue veins • Lightened irises • Fangs • Long fingernails • Blood stains fade • Hair appears beautiful
Buffy the Vampire Slayer (1997) Television Series	All vampire victims are possessed by a demon, their souls and conscience gone. They become remorseless killers, who love their condition. One vampire, Angel, is the victim of a curse that has returned his soul. He cares and no longer drinks human blood. He struggles with his condition, trying to live and act as a human. He is ashamed by his bloodlust, wrestling against his urge to feed.	• Vampire (male) • Victim (male)
Blade (1998)	When a vampire bites a victim and drains all or nearly all the blood, the victim will turn, or become a vampire	• Vampire (male) • Victim (female) • Needle injection to

Movie	Syntax	Semantic Elements
	in a matter of hours. One victim, Karen, is able to delay the transformation through an injection of garlic to the neck. Another victim, Curtis, transforms into a zombie, his skin becoming pale with gaping wounds all over his body. Blade struggles with his infection through the film. He takes a serum through injection to the neck to control his thirst for blood.	the neck (garlic or serum) • Pale skin and gaping wounds
Underworld (2003)	The victim experiences memory transference from the attacking lycan in the form of flashbacks. A similar memory transference occurs when a vampire uses its blood to awaken a dormant vampire.	• Vampire (female) • Lycan (male) • Victim (male) • Flashes of memory

The Expert

THE EXPERT covers the character's appearance, disposition, and mannerisms.

Movie	Syntax	Semantic Elements
Dracula (1931)	The expert, Van Helsing, is seen as a scientist. He knows all the lore of the vampire, and is prepared to beat the creature. He uses a cross against the vampire and a makeshift stake in the creature's destruction.	• Professor • Older man • Glasses • Test tubes • Grey/white hair • Hungarian accent • Debate in drawing room setting • Cross
Dracula's Daughter (1936)	Two experts are present: Van Helsing and Dr. Garth. The doctor employs logic to disavow the vampire's existence, thus undermining her power. The doctor has his own ability to hypnotize.	• Professor or doctor • Older man or romantic lead • Test tubes and lab equipment • Professor has Hungarian accent • Debate in study setting
Son of Dracula (1943)	Two experts are present: Professor Lazlo and Dr. Brewster. Professor Lazlo has accumulated knowledge on the vampire. Dr. Brewster is only the town doctor, but takes an active role, breaking the law in order to track	• Professor or doctor • Older man • Glasses • Grey/white hair • Books (reads Bram Stoker's Dracula)

Movie	Syntax	Semantic Elements
	down the vampire. Both are scientists, and debate the opposition of superstition and science. The professor uses a cross against the vampire.	• Professor has Hungarian accent • Debate in study setting • Cross
Return of the Vampire (1944)	Two experts are present: Dr. Saunders (who dies) and Lady Jane Ainsley. Lady Jane reads Armand Tesla's book, and quotes it often. She and Dr. Saunders debate superstition versus science in the study. Later the Commissioner of Scotland Yard takes up this debate. Both experts stake the vampire, and Lady Jane uses a cross against him.	• Doctor or professor • Young lady or older man • Microscopes and lab equipment • Books (reads Tesla's book) • Debate in study setting • Metal spike • Cross
El Vampiro (1957) [The Vampire— 1958]	The expert, Henry, is a thinly veiled romantic hero. He openly disbelieves the existence of the supernatural, and only gains knowledge through the maid, Aunt Mary, and a book. He has a final confrontation with the vampire in the form of a sword fight.	• Doctor • Young man (romantic lead) • Books (reads account of fist vampire's death) • Debate in bedroom
Horror of Dracula (1958)	Technically there are two experts, Van Helsing and Jonathan. Van Helsing picks up the battle after Jonathan is turned into a vampire. Van Helsing is polite in company, but very physical when chasing a vampire. He explains vampire lore in the study. He is prepared for the vampire, bringing along a bundle of stakes, a mallet, and a cross. He finally destroys vampire.	• Doctor • Older man • Books (reads journal from first vampire hunter) • Debate in study • Wooden stakes and mallet • Cross
Dark Shadows (1967) Television Series	The expert, Dr. Julia Hoffman, confronts the vampire early on, and offers to help him. She seeks a cure for his condition, even protecting him from people who would expose him. Ultimately she falls in love with the vampire.	• Doctor • Older woman • Books (studies up on Collins family) • Works alongside vampire
Blacula (1972)	The expert, Dr. Gordon Thomas, is physically active in destroying the vampires. He breaks the law, digging one up, and leaps at another with stake in hand. He is prepared with a cross, and continually confronts the vampire, attempting to destroy him.	• Doctor • Older man • Books (studies books from library) • Debate in police office • Wooden stakes • Cross

Movie	Syntax	Semantic Elements
Dracula (1974)	The expert, Dr. Van Helsing, smugly explains the aspects of vampirism to the other characters. He actively seeks the vampires, coming prepared with stakes, a mallet, and a cross.	• Doctor • Older man • Mustache • Debate in study • Wooden stakes and mallet • Cross
Dracula (1979)	The expert, Professor Abraham Van Helsing, attempts to confront the vampire and destroy him. He is prepared with a long stake and various crosses. He helps to destroy the vampire.	• Professor • Older man • Books (studies book on vampire bat) • Debate in stables • Wooden stake • Cross
Salem's Lot (1979) Television Mini-series	There are multiple experts, starting with Mark Petrie, a young boy who has a collection of horror toys and science equipment. The next expert is Jason Berk, a local high school teacher. He uses a cross and studies up on vampires. When he has a heart attack, the hero, Ben Mears, takes over. Ben and Mark finally destroy the main vampire.	• School teacher or writer • Older man or young boy • Books (multiple library books) • Debate in study • Wooden stakes and hammer • Holy water • Cross
Fright Night (1985)	There are two experts, both inexperienced. The older, Peter Vincent, is a washed up actor who played a vampire killer in movies. He is well equipped, but timid and cowardly. The younger, Charley Brewster, is naïve but brave. He charges headlong into battling the vampires. An ongoing debate centers on the sanity of Charley and his belief in vampires. Both experts confront and ultimately destroy the vampires.	• Older man or younger teen • Movies (from a television show) • Wooden stake • Cross
The Lost Boys (1987)	There are three experts, the Frog brothers, and Sam. Sam quickly learns about vampires from a comic book. These experts are involved in testing the vampires, and destroying some of the lesser vampires.	• Very young teenage boys • Books (read or sell vampire comics) • Wooden stake • Holy water
Near Dark (1987)	The hero's father, Loy Colton, fulfills some aspects of the expert. He follows the vampires, tracking them across the country. He ultimately saves two vampires through a transfusion of blood.	• Doctor • Older man • Lab equipment

Movie	Syntax	Semantic Elements
Bram Stoker's Dracula (1992)	The expert, Abraham Van Helsing, states that he has pursued Dracula all his life. He is a professor of obscure diseases, and immediately goes to work tracking down the vampire. He personally destroys all the vampire brides, and exorcises the vampire's grave dirt. He is prepared with crosses, wooden stakes, holy water and holy wafers.	• Professor • Older man • Gray/white hair • Hungarian accent • Books (reads *Vampyre* about Vlad Dracula) • Wooden stake • Cross • Holy water • Holy wafers • Debate in courtyard
Interview with the Vampire (1994)	There is no human expert who hunts vampires. There is, however, an on-going debate over the existence and purpose of being a vampire. As Louis seeks information, either Lestat or Armand dole out some answers.	• Debate in various locales
Buffy the Vampire Slayer (1997) *Television Series*	The role of expert has been separated into a research component, Giles, and a physical component, Buffy. Buffy actively tracks down the vampires, dispatching them easily with martial arts attacks and stakes. Giles, on the other hand, seems helpless in a fight, preferring to study up on the creatures, offering advice and strategies. The two debate over the roles of the vampire killer, called the slayer, as well as the black and white nature of vampires. Buffy falls in love with Angel, fighting alongside him.	• Librarian or high school student • Older man or teenager • Glasses • British accent • Books (reads many books, including *Vampyre*) • Wooden stake • Holy water • Debate in library
Blade (1998)	The role of expert is separated, with Blade taking the role of physically subduing the vampires, while Abraham Whistler creates the weapons and researches the vampires. Added to this is Dr. Karen Jenson, a hematologist. She pursues a cure for vampirism. Blade is a vampire hunting vampires and he is equipped with an array of weaponry.	• Vampire, older man, or young woman • Doctor • Books (computer translated text) • Silver stakes • Vampire mace (silver nitrate and garlic) • Shotgun (silver shots) • Automatic pistol (silver hollow point filled with garlic) • Katana sword (silver) • Boomerang (silver) • Ultraviolet light (oversized flashlight) • Debate in warehouse

Movie	Syntax	Semantic Elements
Underworld (2003)	All vampires and lycan take on the role of slayers. They are armed and trained to destroy their enemy.	• Vampire or lycan (werewolf) • Automatic pistol (silver or specialized bullets)

The Cross

THE CROSS shows the effect of a crucifix or cross-shaped object on the vampire, as well as how the cross appears in the film.

Movie	Syntax	Semantic Elements
Dracula (1931)	The expert casually presents the cross. The vampire responds by throwing his arm up and averting his face, hiding behind his cape.	• Vampire • Expert • Small crucifix • Cape
Dracula's Daughter	The vampire and servant avert their faces from the cross.	• Vampire or servant • Cross of two sticks tied together
Son of Dracula (1943)	The vampire either backs away with a look of fright or averts his face, hiding behind his cape.	• Vampire • Expert • Cross (either small or shadow cast by moon) • Cape
Return of the Vampire (1944)	The expert reveals the cross, which glows. The vampire responds by throwing his arm up and averting his face, hiding behind his cape.	• Vampire • Expert • Cross (small necklace or crucifix) • Cross illuminated by light (glowing) • Cape
El Vampiro (1957) [*The Vampire*— 1958]	Crosses abound in the film. When encountered by chance, the vampire grimaces, and hides behind a cape. Other times, the vampire simply looks away.	• Vampire • Cross (large and small, manufactured or woven) • Cape
Horror of Dracula (1958)	The expert uses the cross to drive back an infected victim. She grimaces and backs away. When the cross is pressed to her forehead, it burns a mark. Later, when a cross is dropped into an infected victim's hand, it leaves a burn mark. At the end, the expert keeps the vampire at bay with two candlesticks formed into a cross.	• Vampire • Infected victim • Expert • Cross (small or makeshift) • Vampire stares at cross • Sizzling sound • Vampire screams • Cross shaped burn mark on skin

Movie	Syntax	Semantic Elements
Dark Shadows (1967) Television Series	Not applicable	Not applicable
Blacula (1972)	The expert presents the cross to a lesser vampire, who raises her hands to block it. He uses it to drive her back.	• Lesser vampire • Expert • Cross (large)
Dracula (1974)	The expert presents the cross to the vampire. The new vampire bride shields her eyes and flees. The lead vampire merely winces and averts his eyes. When an infected victim grasps a cross, it sizzles and smokes in her hand. She flings it away leaving the palm reddened and burned.	• Vampire • Infected victim • Expert • Cross (large) • Cross reflects light • Vampire averts eyes • Sizzling sound • Smoke • Vampire screams • Red burn on skin
Dracula (1979)	The cross has various effects on the vampires. For the main vampire, when presented a small cross by the expert, he backs away. When presented a plain wooden cross by another character, he grabs it. The cross bursts into flame. When a cross is presented to a vampire bride, she ignores it until pressed to her forehead. Then it sizzles and she screams and flees. Finally, when the cross is presented to the vampire's lover, she at first stares at it, and faints. Then she revives and kisses the cross, which has no ill effects.	• Vampire • Expert • Cross (large, small, plain, crucifix) • Vampire either grabs cross, stares at cross, or averts eyes • Cape • Sizzling sound • Smoke • Fire • Vampire whimpers
Salem's Lot (1979) Television Mini-series	On the lesser vampires, simply presenting the cross forces them backward. The vampires either hide their faces or are defiant of the cross, but all move away from it. The cross is ineffective on the main vampire because the holder has little faith. The vampire grabs it and tosses it aside. The expert creates a makeshift cross from two tongue depressors and blesses it with a prayer. When touched to a lesser vampire's skin, it burns.	• Vampire • Expert • Cross (small, makeshift) • Lesser vampires move away, while it has no effect on the main vampire • Sizzling sound • Smoke • Vampire screams • Cross shaped burn mark on skin
Fright Night (1985)	On the lesser vampires, merely presenting the cross is enough to keep them at bay. They shield their eyes, whimper, and attempt to flee. Touching the cross to the vampire's	• Vampire • Expert • Cross (large, small, plain, or crucifix) • Vampire either stares

Movie	Syntax	Semantic Elements
	skin burns. On the master vampire, the expert must have faith to make the cross work properly. Without faith, the vampire can touch the cross with no ill effects.	at cross or covers face with arm • Sizzling sound • Smoke • Vampire whimpers • Cross shaped burn mark on skin
The Lost Boys (1987)	The cross is replaced by holy water, with the same effects. When placed on the vampire (splashing water or spraying through a squirt-gun) the skin sizzles and smokes.	• Vampire • Expert • Holy water (bathtub or squirt-gun) • Sizzling sound • Smoke • Burn marks on skin
Near Dark (1987)	Not applicable	Not applicable
Bram Stoker's Dracula (1992)	When faced with a cross, the vampire growls or hisses and backs away. When a vampire bride encounters a cross, she hisses and it melts away. When a cross is presented to the main vampire, it bursts into flame. When the expert throws holy water or touches the skin with a holy wafer, the vampire burns. This is accompanied by a sizzling sound and smoke. A reddened mark is left on the skin.	• Vampire • Expert • Cross (crucifix) • Holy water or wafer • Sizzling sound • Smoke • Burn mark on skin • Fire • Cross melts • Vampire growls or hisses and backs away
Interview with the Vampire (1994)	Not applicable	Not applicable
Buffy the Vampire Slayer (1997) Television Series	The cross has its most potent effect when placed against the vampire, where it sizzles and smokes, burning the skin. Holy water is also used for the same purpose. The vampire does not seem adversely affected by a presented cross. The cross only prevents the vampire from advancing.	• Vampire • Expert • Cross (simple silver) • Holy water • Sizzling sound • Smoke • Cross shaped burn mark on skin • Vampire screams and hides wound
Blade (1998)	The cross is replaced by a liquid called 'vampire mace.' When squirted on the vampire, it causes pain and the vampire to explode.	• Vampire • Expert • Vampire mace (in mace spray) • Vampire explodes
Underworld (2003)	The cross is replaced by silver bullets. When a lycan pulls a silver slug from	• Lycan (werewolf) • Vampire

Movie	Syntax	Semantic Elements
	its body, the fingers smoke and sizzle.	• Specialized bullets (silver) • Skin smokes on contact

The Vampire

THE VAMPIRE covers the character's appearance, disposition, and mannerisms.

Movie	Syntax	Semantic Elements
Dracula (1931)	The vampire, Dracula, is an aristocrat and for most of the film, he is distant and silent, controlling from afar.	• Pale face • Dark full lips • Black cape • Hungarian accent • Ring with crest
Dracula's Daughter (1936)	The vampire, Marya Zaleska, is an aristocrat and easily fits in with society,changing her clothes in nearly every scene. The vampire struggles with her condition. She believes her will can overpower the darkness of her desire. She ultimately fails.	• Pale face • Dark full lips • Black cape • Hungarian accent • Ring with crest
Son of Dracula (1943)	The vampire, Alucard, is an aristocrat, but haughty and demanding.He angers easily, turning to threats or physical attacks.	• Slightly graying hair • Mustache (pencil) • Black cape • Ring with crest
Return of the Vampire (1944)	The vampire, Armand Tesla, is an aristocrat and highly dignified. In society, he is polite to a fault. He avoids physical labor, preferring to have a servant do errands for him.	• Pale face • Dark full lips • Black cape with high collar • Hungarian accent • Ring with tragedy mask
El Vampiro (1957) [*The Vampire*— 1958]	The vampires, Duval and Eloise, are both aristocrats, and extremely dignified to such a point that they ignore trivial incidents (someone fainting).	• Pale face • Dark full lips • Black cape with high collar or black dress with long mantilla • Two upper fangs visible when attacking
Horror of Dracula (1958)	The two vampires, Dracula and his bride, are both physical. Dracula leaps over a table, and at one point, he adopts bloodshot eyes and has blood dripping from his mouth. Yet with	• Pale face • Black cape with high collar or pastel dress • Two upper fangs

Movie	Syntax	Semantic Elements
	company, he can be extremely well mannered.	visible when attacking • Bloodshot eyes • Trickle of blood from the corners of the mouth • Ring with crest
Dark Shadows (1967) Television Series	The vampire, Barnabas Collins, appears quite normal and sociable in public. Privately, and with certain persons, he expresses remorse over the death of his love, Josette, and melancholy towards his existence as a vampire.	• Black overcoat with high collar • Two upper fangs visible when attacking • Ring with black onyx • Silver and gold cane with wolf's head
Blacula (1972)	The vampire takes on two forms, social and predatory. The social vampire is Mamuwalde, and he appears suave, kissing hands. This version longs to be reunited with his lost love, displaying all the aspects of a romantic hero. The predatory vampire is Blacula, and when attacking victims, he grows hair on his cheeks, and eyebrows. He bares fangs that are visible even with the mouth closed. He is very physical and strong, easily crushing men's throats, lifting one man and tossing him down a flight of stairs. The lesser vampires, those infected by Blacula, have pale faces (either white or green) and shaggy hair. They are always bloodthirsty.	• Pale face • Mustache • Bushy eyebrows • Widow's peak • Hairy cheeks • Black cape with high collar • Black tuxedo jacket • Two upper fangs visible when attacking • Blood leaking from eyes • Blood on lips
Dracula (1974)	The vampire, Dracula, takes two forms: physical and sentimental. When with his lost love, the vampire is tender and passionate. With others he is abrupt and haughty. When fighting adversaries, he employs his physical strength to choke or toss men aside. He bares his fangs when attacking or when angered.	• Pale face • Black cape • Two upper fangs visible when attacking
Dracula (1979)	The vampire, Dracula, appears normal throughout the film. He is courteous and suave. His movements are purposeful with no unnecessary gestures. He wears a black cape and white shirt that opens on the front.	• Pale or normal skin tone • Black cape • No fangs or two upper fangs visible when attacking

Movie	Syntax	Semantic Elements
	The vampire brides have pale skin and fangs visible when attacking victims. Blood drips from their lips.	• Normal eyes or black colored eyes • Normal mouth or blood from mouth
Salem's Lot (1979) Television Mini-series	The main vampire, Kurt Barlow, does not speak through the film. He merely growls and appears more animal than human. His skin is blue, with pointy ears, a bald head, long white fingernails, and a mouth full of sharp fangs. The victims turned vampire have pale skin and eyes that reflect yellow in the dark. They have two fangs and seem only intent on attacking their victims. They move slowly, either floating through the air, walking, or crawling.	• Pale or bluish skin • Lesser vampires have two fangs, the main vampire has a mouth full of fangs • Reflective yellow eyes • Long white fingernails • Pointed ears
Fright Night (1985)	The main vampire, Jerry Dandridge, is dressed in contemporary clothes, a grey trench coat and red scarf. He is polite to adults and his lover. When angered or attacking, he physically transforms, gaining 'wolf eyes,' claw-like hands, and a mouthful of fangs. Even in this state, he can be calm and purposeful, using his strength sparingly. The victims are either dressed in street clothes, Evil Ed, or a long flowing dress, for Amy.	• Gray trench coat • Red scarf • Three sets of fangs (upper and lower) when attacking • Wolf eyes when attacking • Long fingers with sharp nails when attacking • Mottled skin when attacking
The Lost Boys (1987)	Although there is a head vampire, Max, the leader of the gang, David, serves as the chief villain. He plays cruel jokes on the hero, and tests him through an initiation. The hero, Michael, at first seems destined for vampirism. He drives a motorcycle, buys a leather jacket, and considers piercing his ear. Later he struggles against the urge to feed on blood.	• Street clothes • Motorcycle • Pierced ears • Long hair • Double fangs (upper) when attacking • Wolf eyes when attacking • Raised forehead when attacking • Pale skin when attacking • Long fingernails when attacking
Near Dark (1987)	The vampires, led by Jesse, appear as a family. There is the mother, Diamondback, the brother, Severen, the sister, Mae, and the little boy, Homer. All these vampires are dressed in ragged street clothes. When hiding	• Street clothes • Blankets • Guns (six-shooter pistol) • Spurs • Cowboy boots

Movie	*Syntax*	*Semantic Elements*
	from the sun, they huddle under thick blankets. These vampires are ruthless and bloodthirsty, easily killing victims for their blood. Some vampires, like Mae, have difficulty with vampirism. She resists biting the hero because she is in love with him.	
Bram Stoker's Dracula (1992)	The vampire, Dracula, assumes many different forms. As an old man, he has wrinkled pale skin and long white hair. He is courteous, but quick to be insulted, growling. When attacking, he becomes part wolf, his body developing a thick coat of black hair. In this form he is very animalistic, succumbing to his lustful desires. When in London, he appears as Prince Vlad, with only slightly pale skin. When angered or upset, he ages, developing the nose of a bat and pale skin. Finally, Dracula assumes the shape of a giant, green bat. In all these forms, the vampire can grow fangs. When in wolf or bat form, he has a mouth full of blood and sharp teeth. The vampire brides have pale skin and can grow a set of fangs. The brides seduce their victims.	• A variety of rich robes or suits • Pale wrinkled skin • Long white hair • Long fingers and nails • Hairy palms • Fangs grow when attacking • Red colored eyes • Bat shaped nose • Body covered in hair when attacking • Mouth filled with blood • Tears of blood
Interview with the Vampire (1994)	All the central characters are vampires, and even though two are transformed humans, they spend the bulk of the film living with the condition of vampirism. All the vampires maintain the personalities they possessed as humans. The various vampires express attitudes as diverse as characters from any other genre. Physically, these vampires always maintain a beautiful appearance. When hair or skin is cut, it grows back or heals immediately. Their skin is cold and pale, yet after drinking blood, it warms. The vampires can float or fly and posses lightning quick reflexes.	• Various period clothes • Pale skin with visible blue veins • Lightened irises • Fangs • Long fingernails • Beautiful long hair
Buffy the Vampire Slayer (1997) Television Series	The vampires are bloodthirsty killers. Most can appear normal right up to the moment of attack. All the vampires are skilled in martial arts combat, using kicks and punches to	• Various street clothes • Fangs • Pale skin • Raised forehead and sunken eyes

Movie	Syntax	Semantic Elements
	subdue their victims. The vampires are highly overconfident, relying on their strength. One vampire, Angel, appears human most of the time. He struggles with the condition of vampirism.	
Blade (1998)	The vampires are separated into two groups, the pure blood vampires and the turned vampires. The pure blood vampire is always seen in suits, and tends to be older. The turned vampire is dressed in fashionable clothing, is younger, and more aggressive. These vampires look like other humans most of the time. One vampire, Blade, struggles with the condition of vampirism. He also hunts the other vampires.	• High fashion clothes or suits • Fangs • Pale skin (very slight) • Long fingernails (appear when needed)
Underworld (2003)	The creatures are separated into two groups: the dominant vampires, and the scruffy lycans. The vampires are always seen in slick outfits, while the lycans dress in ruffed up street clothes. Although the lycan can transform into wolf form, both species appear human most of the time.	• High fashion or ragged clothes • Fangs (slight) • Pale skin (very slight) • Lycan wolf form: animal head, black skin, canine fangs and legs, with claws

The Destruction

THE DESTRUCTION deals with how the vampire is ultimately done in.

Movie	Syntax	Semantic Elements
Dracula (1931)	The expert finds the vampire in his coffin. He pounds a stake into the heart once (not seen on screen). A groan accompanies the strike as the vampire dies.	• Vampire • Expert • Piercing instrument (wooden stake ripped from coffin lid) • Pounding instrument (crowbar) • One strike • Coffin
Dracula's Daughter (1936)	The servant shoots the vampire through the heart. This is viewed on screen and we see the vampire die.	• Vampire • Servant • Piercing instrument (wooden arrow shot from a bow)

Movie	Syntax	Semantic Elements
Son of Dracula (1943)	The romantic lead burns the coffin. Sunlight ultimately kills the vampire. The vampire falls woodenly to the ground, his flesh vanishes leaving only bone. A second coffin, and vampire, is also burned.	• Vampire • Romantic lead • Fire • Sunlight • Skin disappears leaving bone
Return of the Vampire (1944)	The vampire is killed, revived, and killed again. He is first killed in his coffin with a metal spike administered by both experts. Later, the servant drags him into sunlight, which he shuns, but it seems to have no other effect. The servant then pounds a metal spike into the vampire's heart three times with a brick. After this, the vampire's flesh melts away.	• Vampire • Expert • Servant • Piercing instrument (metal spike) • Pounding instrument (hatchet or brick) • Three strikes • Coffin • Sunlight • Skin melts off leaving bone
El Vampiro (1957) [*The Vampire*— 1958]	A 'mad' character destroys both vampires. She chokes one vampire into either death or unconsciousness. Then finds a wooden stake and jams it into the heart (seen on screen). After the master vampire is destroyed, the first vampire withers away to bone.	• Vampire • 'Mad' character • Choking • Piercing instrument (wooden stake broken from chair) • Pierced heart • Coffin • Flesh ages revealing bone
Horror of Dracula (1958)	The expert finds the vampire in a coffin and hammers the stake through the heart with three strikes. At the end, the expert pulls down the curtains and destroys the main vampire with sunlight. The vampire's body withers to dust.	• Vampire • Expert • Piercing instrument (prepared small wooden stake) • Pounding instrument (mallet) • Three strikes • Pierced heart • Coffin • Sunlight • Flesh ages revealing bone
Dark Shadows (1967) Television Series	The vampire is never destroyed, only immobilized. His mortal father can't bring himself to drive a stake through his son's heart, so he chains the vampire inside a coffin.	• Vampire • Father • Coffin • Chains
Blacula (1972)	Many of the lesser vampires are destroyed by the expert either hurling	• Vampire • Expert

Movie	Syntax	Semantic Elements
	burning lamp oil or using a stake pounded through the heart three times. The expert does not accomplish the destruction of the main vampire. Blacula sacrifices himself, climbing up stairs, and exposing himself to sunlight. His skin shrivels and smokes as maggots crawl out of his orifices. The flesh fades to bone.	• Piercing instrument (prepared or makeshift wooden stake) • Pounding instrument (shovel) • Three strikes • Pierced heart • Coffin • Sunlight • Flesh ages revealing bone
Dracula (1974)	The expert uses a large wooden stake and pounds it through the heart with a mallet in three strikes. Another vampire is pushed into a pit and impaled on a stalagmite. The main vampire is disposed of using a combination of sunlight and a pierced heart. The expert pulls down the curtains, which causes the vampire to weaken. Finally the expert uses a spear jammed through the heart with three thrusts.	• Vampire • Expert • Piercing instrument (prepared large wooden stake, stalagmite, or spear) • Pounding instrument (mallet) • Three strikes • Pierced heart • Coffin • Sunlight
Dracula (1979)	The vampire bride is run through with a stake long enough to function as a spear. The main vampire, transformed as a bat, bursts into flames when struck by sunlight. When hauled up into sunlight by a hook, the vampire ages rapidly, his skin burning.	• Vampire • Expert • Piercing instrument (very long stake) • Pierced heart • Sunlight • Fire • Skin and hair ages and flesh burns
Salem's Lot (1979) Television Mini-series	One scene shows a lesser vampire seeming to vanish after having a cross touched to the forehead. The main vampire is killed by repeatedly pounding a stake into the heart. The vampire growls and struggles, but ultimately succumbs. Later the skin is shown to have melted off the bone. The remaining vampires are dispatched by burning the houses with them inside.	• Vampire • Expert • Cross • Vampire vanishes • Piercing instrument (prepared wooden stake) • Pounding instrument (hammer) • Multiple strikes • Pierced heart • Coffin • Skin melts off revealing bone • Fire

Movie	Syntax	Semantic Elements
Fright Night (1985)	The expert uses a stake to pierce the heart of the vampire. However, if the vampire can remove the stake, he will be revived. Sunlight causes the vampire to burst into flame. When hit full on, the vampire sprouts green flame and the skin tears away from the bone. The skeleton transforms into a bat-like demon that explodes and vanishes. The lesser vampires revert to normal.	• Vampire • Expert • Piercing instrument (broken table leg or pencil) • Pierced heart • Sunlight • Fire • Skin tears off revealing bone • Skeleton explodes and vanishes
The Lost Boys (1987)	The experts destroy all of the lesser vampires mostly through staking. One vampire is thrown into a bathtub of holy water and disintegrates. All the vampires struggle when they die. The head vampire explodes in a ball of fire.	• Vampire • Expert of hero • Piercing instrument (wooden stake or arrow) • Pierced heart • Sunlight • Holy water • Explosion of fire
Near Dark (1987)	Indirect sunlight causes the vampires to smolder and smoke. The skin burns, turning black. When a direct beam of sunlight strikes the vampire, flames erupt, charring the skin. Finally the vampire explodes, sending body parts and fire everywhere.	• Vampire • Sunlight • Smoke • Black, charcoal colored skin • Explosion of fire
Bram Stoker's Dracula (1992)	The expert cuts the head off the body, destroying the brides. One bride is staked first using a metal spike and hammer. The main vampire has his throat cut, and a knife thrust into his chest. His lost love finally pushes the knife all the way through, killing the vampire. His skin returns to a normal hue, and the burn mark vanishes from his victim. She finishes the job by using the knife to chop off the head.	• Vampire • Expert or lover • Piercing instrument (metal spike or knife) • Pounding instrument (hammer) • Pierced heart • Slashing instrument (knife or sword) • Severed head
Interview with the Vampire (1994)	Various methods are used to destroy a vampire. Lestat becomes incapacitated by drinking "dead" blood. His throat is then slit, and his body withers, the skin shrinking right to the bone. Later, after his revival, Lestat appears to have rotted, his skin and clothes filthy. When set on fire, the vampires writhe and attempt to escape the flames	• Vampire • Slashing instrument (knife or scythe) • Skin becomes sunken around bones or appears rotted • Fire • Sunlight • Smoke

Movie	Syntax	Semantic Elements
	(often flying). Many of these burning vampires are subsequently cut open or beheaded. Finally, when exposed to sunlight, the skin smokes and burns. The bodies transform into a fine ash that disintegrates on touch.	• Skin becomes a fine ash
Buffy the Vampire Slayer (1997) Television Series	The expert almost exclusively destroys the vampires using a stake. She jams the stake through the heart in one quick gesture. The vampire then collapses to the ground, where it quickly disintegrates, exploding into a puff of black dust. One vampire is destroyed with a thrown cymbal, severing the head.	• Vampire • Expert or vampire • Piercing instrument (prepared or makeshift wooden stake) • Pierced heart • Slashing instrument (cymbal) • Vampire explodes into a pile of dust
Blade (1998)	The experts use a variety of weapons, mostly silver, to dispose of vampires. The silver weapons must pierce the vampire's heart or head. When accomplished, the vampire's flesh quickly burns into ash, and the bones disintegrate. Additionally, if the vampire is slashed through the torso or beheaded, it is also destroyed. When exposed to ultraviolet light, the vampire's flesh burns, turning black, finally killing the vampire. When sprayed in the face with vampire mace, the vampire chokes, and the head finally explodes. When injected with an anticoagulant, the vampire's body bloats grotesquely, finally exploding. When exposed to sunlight, the vampire's skin sizzles and smokes. Finally the flesh breaks apart, and lights on fire. The vampire screams before exploding.	• Vampire • Expert (vampire or human) • Piercing instrument (silver stake, sword, or needle) • Pierced heart or head • Slashing instrument (sword, boomerang, or garrote) • Projectile (silver shot or silver hollow point rounds with garlic) • Vampire burns into ash and bones disintegrate • Ultraviolet light • Skin smolders and turns black • Vampire mace (silver nitrate and garlic) • Vampire's head explodes • Injected anticoagulant (EDTA) • Vampire bloats then explodes • Sunlight • Skin sizzles • Smoke and fire

Movie	Syntax	Semantic Elements
Underworld (2003)	Most vampires (and lycans) are dispatched with bullets from machineguns or pistols. Most simply fall to the ground, not to be seen again. Ultraviolet bullets cause vampires to burn up and smoke, revealing a blue light from inside the body. The silver nitrate bullets act like a poison on the lycan. The veins quickly darken as the creature stiffens in pain.	• Slashing instrument (sword) • Projectile (silver slugs or hollow point rounds with ultraviolet light or silver nitrate) • Vampire burns revealing blue light • Lycan's veins turn dark purple as silver nitrate spreads • Sunlight • Skin sizzles • Smoke and fire

WORKS CITED

Books, Articles and Web Sites

The 80's Movie Rewind. Copyright 2005, Fast-Rewind. 17 October 2005 < http://www. fast-rewind.com >.

Altman, Rick. *Film/Genre.* London: British Film Institute, 1999.

Clark, Mark. *Smirk, Sneer and Scream: Great Acting in Horror Cinema.* Jefferson: McFarland, 2004.

Cook, Pam, and Mieke Bernink, ed. *The Cinema Book: 2nd Edition.* London: BFI, 1999.

Crane, Jonathan Lake. *Terror and Everyday Life: Singular Moments in the History of the Horror Film.* Thousand Oaks: Sage Publications, 1994.

Dark Shadows Love Story. Douglas Hayes. 10 June 2005 <http://members.tripod.com/ ~DouglasHayes/DSstory.html>.

Dawkins, Richard. *The Selfish Gene.* Oxford: Oxford University Press, 1989.

Dyer, Richard. "Dracula and Desire." *Sight and Sound.* Jan. 1993: 8–15.

Hardy, Phil, ed. *The Overlook Film Encyclopedia.* New York: The Overlook Press, 1995.

Hayward, Susan. *Key Concepts in Cinema Studies.* London: Routledge, 1996.

Hogan, David J. *Dark Romance: Sexuality in the Horror Film.* Jefferson: McFarland, 1997.

The Internet Movie Database. Copyright 1990–2005, Internet Movie Database, Inc., an Amazon Company. 20 May 2005 <http://www.imdb.com>.

Landau, Diana, ed. *Bram Stoker's Dracula: The Film and the Legend.* New York: Newmarket Press, 1992.

Melton, J. Gordon. *The Vampire Book.* Detroit: Visible Ink Press, 1999.

Paul, Louis. *Italian Horror Directors.* Jefferson: McFarland, 2005.

Rickels, Laurence A. *The Vampire Lectures.* Minneapolis: University of Minnesota Press, 1999.

Scott, Kathryn Leigh. *The Dark Shadows Companion: 25th Anniversary Collection.* Los Angeles: Pomegranate Press, Ltd., 1990.

Skal, David J. *Hollywood Gothic: The Tangled Web of Dracula from Novel to Stage to Screen.* New York: W. W. Norton and Company, 1991.

Vampyres Online: The Vampire Movie Database. Ed. Roesler, Jan, and Flindt, Matze. 6 May 2005 <http://www.vampyres-online.com/index2.html>.

Wolf, Leonard. *Horror: A Connoisseur's Guide to Literature and Film.* New York: Facts On File, 1989.

Films

Angel." *Buffy the Vampire Slayer.* By David Greenwalt. Videocassette. Twentieth Century Fox Home Entertainment, 1998.

"Harvest, The." *Buffy the Vampire Slayer.* By Joss Whedon. Videocassette. Twentieth Century Fox Home Entertainment, 1998.

"Welcome to the Hellmouth." *Buffy the Vampire Slayer.* By Joss Whedon. Videocassette. Twentieth Century Fox Home Entertainment, 1998

Blacula. Dir. William Crain. Perf. William Marshall. DVD. MGM Home Entertainment, 2004.

Blade. Dir. Stephen Norrington. Perf. Wesley Snipes. DVD. New Line Home Entertainment, Inc., 2001.

Bram Stoker's Dracula. Screenplay by James V. Hart. Dir. Francis Ford Coppola. Perf. Gary Oldman. DVD. Columbia, 1997.

Dark Shadows: DVD Collection 1. By Dan Curtis. MPI Home Video, 2002.

Dark Shadows: DVD Collection 2. By Dan Curtis. MPI Home Video, 2002.

Dark Shadows: DVD Collection 3. By Dan Curtis. MPI Home Video, 2002.

Dark Shadows: DVD Collection 4. By Dan Curtis. MPI Home Video, 2003.

Dracula. Dir. John Badham. Perf. Frank Langella. DVD. Universal Studios, 2004.

Dracula. Dracula: The Legacy Collection. Dir. Tod Browning. Perf. Bela Lugosi, and Edward Van Sloan. DVD. Universal Studios, 2004.

Dracula. Screenplay by Richard Matheson. Dir. Dan Curtis. DVD. MPI Home Video, 2002.

Dracula's Daughter. Dracula: The Legacy Collection. Dir. Lambert Hillyer. DVD. Universal Studios, 2004.

Fright Night. Dir. Tom Holland. DVD. Columbia Tristar Home Video, 1998.

Horror of Dracula. Dir. Terence Fischer. Perf. Peter Cushing, and Christopher Lee. DVD. Warner Home Video, 2002.

Interview with the Vampire. Dir. Neil Jordan. Perf. Tom Cruise, and Brad Pitt. DVD. Warner Home Video, 2000.

Lost Boys, The. Dir. Joel Schumacher. DVD. Warner Home Video, 1998.

Near Dark. Dir. Kathryn Bigelow. DVD. Anchor Bay Entertainment, Inc., 2002.

Return of the Vampire, The. Dir. Lew Landers. Perf. Bela Lugosi. Videocassette. Columbia Tristar Home Video, 1985.

Salem's Lot. Dir. Tobe Hooper. DVD. Warner Home Video, 1999.

Son of Dracula. Dracula: The Legacy Collection. Dir. Robert Siomak. Perf. Lon Chaney Jr. DVD. Universal Studios, 2004.

Underworld. Dir. Len Wiseman. Perf. Kate Beckinsale. DVD. Tristar Home Entertainment, 2004.

Vampire, The [El Vampiro]. Dir. Fernando Méndez. Perf. Germán Robles. Videocassette. The I. S. Filmworks, 1957.

INDEX

Numbers in **boldface** indicate photographs.